PORT AND FILM

The ... become one of commercial cinema's most recognizable genr ... boxing films such as *Raging Bull* (1980) to soccer-themed box o ... ike *Bend it Like Beckham* (2002), the sports film stands at the in ... our most important cultural forms. This book examines the sc ... nd ideological significance of representations of sport in film ir ... n essential guide for all students and enthusiasts of sport, film, n ... ure.

Sport ... aces the history of the sports film, from the beginnings of cinema in ... '0s, its consolidation as a distinct fiction genre in the mid 1920s in Holly... od films such as Harold Lloyd's *The Freshman* (1925), to its contemporary manifestation in Oscar-winning films such as *Million Dollar Baby* (2004) and *The Fighter* (2010). Drawing on an extensive range of films as source material, the book explores key issues in the study of sport, film and wider society, including race, social class, gender and the legacy of 9/11. It also offers an invaluable guide to 'reading' a film, to help students fully engage with their source material. Comprehensive, authoritative and accessible, this book is an important addition to the literature in film and media studies, sport studies and cultural studies more generally.

Seán Crosson is Programme Director of the MA in Film Studies: Theory and Practice in the Huston School of Film & Digital Media at NUI, Galway. He has published widely on film, focusing in particular in recent years on the representation of sport in film. His previous publications include (as co-editor) the collection *Sport, Representation and Evolving Identities in Europe* (Peter Lang, 2010) and a special ... e Media in Ireland' (2011).

Frontiers of Sport

Series editor: Alan Bairner
Loughborough University, UK

Sport is ubiquitous in the modern era. As such, it is engaged with by exponents of other academic disciplines and professional groups. This innovative series explores the close relationships that exist between sport and other disciplines and professions, and traces the theoretical and professional boundaries that they share. Each book in the series introduces the key themes, topics and debates that define a particular discipline and its engagement with sport – such as sport and sociology, or sport and politics – offering an invaluable overview for all students and scholars working in sport and each mainstream discipline.

Available in this series:

Sport and Sociology
Dominic Malcolm

Sport and Film
Seán Crosson

SPORT AND FILM

Seán Crosson

Routledge
Taylor & Francis Group

LONDON AND NEW YORK

First published 2013
by Routledge
2 Park Square, Milton Park, Abingdon, Oxon OX14 4RN

Simultaneously published in the USA and Canada
by Routledge
711 Third Avenue, New York, NY 10017

Routledge is an imprint of the Taylor & Francis Group, an informa business

The author wishes to acknowledge with gratitude support received
from the James Hardiman Library Special Research Fund of the
National University of Ireland, Galway.

This publication was grant-aided by the Publications Fund of
National University of Ireland, Galway.

British Library Cataloguing in Publication Data
A catalogue record for this book is available from the British Library

Library of Congress Cataloging-in-Publication Data
Crosson, Seán.
  Sport and film / Seán Crosson. – 1st ed.
      p. cm.
  1. Sports in motion pictures. I. Title.
  PN1995.9.S67C76 2013
  791.43´6579-dc23   2012043000

ISBN: 978-0-415-56992-7 (hbk)
ISBN: 978-0-415-56993-4 (pbk)
ISBN: 978-0-203-85842-4 (ebk)

Typeset in Bembo
by HWA Text and Data Management, London

MIX
Paper from
responsible sources
FSC
www.fsc.org   FSC® C018575

Printed and bound in Great Britain by MPG Printgroup

CONTENTS

FIGURES

ACKNOWLEDGEMENTS

The research and writing of this book would not have been possible without the support of friends and colleagues in the National University of Ireland, Galway and further afield. Since joining the staff of NUI Galway, I have been the fortunate beneficiary of a positive research support culture including as a recipient of the University's Millennium Minor Project fund which facilitated my initial research in the area of sport and film. NUI Galway also generously contributed to the publication of this book through the Grant-in-Aid of Publications Fund and through the James Hardiman Library Special Research Fund. I would also like to acknowledge the support of colleagues within the School of Humanities and across the College of Arts, Social Sciences and Celtic Studies in the University in particular Philip Dine for his invaluable advice and collaboration on previous sport-related symposia and publications. Within the Huston School of Film & Digital Media where this research was undertaken I am grateful to my colleagues Rod Stoneman, Tony Tracy, Conn Holohan and Dee Quinn for their support in the development of my research. Others who assisted in the completion of this book and to whom I am also grateful include Charles Barr, Marcus Free, Charles I. Armstrong, Liam Burke, Joshua Wells, Simon Whitmore, John Hodgson and Kyle Duggan at Routledge, Amba Horton and Cheryl Thomas at Kobal, Darragh Crosson (for helping me track down those hard to find films), Alan Bairner, Mike Cronin, Dónal McAnallen, David Doyle (for first suggesting I look at the area of sport and film), Ruth Barton, Vincent G. Munley, Paul Rouse, Anna Bold, Garrett Shea, Tommy McNulty, Nick J. Watson, Richard Holt, Werner Huber, Bruce Babington and Joseph McBride. I would also like to thank my parents for their support down through the years and my partner Anne Karhio for her patience and encouragement during the research and completion of this book.

INTRODUCTION

Why sport and film?

> Its drama, its personalities and its worldwide appeal means sport is the new Hollywood.
>
> Bell and Campbell (1999, p. 22)

Sport has developed over the twentieth century and into the twenty-first to become one of the most important and influential of contemporary cultural practices. While sport may appear to many as a trivial distraction, it has grown to have huge economic, cultural and on occasion political importance in people's lives. Indeed, sport has evolved into a popular metaphor for life itself. There are few other cultural practices that have provided as many idioms now used widely in everyday life and outside the sporting contexts in which they first emerged, particularly in the English language. These idioms have come from a variety of sports including horse-racing ('down to the wire', 'home stretch'), baseball, rugby, or American football ('drop the ball'), cricket ('hat-trick'), and association football ('move the goalposts'). Many have emerged from boxing, including 'come out fighting', 'down and out', 'out for the count', 'the gloves are off', 'go the distance', 'have someone in your corner', 'heavy hitter', 'heavyweight', 'hit below the belt', 'infighting', 'K.O.', 'lightweight', 'on the ropes' and 'saved by the bell'.

While boxing has arguably provided more idioms than any other sport to the English language, it is also the sport that has featured most commonly in film. Filmmakers have commented on the allegorical role of boxing with Martin Scorsese describing boxing as basically

> just an allegory for the theatre of life ... you get in the ring and you try to survive or you're on the attack, you're on the defensive, you're on

the offensive, to many people in life … life is that struggle, and there's a struggle everyday in one way or another.

(2004)

This theme of struggle, and the perceived role of sport as a means of overcoming, has been one of the most popular subjects of the sports film.

Despite the emergence of later audio-visual forms such as television and the internet and their popularisation during the late twentieth century, the cinema, in common with sport, also occupies a prominent role in people's lives today. While other audio-visual platforms may have contributed to the decrease in the numbers that attend the cinema regularly in the West, elsewhere cinema attendances continue to grow with audiences in excess of 65 million people attending the cinema weekly in India (Wright, 2006, p. 1). There are also signs in the West that cinema attendances are increasing. Indeed, given the fragmentation of audiences through the emergence of cable and satellite television and the exponential growth of television channels, cinema provides one of the few contemporary forms that still attracts huge audiences to a single cultural product. The success in 2010 of the film *Avatar*, the most commercially successful film of all time, indicates both the continuing popularity of the cinematic experience and its engagement of a mass, undifferentiated audience in a manner unusual in today's fragmented cultural milieu.

In some ways there are obvious attractions to sport that would seem at face value to make it the ideal subject for film. Sport attracts huge attention and is one of the most popular cultural practices internationally providing a crucial source of personal, communal, national and occasionally international identification. In its myriad forms, it offers both participative and viewing possibilities for billions daily. It crosses from the recreational to the political and has a unique ability to effect individual and collective actions. Indeed, as will be considered in Chapter 6, sport can have a powerful role in affirming national identities and furthermore can have nationalistic and political reverberations beyond the sporting events themselves as evidenced most famously in the four-day war – often referred to as the 'Football War' – that broke out between Honduras and El Salvador in July 1969, the catalyst for which was the qualifying games for the 1970 FIFA World Cup the previous month between these two countries, and their representation in each country's media (Kapuscinki, 1990). The extent of the sponsorship by leading sporting, food and drink, and clothing companies of major sporting events is indicative of its importance commercially not to mention the huge role that sport plays in the media internationally such that, as Boyle and Haynes contend, '[s]port and the media are now integral components of what we often called the entertainment or cultural industries' (2000, p. xi). There are also aesthetic and structural parallels, as Chapter 1 outlines, between sport and film including the ability of both to evoke intense emotional responses and to possess dramatic possibilities realised in film through the manipulation of its various fundamentals including cinematography, sound and editing.

Modern sport and the cinema both emerged contemporaneously towards the end of the nineteenth century. The first modern Olympic Games were held in Athens in April 1896, only four months after the Lumière brothers gave the first public screening to a paying Paris audience of their new invention, the 'cinématographe'. It is significant that these two pivotal events in modern cultural history occurred in the space of less than half a year. The beginnings of the art form that would eventually become popularly known as 'film', 'the movies' or 'the cinema' is inextricably linked with sport. Indeed, sport, as a widespread cultural practice with a well-established following internationally, had a vital role in popularising the new medium of film, a topic explored further in Chapter 2.

The development of both sport and film also reflected the substantial changes that the Western World in particular was undergoing in the late nineteenth century. As the industrialisation and modernisation process developed apace and Western countries became increasingly urbanised, the need to provide structured leisure for such rapidly changing societies became evermore pressing. As noted by Johnny Waterson and Lindie Naughton,

> Sport as we know it is a Victorian invention, a by-product of the move off the land. Town life, by its very nature, created rules and couldn't afford to be governed solely by the weather and the seasons. There was also less space and in the cramped towns of the nineteenth century, sporting activities became restricted to strictly confined areas. Later, as the working hours became shorter, Victorians began looking for something to do in their time off. The result was a dramatic growth in all kinds of activities and 'hobbies' from the Salvation Army and brass bands, to music halls and horse racing.
>
> (1992, p. 3)

For many people, sport in its various forms particularly as it became codified and commercialised, provided a crucial source of both participative and entertainment possibilities.

Understandings of sport also changed significantly during the eighteenth and nineteenth centuries. As Ikuo Abe has observed, the description of 'sport' in English and American dictionaries was confined principally to the predominantly upper-class 'skills in the field, like riding and hunting' until the 1880s and 1890s when this term began to be applied more generally to athletic 'or physically competitive activities' (1988, pp. 3, 24). The changing application of the term reflected what Norbert Elias has described as a process of 'sportization' (Elias, 1986, p.151) involving the codification of sports during the mid- to late-nineteenth century as institutionalisation and bureaucratic organisation along with 'rational calculation in the pursuit of goals, emphasis on task performance, and seriousness' would come to 'distinguish sport from other types of physical activities such as play, recreation, and games' (Nixon, 1984, p. 13).

The institutionalisation of sport, including the formalisation of rules, and the establishment of national and regional sporting associations and authorities was also part of an attempt to control and ameliorate concerns and suspicions regarding sporting activities themselves. Sport was viewed with considerable suspicion in the nineteenth and early twentieth century, particularly among the Establishment of Europe and the United States who often regarded it as a valueless distraction associated with a range of vices including drinking, gambling and violence and 'at worst a manifestation of cultural decline and barbarism' (Gruneau, 1993, p. 86). However, the very development of modernity and capitalism, and the attendant problems they gave rise to, including the fragmentation and attenuation of traditional communities and beliefs, contributed to a re-evaluation of sport and the role that it might play in society. In this context, issues of personal and social advancement became increasingly important and sport was deemed to have an important role to play in their development. Sport's role in these respects has been traced through the influence of British public schools and imperialism, and French romanticism in the nineteenth century (Holt, 1990, pp. 74–85).

In the United States, the growing realisation of the importance of sport has been linked to fears around national weakness and a belief in the ability of sport to produce men of action (Streible, 2008, p. 11). Particularly from the 1850s onwards, with the advent of intercollegiate competitions in boat racing and subsequently baseball, athletics and American football, sport came to play an increasingly prominent role in American society and culture. For those in positions of authority, sports became much more than diversions from study; as in the development of sport in the British public school system, they were promoted as a means of instilling discipline and imparting leadership and an appreciation of the value of teamwork in students while affirming the social barriers that distinguished these students from working-class men (Corn and Goldstein, 1993, pp. 147–148). Sport was also viewed by influential figures such as president Theodore Roosevelt in the 1890s as a means of sustaining the dominance of White Anglo-Saxon men at a time when immigrants, African Americans and women played more prominent and influential roles in American life (Umphlett, 1984, p. 34).

However, there were further impulses at work that were related to the very nature of capitalism itself and the discontinuities and disruptions it gave rise to. For Marxists in particular, sport has often been viewed warily as a crucial part of the ideological state apparatus through which ideology[1] interpellates individuals as subjects within the social system (Althusser, 1972, p. 173). For Louis Althusser, sport was one of the ideological state apparatuses or 'number of realities which present themselves to the immediate observer in the form of distinct and specialized institutions' (1972, p. 143). These apparatuses are particularly effective because they do not function primarily by force but rather through ideology creating individuals as 'self-recognized cultural subjects' (Tudor, 1997, p. xvii).

One of the most influential political thinkers for Marxist readings of sport and society, including the work of Louis Althusser, is the Italian political philosopher Antonio Gramsci. Arguably Gramsci's greatest contribution to the evolution and nuancing of Marxist thought was his analysis of the role ideology plays in society. Rather than seeing the functioning of power in society as being principally the result of force and coercion, Gramsci saw power functioning in much more subtle ways through ideological control that maintained and prolonged the prevailing structures of domination and subjugation. Power, Gramsci contended, was maintained by two forces in society, direct domination through coercive forces such as the army and police, or the more subtle, though equally, if not more effective, processes of ideological control that saw people give their consent to systems that ultimately contributed to their repression. For Gramsci the second element was crucial to the maintenance of control in any society as coercion was rarely sufficient to such a task (Gramsci, 1971).

For Gramsci a fundamental aim of a State is 'to raise the great mass of the population to a particular cultural and moral level, a level (or type) which corresponds to the needs of the productive forces for development, and hence to the interests of the ruling class' (1971, p. 258). A crucial concept in this respect for Gramsci was cultural hegemony which referred to the maintenance of control of one social class over others through the diffusion of a complete system of beliefs, ethics, values and ways of thinking throughout particular societies that ultimately becomes the 'organising principle' that supports the existing power structures. These ideas on all aspects of life ultimately work to support the ruling elite and become accepted as the prevailing 'common sense' (Boggs, 1976, p. 39) or, as Geoffrey Nowell-Smith contends, 'the way a subordinate class lives its subordination' (cited in Alvarado and Boyd-Barrett, 1992, p. 51).

What Gramsci described as 'common sense', Roland Barthes referred to as 'bourgeois norms' (1957, p. 140) while for Althusser it was 'obviousness' (1972, p. 171), a crucial tool in the maintenance of hegemonic power. However, as Gramsci observed, 'common sense is not something rigid and immobile, but is continually transforming itself' (Gramsci, cited in Hall, 1982, p. 73). Drawing on Gramsci's ideas, John Fiske summarises that

> Consent must be constantly won and rewon, for people's material social experience constantly reminds them of the disadvantages of subordination and thus poses a threat to the dominant class ... Hegemony ... posits a constant contradiction between ideology and the social experience of the subordinate that makes this interface into an inevitable site of ideological struggle.
>
> (1992, p. 291)

It is in this context that sport, film and the media more generally play a central role both as a means of maintaining hegemonic power but also as sites revealing the tensions inherent in its maintenance. The codification and development of sport in the late nineteenth century reflected the functioning of hegemonic forces in society at that time concerned with affirming and promoting particular values more generally but 'in ways that privileged the material resources, cultural competencies, and preferred beliefs of European and North American males from a particular class' (Gruneau, 1993, p. 97). As such, the codification of sport could be viewed as part of a desire to control and provide continuity for societies in a period marked by considerable discontinuity. While the old certainties of place, identity and religion were increasingly problematised with the rapid escalation of modernisation, sport contributed to their reconstruction. As new communities emerged in the rapidly growing urban centres, sport provided people with a sense of identity through their identification with particular athletes and teams and a sense of belonging and community through sharing their sporting experiences with others. Sport, in a manner comparable to religion historically, over time became 'loaded with symbolism, imagery, myths, rituals; in short, the meaning-making apparatus that we associate with any other area of cultural life' (Cashmore, 2000, p. ix).

Film too would come to hold a crucial role in people's lives. Indeed, Andrew Sarris has described most Hollywood films by the 1930s as 'semi-religious light shows built around the rituals of family and courtship' (1998, p. 15). This focus on the ritual function of film has preoccupied one major strand of critical discourse concerning the emergence of genres in cinema (discussed further in Chapter 3) with Rick Altman contending that

> By choosing the films it would patronize, the audience revealed its preferences and its beliefs, thus inducing Hollywood studios to produce films reflecting its desires. Participation in the genre film experience thus reinforces spectator expectations and desires. Far from being limited to mere entertainment, filmgoing offers a satisfaction more akin to that associated with established religion.
>
> (1984, p. 9)

The satisfaction found by audiences in film has been described by Richard Dyer (1977) as a 'utopian sensibility', a sensibility that is shared by followers of sport. Sport maps a utopian space beyond the challenges of everyday life. While sport evolved in form and practice during the nineteenth century, it maintained and developed a central powerful appeal. Sport provides utopian possibilities that can transcend the sometimes tarnished and challenging present, and past, circumstances of those who engage in sporting activities or follow those who are. Indeed, the origins of one of the largest global sporting events, the Olympic Games, lay precisely in a belief in the utopian potential of sport. For the founder of the modern Olympics, Baron Pierre de Coubertin, 'sports were offered as a peaceable lingua franca, a means by which the people of different nations could communicate and cooperate in a manner that would lessen the likelihood of war between "alien" entities' (Rowe, 1998, p. 352).

Drawing on the definition offered by Dyer in his influential essay on 'Entertainment and Utopia', this study suggests that it is the utopian sensibility that both sport and film offer, as popular forms of entertainment, that are their most seductive qualities. As Dyer observes,

> Entertainment offers the image of 'something better' to escape into, or something we want deeply that our day-to-day lives don't provide … Entertainment does not, however, present models of utopian worlds … Rather the utopianism is contained in the feelings it embodies. It presents, head-on as it were, what utopia would feel like rather than how it would be organized. It thus works at the level of sensibility, by which I mean an effective code that is characteristic of, and largely specific to, a given mode of cultural production.
>
> (1977, p. 373)

In commentary on sport by those long engaged – and possibly obsessed – by it, one encounters descriptions that repeatedly affirm the powerful utopian feelings sport evokes. As Nick Hornby writes in his book *Fever Pitch* as a fan of English association football club Arsenal:

> please, be tolerant of those who describe a sporting moment as their best ever. We do not lack imagination, nor have we had sad and barren lives; it is just that real life is paler, duller, and contains less potential for unexpected delirium.
>
> (1992, p. 6)

Similarly, for Chief Sports Writer of *The Times*, Simon Barnes,

> Sport is such stuff as daydreams are made of, for sure; but it's also the stuff of real dreams … Like dreams, sport can bring us the most ecstatic and profoundly felt pleasures, and can also bring us matters so complex and confusing that we don't know how to react to them. Sport can deliver those moments we thought only possible in fiction or daydream, but with a visceral intensity that no amount of private musing can rival.
>
> (2006, p. 166)

For followers of individual athletes or teams, competition and the possibility of victory – and its enjoyment – allows them to step outside what may be challenging, or possibly unsatisfactory lives, to experience intense emotions rarely found elsewhere. This experience can be brief, and may only last for the duration of a single competitive event, but nonetheless for millions of people engaged with sport, it is very real. It is, as Dyer describes, a feeling, but one, as Barnes continues, of 'visceral intensity', and few cultural forms have the emotional impact on people's lives of sport, a factor exploited readily by directors of sports films. This is particularly evident in the frequent, and often highly emotionally manipulative, final fight, game, or race scene found at the climax of so many sports films.

Indeed, film has a powerful ability, inherited and developed by other audio-visual forms such as television and the internet, to preserve, elevate and slow down the utopian moment in sport; not just to capture it for perpetuity, but to transform that moment. As André Bazin noted, the photographic image 'embalms time' and film adds to this property 'the image of their duration, change mummified as it were' (1960, p. 8). As a seductive and powerfully influential form, film's fundamentals – including as discussed in Chapter 1, narrative, mise-en-scène, cinematography, editing and sound – provide powerful tools for exploiting sport's utopian sensibilities.

Hollywood sports films in particular, which have been most influential for the form internationally and constitute the largest number of such films produced, are characterised by this utopian sensibility. As David Rowe has summarised in Hollywood sports films customarily 'all manner of social, structural, and cultural conflicts and divisions are resolved through the fantastic agency of sports' (1998, p. 355). What these films frequently offer is an idealised view of sport providing an overly simplistic solution to real social problems. However, this trajectory also includes a commitment to the social structures that have ultimately perpetuated social inequality. As Aaron Baker has argued in his study of the American sports film, drawing on the work of Richard Dyer,

> the conservatism of utopian entertainment comes from the way it offers representations of a better life if we just follow the rules and try harder. In other words, not only does such utopian entertainment avoid suggesting specific ways to change the current social reality, it promises us happiness by adhering to the status quo … this utopian response only works if one ignores – as entertainment almost always does – how social identities such as race, class, gender, and sexuality complicate self-definition. On the contrary, the acknowledgement of social forces in the constitution of identity makes evident that the opportunity, abundance, and happiness in utopian narratives are not there for everyone to the same degree. Even when sports movies acknowledge the disadvantage of racism, sexism, or class difference (homophobia is still widely ignored), individual performance is generally held up as the best way to overcome this influence.
>
> (2003, p. 13)

Despite this predominant 'utopian narrative', mainstream sports films nonetheless reveal recurring tensions and contradictions. While many of these films may ultimately affirm the American Dream of opportunity, upward social mobility and material success (discussed further in Chapter 4), they also contain elements that have the potential to unsettle or destabilise this trajectory. This is a feature of populist entertainment more generally whereby its polysemy or strategic ambiguity provides multiple points of identification only to ultimately attempt to contain these in the interests of affirming hegemonic values and order. As noted by Slavoj Žižek,

To work, the ruling ideology has to incorporate a series of features in which the exploited majority will be able to recognize its authentic longings. In other words, each hegemonic universality has to incorporate at least two particular contents, the authentic popular content as well as its distortion by the relations of domination and exploitation ... How did Christianity become the ruling ideology? By incorporating a series of crucial motifs and aspirations of the oppressed – truth is on the side of the suffering and humiliated, power corrupts, and so on – and rearticulating them in such a way that they became compatible with the existing relations of domination.

(1997, pp. 29–30)

Hence, mainstream sports cinema may depict racial, social class or gender issues, as part of its appeal to a mass audience, but these issues are rarely engaged with critically or provided with a social or historical context. Rather, they are used to appeal to the 'authentic longings' of the marginalised, as a means to ultimately affirm the structures that perpetuate their marginalisation. This tendency is found particularly in the most commercially successful sports films, a theme explored in more detail in Chapters 4 and 5.

The following six chapters and conclusion will provide an overview of the historical development and ideological importance of the sports film. While the focus will principally be on mainstream fiction films that have emerged from the United States, and Hollywood in particular, given the influence and popularity of work emerging from that source, consideration will also be given to sports films that have arisen from other national contexts in Chapter 6. As an introduction to the subject, this book is far from comprehensive with regard to either sports films or the examination of pertinent themes therein. It is unlikely that any single volume could accomplish this task. Indeed, there is at least material for a single monograph (and possibly several) dedicated to each of the themes considered, and others not, in this book. The Internet Movie Database (IMDb) lists over 1,000 sports feature films produced in the United States alone with almost 750 more produced internationally. These figures relate to fiction films only; details of in excess of 2,800 sport-themed documentaries are available on IMDb though this is likely to be a considerable underestimate of the total given the popularity of sports-themed documentaries on television internationally.

Therefore, this book examines but a small fraction of the total. The themes examined in this book are also by no means exhaustive. Other themes that deserve consideration include sexuality, religion and disability to name but three; while aspects of each are touched upon in this study, their prominence and complexity merit more substantial and in-depth consideration. Furthermore, a dedicated study of the sports documentary film – touched on in Chapter 3 – is well overdue. However, from the hundreds of sports films viewed during the research towards the completion of this book, this study attempts to chart some of the recurring features and themes found across these works. The films chosen to examine, particularly in Chapters 4–6, are among the most commercially and/or critically successful sports films produced; their popularity challenges scholars to consider not just the reason for their appeal but also what function these films may play in popular culture. As scholars of both media and cultural studies have contended, film is a significant mediator of social relations through the naturalisation of cultural norms including those concerning race, social class and gender (Croteau and Hoynes, 2003; Schirato and Webb, 2004; Boyle, Millington, and Vertinsky, 2006, p. 110). Sport has also been recognised as playing a crucial and comparable role in each of these areas (Jones, 1992; Gruneau, 1999; Scraton and Flintoff, 2002; Smith, 2009). A central argument returned to repeatedly in this book – whether in terms of its analysis of race and social class (Chapter 4), or gender (Chapter 5) – is the important role the sports film plays in the affirmation of the American Dream ideology and the maintenance of patriarchal hegemony. This dream is by no means confined to the United States; as Chapter 6 contends, such has been the popularity and influence of Hollywood cinema that sports films that have emerged in other national contexts frequently share characteristics with American films, including the utopian trajectory found therein. However, Chapter 6 will also consider instances that challenge both the utopian trajectory and hegemonic national structures. The phenomenon of the post-9/11 Hollywood sports film will be considered in the concluding chapter; the films examined here provide a useful case study to summarise the continuing appeal and importance of the mainstream sports film in popular culture today.

1

READING THE SPORTS FILM

To raise the issue of how to 'read film', may appear to some superfluous. Film seems so accessible and immediate a form that the notion that people require guidance in understanding its message, or 'language', may appear both patronising and peculiar. Indeed, the seeming simplicity of film and its apparent lack of ambiguity when compared with other art forms have contributed considerably to its popularity. Allied to this has been the driving force within commercial film-making practice since its first appearance: greater verisimilitude, or the ability to represent the world as we know it as closely as possible to its actual appearance in reality. As James Monaco has noted, the placing of film among the recording arts reflects its ability to 'provide a more direct path between subject and observer' (2000, p. 27). However, film's popularity is not just because of its ability to render reality as we know it; films have been carefully designed to evoke responses from viewers, a process that has developed substantially since the first moving picture images flickered across screens in the mid-1890s. These designs are dependant on decisions regarding the form and style of a particular film, decisions that encompass stylistic techniques crucial to the realisation of film including narrative, mise-en-scène, cinematography, editing and sound. Decisions on each of these techniques are themselves influenced by financial, social, cultural and sometimes political considerations. Furthermore, due to its powerful potential to affect viewers by dynamically engaging their expectations and emotions, film can itself have an impact in some or all of these areas. Indeed, given all of this, commercial cinema in general, and Hollywood cinema in particular, might be more correctly described in Rick Altman's terms as 'a deceptively obvious cinema' (1999, p. 135).

Form and style in film

Film's success and its engagement of audiences depend on the successful creation of a pattern, or form, by those responsible for the production of a film. This pattern can be described as a film's form and it responds to, and exploits, the natural human inclination to seek a structured experience in what we encounter (Bordwell and Thompson, 2010, p. 56). To understand form in film, therefore, an important starting point is those who perceive the films themselves, the audience. Films encourage, or cue, us to make connections, identify significant moments and recognise important references and often our enjoyment, or otherwise, of a film will depend on how well a particular film succeeds in doing so. The attraction of sport, therefore, for filmmakers is immediately apparent as one of the most popular cultural practices, in all its various forms, in everyday life across the world. Indeed, as Poulton and Roderick observe, 'sport offers everything a good story should have: heroes and villains, triumph and disaster, achievement and despair, tension and drama. Consequently, sport makes for a compelling film narrative and films, in turn, are a vivid medium for sport' (2008, p. 107).

A film's form can be described as 'the overall system of relations that we can perceive among the elements in the whole film' (Bordwell and Thompson, 2010, p. 57). This system is composed of narrative elements (the film's story) and stylistic elements, including a film's mise-en-scène, cinematography, editing and sound. It also depends on audience expectations as audiences naturally seek some sense of order, coherence and continuity in cultural forms including film. Films, however, play with audience expectations regarding formal patterns and sometimes a film's success is contributed to by the manner in which it departs in surprising or unexpected ways from established formal conventions. Over time, dominant styles or traditions emerge in films, sometimes coalescing into rules or conventions that dictate much of what happens in a particular film. These conventions are crucial to the emergence of film genres, such as the sports film genre, marked by familiar and recurring tropes, characters and locales and recurring patterns of storytelling. This includes the familiar final big game or athletic contest found towards the end of many sports films. Films and filmmakers are also influenced by previous films and patterns of storytelling, as well as patterns found in other art forms. An audience's prior experience and familiarity with specific conventions in film will cue them as well to respond in particular ways to subsequent films.

Narrative

A crucial part of a film's form is its narrative. Film narrative can be described as 'a chain of events linked by cause and effect and occurring in time and space' (Bordwell and Thompson, 2010, p. 79). This approach to narrative is commonly associated with Hollywood film, though, as we will see below, there are alternate ways of understanding how narrative functions within Hollywood, and particularly genre, film. Narrative is composed principally of two elements, story and plot. While the story refers to all the events, both those screened in the film and inferred by it, the plot refers only to what we are visibly and audibly presented with within the film itself. One of the most basic narrative patterns found in many artworks is the three-act structure. It is a structure that can be found as far back as Greek theatre and the writings of Aristotle who described a good story as having a beginning, a middle and an end. These sections comprised a work's *exposition* – its opening in which characters and background information are introduced as well as, later on, the main *conflict* that provides the central concern of the second part (or middle) of the film before moving towards some *resolution* in the final part (the end) (Sikov, 2010, p. 105). This very loosely defined structure has been modified to describe films with Richard Barsam suggesting a five-part structure as characteristic of commercial, and particularly Hollywood, cinema. This includes *exposition, rising action* ('the principal conflict develops and may be complicated by the introduction of related secondary conflicts'), *climax* ('the turning point'), *falling action* ('the principal conflict moves towards resolution') and *denouement* ('everything is made clear and no questions or surprises remain') (2007, p. 59). Codified sport provides a very appropriate and attractive subject for such a structure with most sporting contests – from basketball, to association football, American football or baseball – containing within them elements of this structure. This includes exposition, with the introduction of both teams and players at the beginning of games both in match programmes and by announcers and commentators at the games themselves and through the media; rising action, as the game develops and the key conflicts emerge between individual players and the teams as a whole; the climax of a game can come with the scoring of a crucial penalty in a soccer game or a touchdown that turns the game in favour of one team or another; the falling action frequently follows this as one team consolidates their winning position; while the denouement arrives at the end of the game when the winners or losers are clearly identified on the scoreboard. As with film, this pattern is not always precisely followed, and a sporting contest, much as with a film, may have several climaxes – or its climax may occur towards the end rather than in the middle, of the film. Alternatively, some films may refuse the denouement and leave the ending open-ended with no clear resolution, much as some sporting events may not result in clear winners or losers but in a drawn contest. However, this structure remains remarkably popular in both Hollywood films and in sporting contests. Film and sport both provide familiar narratives and structures but it's the ability to rework and the possibility of surprising twists and turns that are among the main attractions for audiences of both.

A film's narrative is a crucial part of its appeal. Prior familiarity with the story to be found in the film can be an added attraction for audiences, as in biopics of sporting heroes such as Lou Gehrig (*The Pride of the Yankees* (1942)), Muhammad Ali (*Ali* (2001)), or Maurice Richard (*Maurice Richard* (2005)). Beyond stories we are familiar with, we may also have expectations about the theme of the narrative, how the narrative will be structured or the types of incidents we may encounter in a particular film, often flagged by the titles of film genres such as comedy, thriller or musical. The sports film genre will be considered in more detail in Chapter 3 but for the moment it is worth noting a significant parallel between genre – a crucial aspect of popular filmmaking – and sport. Much as sport has been described as taking place 'within limits set in explicit and formal rules governing role and position relationships' (Edwards, 1973, pp. 57–58), Thomas Schatz has defined film genre as 'a specific grammar or system of rules of expression and construction and the individual genre film as a manifestation of these rules' (1991, p. 644). However, as noted above, it is the ability of individual genre films to rework the expectations of the genre that can often be among the most appealing characteristics of individual films, much as the enjoyment of sport depends significantly, for spectators, on its unpredictability.

Crucial to the development of most commercial film narratives is causality. Why did Rocky fight for the world heavyweight title? Because Apollo Creed wanted to give a no-hoper a crack at his crown after his intended opponent pulled out of a heavyweight bout due to injury. In most films, it is the characters that are the agents of cause and effect. As in real life, we seek to identify traits of characters in films, traits that often have a crucial bearing on the action in the film. As Bordwell and Thompson observe, most 'patterns of plot development depend heavily on the ways that causes and effects create a change in a character's situation. The most common general pattern is a *change in knowledge*' (2010, p. 91). A very popular pattern of development in Hollywood and commercial film is the goal-orientated plot in which a character or characters attempt to achieve specific goals or outcomes. This goal or 'heroic quest' structure, has a precedent in ancient Greek ritual drama and sacred games (Edinger, 1976, p. 68; Tudor, 1997, p. 6) and has been identified by David Mosher as contributing to 'a romantic impulse that is the essence of both sport and culture' (1983, p. 16). Furthermore, many sports films lead 'to a climactic struggle between hero and villain and conclude with the exaltation of the hero' (Mosher, 1983, p. 16). Sport, therefore, provides an obvious setting to find such goal-orientated characters. Whether based on individual athletes, or teams, most sports films are focused on the attempts of the central protagonists to achieve a particular goal – Olympic glory (*Chariots of Fire* (1981)), Grand National victory (*National Velvet* (1944)) or the state championship (*Hoosiers* (1986)) to name but a few – providing appealing material for one of the most popular and recognisable plot patterns in commercial film. A goal-orientated plot is also often combined with others, including those provided by time and space as in the documentary *Hoop Dreams* (1994) which is structured around the high school careers of its two main protagonists and their attempts to become professional basketball players.

Specific expectations are created as a result of patterns of plot development. The decline of a boxer, for example, is often marked by his physical and sometimes moral deterioration between fights and we are cued to expect his eventual defeat in the ring. When a sporting contest is announced in a film, we anticipate its eventual occurrence and the attempts of the central protagonists to achieve victory, as in the announcement of the upcoming Little 500 race in *Breaking Away* (1979). However, an expected or hoped-for outcome is typically delayed along the way, as in Dave Stoller's (Dennis Christopher) disillusionment in *Breaking Away* with cycling and threat to not enter the Little 500 after being unfairly forced out of an earlier race by a professional Italian team.

Although a huge number of narrative structures are possible, a single tradition of narrative form has dominated fiction filmmaking, a mode referred to as classical Hollywood filmmaking. Though associated with Hollywood, the centre that developed and popularised the form most successfully, the form is found in national cinemas internationally. Even documentary, as identified increasingly by commentators (Morrison, 2004; Arthur, 2005; McDonald, 2007), often draws on conventions associated with this form. A fundamental requirement in this form is that

> action will spring primarily from individual characters as causal agents. Natural causes (floods, earthquakes) or societal causes (institutions, wars, economic depressions) may affect the action, but the narrative centers on personal psychological causes: decisions, choices, and traits of character.
> (Bordwell and Thompson, 2010, p. 102)

A central impetus in this form is the desire of a central character, for example for sporting success, a desire which sets up a central goal which shapes the narrative of the film. In this form, the central character's attempt to achieve his/her goal is not straightforward or unchallenged, and typically an opponent with their own goals and traits is encountered creating a conflict. Again sport provides ready-made material for such a form. The protagonist must engage with this opposition, and hopefully overcome in order to achieve his/her goal. The central dynamic of cause and effect in this form implies change and typically characters undergo some change and development over the duration of the film. Following this trajectory, all other elements, including time and space, are subordinated to the cause–effect chain in the classical Hollywood form.[1]

However, while the cause and effect dynamic is a crucial part of Hollywood film, it isn't the only way of understanding the appeal of these films. Rick Altman has argued that *fertile juxtaposition* is essential to the attraction of Hollywood film. Rather than seeing events in a film as part of a narrative chain, Altman contends that

> we have something more like a puzzle, where each piece is valorized not by a single cause and a single effect, but by several surrounding pieces. Typically treated according to a temporal (and linear) model, Hollywood narrative gains from being seen instead through the more complex and more open spatial model of juxtaposition. More akin to multiple-plot

medieval Grail romances and nineteenth-century serial novels than to the linear psychological novels on which most narrative theory has been based, Hollywood films gain much of their power from a careful interlacing of multiple characters, plots and themes.

(1999, p. 136)

Altman views the structure of Hollywood films as closer to 'the dual-focus configuration of melodrama than to the single-focus arrangement of Aristotelian narrative' and identifies 'generic crossroads' as crucial to their development, whereby rather than 'specific causes leading to necessary effects, culminating in a fully logical conclusion, generic situations offer instead a process of intensification and release'(1999, pp. 154–155). By this, Altman refers to the process whereby films continually offer possible directions in the narrative, routinely adopting unconventional or counter-cultural choices before eventually returning, and reaffirming, the hegemonic order. As he argues,

genres do sometimes deploy cause-and-effect logic, but primarily to cover up their principal strategy of offering an increasingly intense counter-cultural genre pleasure experience, only eventually to reverse that pattern and revert to cultural dominance … Returning to a culturally sanctioned position, the *in extremis* reversal characteristic of genre films produces further spectator pleasure while folding spectators back into cultural norms.

(1999, pp. 155, 165)

As considered later in this study the mainstream sports film also fits within this pattern delineated by Altman, providing the viewer with recurring moments of counter-cultural pleasure – through the depiction, for example, of the corruption surrounding boxing or the immoral actions of athletes – before customarily reaffirming hegemonic cultural norms by the film's conclusion.

While form and narrative are crucial to conceptions of cinema, in order to further understand film, we must go beyond these aspects to explore those techniques that give shape to individual films. These include principally mise-en-scène, cinematography, sound and editing, and the combined and integrated use of such technical choices comprises a film's style.

Mise-en-scène

Mise-en-scène refers to 'the director's control over what appears in the film frame … setting, lighting, costume, and the behaviour of figures' (Bordwell and Thompson, 2010, p. 118). Filmmakers may either use already existing settings or construct a setting appropriate to the film they are trying to make. The former became particularly apparent in the post-World War II period, influenced by the emergence of Italian neo-realism and its use of on-location shooting in films such as *Roma, città aperta* (*Rome, Open City* 1945), while the latter owes a debt to the earliest imaginative film work of French director George Méliès, including the pioneering science-fiction film *Le voyage dans la lune* (*A Trip to the Moon* 1902). With the advent of digital technology, imagined worlds have become more and more significant, particularly in science-fiction films, such as *Rollerball* (2002) and *Real Steel* (2011), each of which depict fictional sports in futuristic imagined contexts.

Lighting is a crucial aspect of mise-en-scène and can be characterised according to its quality, direction, source and colour. Fictional films tend to use more lighting than documentaries to control the look of the film, but usually used subtly in order to suggest that lighting comes from the source evident in the shot and in keeping with the diegesis, the film's story world (Bordwell and Thompson, 2010, pp. 132–134). A film's lighting can create powerful effects for the viewer and should not be underestimated in analyses of films. A pertinent example is the sophisticated use of lighting combined with black-and-white photography found in Martin Scorsese's *Raging Bull* (1980). The film moves between brightly lit and elegant sequences, using high key lighting, to low key lighting scenes of boxing itself in the ring to complement the brutality depicted.

Costumes and makeup also play an important part in adding authenticity to a character within a film – for example, the sharp suits of Jerry Maguire (Tom Cruise) at the beginning of *Jerry Maguire* (1996) are transformed into more casual clothing (Fig. 1.1) as he comes to identify with his working class secretary, Dorothy Boyd (Renée Zellweger), and questions the ethos of the industry of

FIGURE 1.1 *Jerry Maguire* (TriStar Pictures, 1996) (Columbia Tri Star/The Kobal Collection)

which he is part. Indeed, costumes have a particularly important role to play in sports films in distinguishing and identifying prominent characters within particular settings, such as footballers or basketball players.

A further important element of mise-en-scène is staging, the process by which a director controls the movement and actions of the figures in the mise-en-scène. Actors playing roles is the most familiar aspect of staging; their performances include both visual (expressions and appearance) and sound (voice) aspects. Genre films in particular are heavily dependent on familiar stereotypes where characters, as Grant observes, 'are more often recognisable types rather than psychologically complex characters' (2006, p. 17), and hence the popularity of familiar figures such as the Irish cop, the Black servant or, in the sports film, the corrupt promoter and the inspirational coach.

Cinematography

When we examine mise-en-scène we are concerned with *what* is filmed; however filmmakers also have control over *how* a particular scene is filmed through cinematography and the control of the photographic elements of the shot, its framing and its duration. There are a number of aspects to the photographic image itself including the range of tonalities, the speed of motion and perspective. Through his manipulation of film stock, exposure and developing processes, a filmmaker can dictate the visual qualities of the film image. The ability to control speed of motion by filmmakers has a particular relevance to the filming of sport, as evident in the frequent use of slow motion to replay an athlete's performance. Indeed, as Bordwell and Thompson observe, audiences are arguably most 'familiar with freeze-framing, slow-motion, and reverse-motion printing effects from the *instant replays* of sports coverage and investigative documentaries' (2010, p. 173).

Apart from the photographic aspects of the shot, a second important feature of how a film is filmed involves the framing of the shot. It is the frame that defines the image we see in a film in terms of its shape and size and the delineation of onscreen and offscreen space. Finally, as well as manipulating the elements within a shot, the director also controls the length of time a shot lasts for. While short takes – shots of short duration – predominate in commercial filmmaking, the long take is also an important part of filming that can depict the progression of events through time without the intervention of editing.

Sound

While it is important to read films in terms of the visuals we see – an aspect mostly prioritised in analyses and criticisms of cinema – a significant influence on how we engage with film is the sounds we hear, as manipulated and subject to the preferences of directors in fiction film in particular as the visuals. Developments and improvements in sound design and performance since the 1970s have resulted in the complex sound systems found in cinemas today as well as advanced home theatre audio systems that have encouraged audience expectations of increasingly sophisticated soundscapes in films. A film's soundtrack has a crucial impact on perceptions and interpretations of the subject depicted, all the more so as audiences tend to underestimate the role of sound. This is particularly the case with regard to the popular sports film; the emotional and visceral impact of popular films such as *Rocky* (1976), *Miracle* (2004) or *The Blind Side* (2009) owe a great deal to the strategic employment of music, music that may cloud audiences' ability to critically engage with the depictions themselves, an issue explored further in Chapter 4. While sound can actively influence how we interpret images, it can also direct our attention within the image itself or cue us to form expectations. Furthermore, sound can provide similar possibilities to editing in giving wholeness to disparate images and sequences in films through a continuous and coherent soundtrack.

As with many of the visual aspects of film the aural properties also build on expectations people carry from their everyday life. These include the loudness, pitch ('perceived highness or lowness of a sound'), and timbre ('color, or tone quality') of sounds (Bordwell and Thompson, 2010, p. 273). Sound in film also has a spatial dimension as it originates from a source. This source can be diegetic, originating in the film's story world, or it may be non-diegetic, as in the case of most music we encounter in cinema, which usually does not have a source in the world of the film itself.

Editing

Particularly since the emergence of the Soviet school of filmmaking in the 1920s, editing has been viewed as one of the most important elements of filmmaking. Filmmakers have four principal choices in editing, to exploit graphic, rhythmic, spatial or temporal relations between shots. In films featuring sport, editing has a particularly significant role to play. One of the most famous examples here is the diving sequence from Leni Riefenstahl's *Olympia* (1938) which created a beautifully choreographed ballet from the diving competition at the 1936 Berlin Olympics through the manipulation of editing, including playing dives backwards and accelerated cutting.

Defined as 'the coordination of one shot with the next', through effects such as a fade-out (darkening the end of the shot), a fade-in (brightening a shot from black), a dissolve (superimposing the end of one shot over the beginning of the next) or the wipe (replacing one shot with another by a line moving across the screen), film editors create rich effects, as well as subtle, and sometimes more abrupt, changes in a film's development (Bordwell and Thompson, 2010, p. 223). Most commonly shots are joined in film by a cut, whereby one shot is instantaneously replaced by another, a transition often barely perceptible to the viewer in the continuity editing style popularised by Hollywood cinema.

Indeed, a crucial element in the realisation of the classical Hollywood style is editing. As cinema moved from merely capturing aspects of everyday life – in the actuality films of the late nineteenth century – to telling stories in the first decade of the twentieth, a style of editing emerged, assisted by particular approaches to mise-en-scène, cinematography and sound, to ensure narrative continuity. This style became known as continuity editing and was principally concerned with permitting space, time and action to flow as seamlessly as possible over a series of shots. As noted by Bordwell and Thompson,

> All the possibilities of editing ... are turned to this end. First, graphic qualities are usually kept roughly continuous from shot to shot. The figures are balanced and symmetrically deployed in the frame; the overall lighting tonality remains constant; the action occupies the central zone of the screen.
>
> Second, the rhythm of the cutting is usually made dependent on the camera distance of the shot. Long shots are left on the screen longer than medium shots, and medium shots are left on longer than close-ups. The assumption is that the spectator needs more time to take in the shots containing more details ... Since the continuity style seeks to present a story, it's chiefly through the handling of space and time that editing furthers narrative continuity.
>
> (2010, p. 236)

The continuity style dictates a number of spatial and stylistic rules including the construction of the space of scenes along an axis of action known as the 180° line that may not be crossed during a scene; moving the camera at least 30° between successive shots of the same subject; and the exploitation of patterns such as the establishing shot, shot/reverse-shot sequence, eyeline match, re-establishing shot and match on action. By following these dictates, directors can affirm the continuity style and narrative continuity in a film. Rick Altman has argued that the development of this style was due to a concern to 'restore the sensation of presence' to the film-going experience as audiences became increasingly removed physically, and in terms of subject matter, from the themes of individual films. The earliest productions were often focused on filming face-to-face events and were comprised largely of locally shot footage, the screening of which audiences would attend in the hope of seeing themselves or acquaintances on the screen. As noted by Altman, 'moving pictures thus constituted an illustrated extension of the letter and a storable version of face-to-face contact. Initially conceived as memories of real experiences, films were designed to be shown only to friends of the figures on the screen' (1999, p. 185).

However, with the increasing narrativisation of cinema, editing techniques developed to restore the sensation of presence evident in an earlier period. While the camera shot aspects of everyday life in the earliest films, recording what it encountered, gradually the camera came to be located so that it could stand in for a character, and through such characters, for prospective spectators. As Altman observes,

> Through an increasingly complex and standardized pattern of shot/reverse shots and point-of-view shots, narrative films succeeded in providing a specific place for the viewer, albeit not specific to any particular viewer. Eventually codified and consecrated in the Hollywood classical narrative technique of suture, this process simplified the producer's task (it is easier to edit an anonymous viewer into the fabric of every film than to shoot footage of each town on your exhibition route), while directly addressing spectator regret at the loss of presence.
>
> (1999, p. 187)

This technique was complemented by the development of popular film genres, discussed at more length in Chapter 3, which also performed a similar function by providing audiences with familiar and recognisable narratives and characters.

A prominent technique in the Hollywood continuity style is parallel editing or crosscutting, one frequently used in sports films. As Bordwell and Thompson summarise,

> Crosscutting gives us an unrestricted knowledge of causal, temporal, or spatial information by alternating shots from one line of action in one place with shots of other events in other places. Crosscutting thus creates some spatial discontinuity, but it binds the action together by creating a sense of cause and effect and simultaneous time. In *Jerry Maguire*, for example, crosscutting interweaves the action of sports agent Jerry and his rival racing to sign up the same clients.
>
> (2010, p. 248)

Continuity editing is concerned with disguising and effacing the strategies and techniques that go into creating a film. It is a vital part of a film's successful attainment of verisimilitude and is dependent on audiences' prior familiarity with the form. However, this concern with verisimilitude also obscures the political and ideological messages within individual films, further obfuscated by the frequent foregrounding of emotionally charged personal themes.

Sport provides an attractive form for filmmakers exploiting continuity editing in their work. Through live coverage of sporting events on television, audiences have become accustomed to expect the use of continuity editing, moving from one angle to another and matching shots closely to follow the play as it progresses. However, the exploitation of the continuity style in sports films has ideological consequences. This is particularly the case in biopics or films based on actual sporting events where individual performance is prioritised in works that exploit a realist aesthetic while disavowing their constructed nature. As Aaron Baker contends,

These cinematic contests are frequently narrated by announcers in the style of television or radio coverage and shown with a continuity editing style that makes the sequence of shots seem motivated by the logic of the events rather than the choices of filmmakers. For historical sports films this representational style has special resonance because it recalls real events in sports 'history': athletic contests that the audience has witnessed in the past. Heightened realism in scenes in which the star competes is especially important in validating an ideology of agency that assumes that individual performance in these situations counts most in making the athlete what he is.

(2003, p. 13)

Baker's comments suggest the social and cultural significance of films beyond their role as forms of entertainment. Films have meanings and these range from referential to explicit, implicit and symptomatic. While referential meanings refer to the obvious concrete plot features of the film itself, the explicit meaning might be termed the moral or central message of the film. Implicit meanings, however, are less concrete and not directly stated and depend heavily on the interpretation of viewers. Unlike referential and explicit meanings, there can be much variation in the implicit meanings viewers find in a film, but they all respond to potentials inherent in the form of the film itself and larger values in a society. As noted by Bordwell and Thompson,

it's possible to understand a film's explicit or implicit meanings as bearing traces of a particular set of social values. We can call this symptomatic meaning, and the set of values that get revealed can be considered a social *ideology*.

(2010, p. 65)

Symptomatic meanings are crucial to understanding the role of sport in film. Sports-themed films exploit and evoke responses from viewers not just as a result of the powerful effects that film as a form in and of itself can produce, but also from the associations that sport already has in particular societies. Sport in the United States, for example, is associated with a central ideology in American life, the American Dream. As Howard L. Nixon has argued,

The pursuit of the American dream of achievement, mobility, and success continues to be a major driving force in the lives of the majority of Americans ... Sport seems the ideal vehicle for understanding the pursuit of the American dream both because achievement and success are so openly and explicitly emphasized in sport, and because the rags to riches story so often seems to be told by the contemporary mass media with sports figures as the main characters.

(1984, pp. 6–10)

This ideology of the American Dream, explored at more length in Chapter 4, is a powerful and influential belief that is affirmed for many Americans through their experience of sport. Yet, as its frequent description as a 'Dream factory' may suggest, Hollywood films are also associated with the promotion of dreams, dreams that can be all the more powerful when associated with sport. Therefore, to understand and appreciate the role of film and a film's form – and by extension the role sport plays in film – one must consider the social context from which and within which a film emerges and circulates. This has been one of the major concerns of scholars of film particularly since the 1960s and is evident in the development of critical and theoretical approaches to film.

Film theory

Despite sport being one of the earliest subjects of film, in both non-fiction and fiction forms, academic engagement with these representations has been slow to develop. This is partly due to the path that critical and theoretical approaches to film took from early in the twentieth century. Indeed, because of film's initial consideration as a 'lower' form of entertainment, to some extent as considered in Chapter 2 because of its association with perceived 'lesser' sports such as boxing, much of the early writings on film were concerned with advocating for a degree of respectability for this new cultural form. Proponents also argued for film's particularity as a form with a separate aesthetic of its own, beyond those cultural forms and practices with which it was associated. Early theorists such as Vachel Lindsay, Hugo Münsterberg and Rudolf Arnheim sought to identify film's own distinctiveness, as more than just a format for adapting established arts such as literature and theatre (Monaco, 2000, pp. 391–394).

As film theory developed in the twentieth century, like practice, approaches divided roughly along realist and expressionist lines. While the former approach has been concerned primarily with prioritising the raw material captured by the filmmaker, the latter emphasised the expressive possibilities of film as realised by the ability of the filmmaker to manipulate or modify the world captured on film. Indeed, these sensibilities are apparent from the earliest days of cinema and are often associated with the differing approaches to film of pioneering figures such as Auguste and Louis Lumière and George Méliès (Monaco, 2000, p. 395).

In the 1920s and 1930s, expressionist approaches to film remained to the fore. Whether in Hollywood cinema or German Expressionism, filmmakers and theorists of the early twentieth century emphasised the great experience of the cinema above all and were more concerned with various ways of evoking reactions from their audience than with the active involvement, or otherwise, of the spectator in the movie-going experience. As outlined in Chapter 2, sport would have a role to play in this 'cinema of attractions' (Gunning, 1986, pp. 63–70) particularly as it provided ready-made attractions for audience amusement. With the advent of the British documentary school under John Grierson in the 1930s and particularly the influence of Italian neo-realism in the 1940s and

1950s, realism would come to play an increasingly important role both in film practice and in theoretical approaches to film.

In asserting film's distinctiveness as an art form, early theorists placed great emphasis on the role of editing or *montage*, particularly in the Soviet Union in the 1920s and 1930s. Filmmakers such as Vsevolod Pudovkin, Sergei Eisenstein and Dziga Vertov not only produced some of the most significant films of these decades, they were also responsible for an important body of theoretical writing that reflected on the form of film itself and their formalist studies would have profound influence on the development of cinema subsequently. For each of these filmmakers, their ideas concerning film developed particularly from their formative experiences editing found film clips and led to the development of their respective theories of montage, that regarded editing or the '*juxtaposition* of fragments' (Eisenstein, Pudovkin and Alexandrov, 1928, p. 361) as central to the art of cinema.[2] The efforts of these Soviet filmmakers were focused above all – as theorists in the West increasingly would be – on identifying a specific language of film. Indeed, Dziga Vertov's masterpiece *Man with a Movie Camera* (1929) was centrally concerned with 'the creation of an authentically international absolute language of cinema' – as the opening credits to the film declared – a language that would not be dependent on previous art forms in literature, art or the theatre. Vertov was also interested in finding truth through the camera eye; *Kino Pravda* (literally 'cinema truth') was the title of the newsreel he produced for several years in the 1920s and his ideas would be very influential for subsequent international film movements and theorists, above all in France in the 1950s and 1960s.

The 1950s onwards has been a particularly fertile period for the development of film theory. Facilitated by the popularisation of film festivals and societies and the increasing acceptance of film internationally as an academic discipline, a broad and varied range of approaches to film developed drawing inspiration from developments more generally in academia in diverse areas such as psychoanalytic analysis, linguistics, cognitive psychology, social anthropology, Marxism and feminism. Second wave feminists in particular by the 1970s drew on this broad range of disciplines to raise questions regarding the 'male gaze' in mainstream cinema and the often problematic positioning of female characters, issues relevant to the development of the sports film as outlined in Chapter 5.

One of the most influential approaches to emerge in the 1950s and 1960s was auteur theory. In France in this period, filmmakers such as Jean-Luc Godard, François Truffaut, Eric Rohmer and Claude Chabrol in their work and contributions to the seminal journal *Cahiers du cinéma* advocated for the director as the author of their work. 'La politique des auteurs' or auteur theory was described by *Cahier*'s co-founder André Bazin as consisting 'of choosing the personal factor in artistic creation as a standard of reference, and then of assuming that it continues and even progresses from one film to the next' (1957, p. 255). As this approach prioritised the role of the filmmaker above the subject matter of individual films, the sports film would therefore rarely feature as a concern of those critics to adopt this focus.

Structuralist approaches to culture and society also came to prominence in the mid-twentieth century, including in the anthropological work of Claude Lévi-Strauss and it is not surprising that film too would become subject to structuralist readings. Structuralism is an approach that examines the deep structuring logic of cultural practices and products. Its roots are found in the work of Swiss linguist Ferdinard de Saussure who argued that language could be studied as a formal system of differential elements. Closely related to structuralism is semiotics, the theory and study of symbols and signs, particularly as components of language or other communication systems. French theorist Christian Metz pioneered the application of de Saussure's theories to film, arguing that film was a logical entity that could be examined using scientific techniques, a belief he developed in his influential works *Language and Cinema* (1974) and *Film Language: A Semiotics of the Cinema* (1974). A semiotics of the cinema refers to a 'theory of film-as-a-system-of-signs' (Harman, 1975, p. 90) and Metz's approach was concerned primarily with how specific films, particularly narrative feature films, have importance and meaning for audiences (Harman, 1975, p. 90). As he argued '*it was precisely to the extent that the cinema confronted the problems of narration* that, in the course of successive groupings, it came to produce a body of specific signifying procedures' (Metz, 1974b, p. 95).

Metz identified a system of codes and signs in film that have become normalised over time as cinematic conventions understood by both those who produce and those who consume film. Indeed, the existence of film genres is the most recognisable example of how a particular and recognisable 'language' has evolved in cinema, including around the representation of sport. Metz also recognised the manner through which audiences brought their own cultural influences and previous experiences of film to understandings of cinema and how these afilmic cultural significations intrude on films (1974b, p. 140). This focus reflects a movement from the 1960s onwards in film theory from the focus on the film text itself to its perception. As Monaco observes, 'The center of interest has shifted from generative to receptive theories. We are now no longer so concerned with how a film is made as with how it is perceived and what effect it has in our lives' (2000, p. 395).

Genre theory

This concern with audiences is particularly apparent within genre approaches to film, approaches also influenced by structuralism. For Rick Altman

> If it is not defined by the industry and recognized by the mass audience, then it cannot be a genre, because film genres are by definition not just scientifically derived or theoretically constructed categories, but are always industrially certified and publicly shared.
>
> (1999, p. 16)

Two important critical currents came to prominence in the 1960s and 1970s in genre theory. Drawing on the work of Claude Lévi-Strauss in particular, a *ritual* approach emerged that viewed genre as a type of societal self-expression 'directly addressing the society's constitutive contradictions' (Altman, 1999, p. 26). However, an ideological approach also developed, influenced particularly by the work of Louis Althusser that 'demonstrated the ideological investment that governments and industries place in the symbolic and representational systems that they produce' (Altman, 1999, p. 26). While the ritual approach viewed audiences as the principle creators of genres, with their forms emerging from existing social practices, ideological critics saw genres instead as 'the vehicle for a government's address to its citizens/subjects or an industry's appeal to its clients' (Altman, 1999, p. 27). As Altman observes,

> Whereas ritual critics interpret narrative situations and structural relations as offering *imaginative* solutions to a society's real problems, ideological critics see the same situations and structures as luring audiences into accepting *deceptive* non-solutions, while all the time serving governmental or industry purposes. Here too, genres have a particular role and importance, for it is through generic conventions that audiences are lured into false assumptions of societal unity and future happiness.
>
> (1999, p. 27)

This latter approach was particularly influenced by the work of the Frankfurt school of writers such as Theodor Adorno, as well as the work of Roland Barthes who viewed genres and popular culture in general as tools for the maintenance of hegemonic power. This study is informed in particular by Rick Altman's contention that it is possible to see value in both the ritual and ideological approaches in understanding the popularity of genre, and indeed of the sports genre itself; that is, that the existence of a particular genre depends on its ability to serve both a ritual and ideological function for a society:

> Though an individual film may have a single (albeit usually collaborative) author, genres always depend on decoding practices shared by a broad if dispersed community. This double authorship prompts genres to lay claim simultaneously to both positions, both ideological and ritual.
>
> (Altman, 1999, pp. 172–173)

As genre theory grew in influence in film studies, the sports film genre would eventually become the subject of increasing attention, particularly since the early 1980s. From Manchel's *Great Sports Movies* (1980) to Bergan's *Sports in the Movies* (1982), Wallenfeldt's *Sports Movies* (1989), Williams' *Sports Cinema* (2006), Didinger and Macnow's *The Ultimate Book of Sports Movies* (2009) and Edgington, Erskine and Welsh's *Encyclopedia of Sports Films* (2010), successive authors have contributed to the recognition of the sports film genre, a subject considered in more detail in Chapter 3.

Post-structuralism

The emergence of post-structuralism in the 1960s had an important influence on the development of theoretical approaches to film and eventually on the sports film itself. In particular, Roland Barthes' work further moved the focus of examination from the text and its production – be that print, photographic or filmic – to its consumption, arguing famously in his essay 'The Death of the Author' against a focus on authorial intent or the context of a book's production and for the importance of the interpretations of the reader, maintaining that 'a text's unity lies not in its origin but in its destination' (1977, p. 148). For Barthes and other post-structuralists such as Jacques Derrida, a text is composed not of a single or absolute meaning but rather 'of multiple writings, from many cultures and entering into mutual relations of dialogue, contestations' (Barthes, 1977, p. 148). For Derrida, examining a text involved a process of *deconstruction* to reveal the sometimes contradictory and unstable elements within (Johnson, 1980, p. 5).

Among Barthes' most influential publications was his 1957 book *Mythologies*, a work concerned with the meanings and mythologies that become associated with aspects of people's everyday life. The volume included two essays on sport, one on wrestling and one on the annual cycling race, the *Tour de France*. While wrestling for Barthes was not a sport but a 'spectacle of excess' comparable to classical theatre with an audience every bit as sophisticated as that which attended high art events, the *Tour de France* provided

> the best example we have ever encountered of a total, hence an ambiguous myth; the Tour is at once a myth of expression and a myth of projection, realistic and Utopian at the same time. The Tour expresses and liberates the French people through a unique fable in which the traditional impostures (psychology of essences, ethics of combat, magism of elements and forces, hierarchy of supermen and servants) mingle with forms of a positive interest, with the Utopian image of a world which stubbornly seeks reconciliation by the spectacle of a total clarity of relations between man, men, and Nature. What is vitiated in the Tour is the basis, the economic motives, the ultimate profit of the ordeal, generator of ideological alibis.
>
> (1979, p. 87)

As these remarks suggest, Barthes' interest was in how the mythologising of aspects of everyday life disguises their economic origins and ultimate ideological purpose. Barthes was particularly concerned with the manner through which the media depicts elements of everyday life, elevating some aspects to myth while disguising or eliding, as the quote above suggests, other issues, including history. As he wrote, 'Myth deprives the object of which it speaks of all History. In it, history evaporates' (1957, p. 151). This has been a recurring feature of the representation of sport in mainstream cinema where history does indeed, at times, appear to evaporate as narratives elevate individual performance as the principle means of overcoming adversity and achieving success.

Cultural studies

Barthes' writing has been particularly influential for the development of cultural studies. A crucial question for studies of the cinema is whether film is considered principally in terms of its existence as a form or in terms of its function, particularly as it impacts on culture and society. As noted above, formalist approaches have featured prominently in the development of critical approaches to film. However, for the purposes of this study, it is the function of film that is of principle concern particularly when it is combined with sport. It is here that cultural studies provides a useful methodology. Cultural studies draws on aspects of Marxist criticism, particularly as interpreted via the work of writers who emerged from the Frankfurt Institute of Social Research in Germany in the 1920s. Scholars such as Walter Benjamin, Erich Fromm, Siegfried Kracauer, Herbert Marcuse, Theodor Adorno and Max Horkheimer brought together aspects of sociology, politics, psychology and culture to examine the role of cultural products in society under the rubric of Critical Theory. While the origins of cultural studies can be traced to the work of the Frankfurt school, an important catalyst in the popularisation of this approach was the establishment of the Centre for Contemporary Cultural Studies (CCCS) at Birmingham in 1964 under the directorship initially of Richard Hoggart, but particularly his successor, Stuart Hall. Of critical importance to the work of Hall and other scholars emerging from the CCCS has been the writings of Italian political philosopher Antonio Gramsci and particularly his concept of cultural hegemony, discussed in the introduction to this study.

Cultural studies is concerned above all with the political character of culture. It is a methodological approach that allows us to encompass the broad range of issues relevant to sport in film and touched upon in this book, including ideology, race, social class, and gender. A central concern within cultural studies is the meanings particular cultural products, such as film, produce and how they are circulated and received. Cultural studies shares with film studies a concern with the textual analysis of popular forms and the historical context of their creation, and indeed there has been considerable cross-over here in terms of the works theorists in both areas have drawn on for their analysis. However, whereas film studies has tended to focus on the aesthetic value of individual films, cultural studies has been more concerned with the examination of 'the popularity of popular cinema' (Turner, 2000, pp. 196–197), within which we might include mainstream sports films. While individual sports films may be of limited or questionable aesthetic value, their very popularity requires us to examine further their prominence in contemporary society and the reasons for it. The interdisciplinary nature of cultural studies also makes it particularly appropriate to a study encompassing two popular cultural forms such as film and sport and this has been reflected in recent studies of sport in film informed by cultural studies, including Tudor's *Hollywood's Vision of Team Sports: Heroes, Race, and Gender* (1997), Baker's *Contesting Identities: Sports in American Film* (2003), and contributions to the collections *Out of Bounds: Sports, Media, and the Politics of Identity* (Baker et al., 1997), *Visual Economies of/in Motion: Sport and Film* (King and Leonard, 2006) and *All-Stars and Movie Stars: Sports in Film & History* (Leonard, 2008).

A recurring theme returned to in this work is the manner through which popular film displaces the causes of social conflict in works that ultimately attempt to affirm the hegemonic order. Film theorist Robert B. Ray has identified in classical Hollywood film, for example, the displacement of social issues into emotionally charged personal melodrama, a feature also apparent in many mainstream sports films (1985, p. 57). Furthermore, Ray identifies the resolving of contradictions and the overcoming of dichotomies as a central concern of Hollywood cinema where films may feature both an 'official' hero and an 'official' outlaw, the latter allowing audiences to vicariously experience the enjoyment of rebellion while the film as a whole maintains the status quo through the ultimate triumph of the official hero (1985, p. 55). Genre critics such as Robin Wood (1977, p. 720; 1985, p. 201) and Thomas Schatz (1991, p. 699) have also argued that a central concern of genre films is both the enactment of conflict between a dominant and oppositional value system and the eventual elimination or assimilation of the latter. This is a recurring feature of mainstream sports films which engage repeatedly in this process, foregrounding oppositional and counter-cultural elements before almost inevitably attempting to affirm the hegemonic order. Throughout this book, the development of this trope, its occasional contestation, as well as its frequent reaffirmation in mainstream sports films will be examined.

2

EARLY CINEMA AND THE EMERGENCE OF THE SPORTS FILM

The fortunes of the prize ring are apparently interwoven with those of the moving pictures. Without the moving picture your modern prize fight would be shorn of most of its financial glamour and possibilities; without the prize fight the moving picture would not appeal to so many people as it apparently does
'Pictures and Pugilism', *Moving Pictures World*, December 18, 1909[1]

In the late nineteenth century, when the first flickering cinematographic images appeared on screens in New York, Paris and London, film was viewed by many, including one of its pioneers Louis Lumière, as 'an invention without a future' (cited in Wolz, 2004, p. 3). Indeed, the beginnings of moving image technology were as much a product of scientific curiosity as of cultural advancement, a curiosity that had an important sporting significance. In 1870s France, the pioneering gymnast Georges Demenÿ assisted French scientist Étienne-Jules Marey in his early experiments at capturing movement photographically, including serving as the subject for Marey's work (Braun, 1992, pp. 66–67). In the same period in the United States, attempts to capture motion in photography, in the work of English photographer Eadweard Muybridge, were also focused on sport, including images featuring members of the Olympic Athletic Club based in San Francisco engaged in various athletic activities from boxing to jumping (Clegg, 2007, p. 137).

Muybridge's photographs, including those commissioned by American industrialist and politician Leland Stanford of a trotting horse (Fig. 2.1), are today viewed as a forerunner to what would become motion picture technology in the 1890s. However, these efforts were concerned as much with demonstrating the technology used to capture animal and human movements as with the subjects of these depictions. As John Ott contends 'Leland Stanford and his advocates

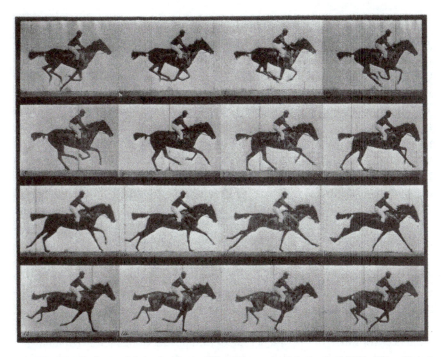

FIGURE 2.1 Eadweard Muybridge's 'The Horse in Motion' (1878) (The Kobal Collection)

publicly staged and disseminated these photographs in order to consolidate, promote, and naturalise the developments of industrial capitalism' (2005, p. 407). The emergence of cinema itself was due to similar impulses and, as will be considered later in this book, the representation of sport in mainstream cinema continues to respond to comparable concerns. The nineteenth century was marked by rapid changes in society influenced by the changing nature of production that the industrial revolution brought: capitalism advanced and technology rapidly developed. The arrival of the train and other modern modes of transportation, including the bicycle and eventually the automobile, facilitated the increasingly swift movement of people over longer distances as well as within the rapidly growing urban communities. The rising availability of mass-produced goods and services revolutionised economies and people's everyday experiences while the advent of the telegraph, the telephone and the radio facilitated communication on a scale never experienced before. These advances in communications in particular would have a considerable influence on the development of sport allowing for its transformation from local pastimes to national obsessions written extensively about in the expanding press, with dedicated sporting publications emerging in countries across the Western World by the end of the nineteenth century. Sport would be prime material, therefore, in the mid-1890s to extend the popularity of this new moving image technology.

In its earliest incarnations, this new invention wooed audiences with its ability to capture aspects of their daily lives with a degree of verisimilitude previously unknown. However, its development beyond a mere 'fad' as Charlie Chaplin described it at one point (cited in Kaufman, 2008, p. 70) depended in its earliest years on its pioneers capturing aspects of popular culture that already attracted significant interest. Studies of intermediality, for example, have noted the crucial role established cultural practices, including sport, played in the earliest years of moving image entertainment before cinema was recognised as an important and distinctive cultural form in its own right, a form that would subsequently influence the development of the practices it depicted (Gaudreault, 2000, pp. 8–15). Indeed, in its earliest incarnations, film comprised above all, as Gunning has observed, a 'cinema of attractions' where actuality films, bringing moments from everyday life and exotic scenes from all over the world, dominated film production up to at least 1906.

Sport played a crucial role in these early days and, as Luke McKernan has observed, 'represented the changeover from film as a medium of scientific study to a medium of entertainment' (1996, p. 109). While the new moving image technology may have attracted audiences for its novelty at its first screenings, it was sport, and particularly boxing in the United States, that continued to attract audiences for much of the first decade of film production. McKernan identifies in the early boxing films 'the very birth of American cinema realism and drama, newsfilm and fakery, commercialism, populism, professionalism, two protagonists battling within the perfect staging, the ring' (1996, p. 110). Indeed, the first feature-length films, the first use of actors and the first commercial cinema exhibitions in the United States were all of boxing films.

The cinema would also play an important role in the modernisation, popularisation and, indeed, legitimisation of boxing, a sport renowned for its corruption and violence in the nineteenth century (Streible, 2008, p. 13). From the production of the earliest 'prize fight' films, legal action against the producers and those involved in the production was always a very real threat, with prize fighting in the late 1890s only legal in one state in the US, New York, where it would also be deemed illegal from 1900 onwards. The *Corbett–Fitzsimmons Fight* (1897), one of the most successful early fight films, was delayed repeatedly, mainly because of objections to boxing itself in several states where it was first proposed it be held and indeed, the eventual arrest of both 'Gentleman' Jim Corbett and Bob Fitzsimmons in an attempt to prevent the fight going ahead.

Much as attempts were made to prevent the Corbett–Fitzsimmons fight from happening in the first instance, efforts were also made to censor the film of it including a proposed bill – that eventually failed – in the United States Congress to ban the distribution or exhibition of fight pictures. Indeed, while boxing is associated with the beginnings of the cinema, it also marks the beginnings of film censorship. In the US, ten state legislatures banned fight pictures as did Canada (Streible, 2008, pp. 62–63) while fight films would also be the subject of some of the first attempts at film censorship internationally. In Ireland, the first major controversy regarding the cinema concerned the screening of the 1910 world heavyweight bout between James J. Jeffries and the African American Jack Johnson which prominent Irish political and religious figures tried to have banned (Rockett, 2004, pp. 31–35). These bans were ineffective, however, given the huge popularity of boxing in this period and, indeed, the challenge of defining what exactly film was, as a very new medium taking various forms. Film pioneer Thomas Edison's own concerns about the impact of prize fights on his reputation led to his subcontracting of fight films from the mid-1890s onwards to companies such as the Kinetoscope Exhibition Company, allowing him to disavow direct involvement in the productions (Streible, 2008, p. 34). Nonetheless, despite legal and moral concerns, such was the popularity of the fight film genre that from the arrival of cinema, most heavyweight champions won their titles in front of motion-picture cameras. Motion pictures also mediated the experience of watching fights and thereby, by screening fights in areas away from the blood and sweat of the original encounter, brought increased success for the fighters themselves and new audiences to boxing, including women.

Concerns regarding the violence and illegality associated with boxing were somewhat diffused through the large number of comic boxing-themed films produced in the early years of the cinema, including *Comedy Set-To* (1898), *Chuck Connors vs. Chin Ong* (1899), *Gordon Sisters Boxing* (1901), *Boxing in Barrels* (1901), *A Scrap in Black and White* (1903), *The Last Round Ended in a Free Fight* (1903), *Prof. Langtry's Boxing School* (1903) and *A Couple of Lightweights at Coney Island* (1904). These films represent the beginnings on film of the knockabout comedy boxing films in which Charlie Chaplin in particular would excel in later decades.

Boxing was not the only sport that provided comic material in the early years of the cinema. While the earliest examples lacked the sophistication of comedy sports films by Chaplin, Harold Lloyd, Buster Keaton or the Marx Brothers in later years, as early as 1899, a short baseball comedy, *Casey at the Bat* (1899), was directed by James H. White for the Edison Manufacturing Company. Anticipating what would become one of the most popular sub-genres of the sports film, the comedy sports film attracted the attentions of some of the leading early directors including Edwin S. Porter who directed a further baseball themed comedy *How the Office Boy Saw the Ball Game* (1906). Indeed, apart from boxing, baseball was one of the most popular subjects in the early silent period of American cinema, reflecting its popularity as the national team sport in the United States in the early twentieth century ('Baseball Films of the Silent Era'; Edelman, 2007, p. 22). Filmmakers attempted to recreate the excitement of the game in film while also giving audiences a chance to see some of their favourite players heroicised on the big screen. Films ranged from newsreel inserts, to cameo appearances in short films to 'highly fictionalized "biographical" features in which scenarists transformed ballplayers into fairy-tale heroes' (Edelman,

FIGURE 2.2 Babe Ruth as himself (on the right) in the popular Harold Lloyd film *Speedy* (Paramount Pictures, 1928) (Paramount/The Kobal Collection)

2007, p. 22). These films tended to elevate rural and pastoral existence and small-town life over the urban and to represent nostalgic narratives for a 'time of innocence, a pre-Jazz Age America that was a nation of small towns and small-town types' (Edelman, 2007, p. 22). Baseball film narratives, however, in the silent era were predictable and the characters simply drawn with baseball stars sometimes featured playing one-dimensional good guys who manage to win the girl and overcome the evil antagonist, as in the 1920 feature *Headin' Home* which starred the legendary baseball player Babe Ruth in the lead role.

Ruth, one of the most prolific hitters in Major League baseball history, featured in a series of films during his time playing in the Majors, particularly after his move from the Boston Red Sox to the New York Yankees in 1919. In these films, Ruth always played himself or characters loosely based on his star persona, including in *Headin' Home, Babe Comes Home* (1927) and the Harold Lloyd box-office hit *Speedy* (1928) (Fig. 2.2). As with other films featuring sporting celebrities, these works exploited Babe's iconic status for their appeal while contributing to his 'ruthian' image and affirming the American Dream in the process. Indeed, as Rader contends, Ruth himself had a unique ability to

> project multiple images of brute power, the natural uninhibited man and
> the fulfilment of the American success dream. Ruth was living proof that

the lone individual could still rise from mean, vulgar beginnings to fame and fortune, to a position of public recognition equalled by few men in American history.

(2008, p. 130)

Headin' Home was an early representative example of the mass-marketing of baseball. It was released as a showcase film and screened in the largest and most prestigious venues of the day, including the 10,000-seater Madison Square Garden (Trimble, 1996, pp. 51–52). The Garden screening was a huge media event, that included, according to contemporary reports, 'a circus-like atmosphere' with 'numerous items being sold during the show, everything from Babe Ruth autographs and records to sheet music for a song called "Oh, You Babe Ruth" which Tim Bryan and his band played over and over again' (Trimble, 1996, p. 52).

Ruth played himself in *Headin' Home* in this entirely fictionalised account of his life in which he rises from humble small-town beginnings in the 'little egg and hamlet in the sticks' Haverlock where he is mocked for his clumsiness, to star player with the New York Yankees. This theme of the seeming simpleton with limited apparent ability overcoming the odds and turning out to be a gifted athlete would be a recurring trope of many subsequent productions, including more recent films such as *Forrest Gump* (1994) and *The Waterboy* (1998). It provides a powerful affirmation again of the American Dream ideology suggesting that even for those of seeming limited intelligence the dream remains a possibility, particularly if they show a talent for sport. While *Headin' Home* is a much sanitised version of Babe's life, depicting him as coming from a loving home – rather than the more difficult childhood he actually experienced in a Baltimore reformatory – the trajectory of rags-to-riches is nonetheless to the fore while the film emphasises Babe's moral character in his supportive relationship with his widowed mother and foster sister 'Pigtails'. These themes were particularly important for audiences in the 1920s. For Patrick Trimble

> *Headin' Home* and its surrounding publicity perpetuated the cultural image of Babe Ruth as an American success story. His individualism and hedonistic sense of self-fulfilment were an affirmation of many of the personal values that were most admired in a cultural celebrity during the 1920's. The public perceived that his humble beginnings created strong moral fiber, while individual ability and courage provided personal growth and financial well-being.

(1996, p. 53)

Other sports depicted during the first three decades of cinema included American football, hockey, athletic meetings, automobile racing, boating events, golf, and fencing. These films were not all American, and while the Edison Manufacturing Company and other American producers chose boxing as the subject of many of their earliest films, in Britain other sports would feature in the work of the pioneers of British film, Birt Acres and Robert W. Paul. Two of their earliest films were *The Oxford and Cambridge University Boat Race* (1895) and *Derby* (1895), the latter including footage of the Epsom horse racing Derby of that year. According to Luke McKernan, *Derby* 'was shown in music halls within a day of the race having been run, and its ecstatic reception announced the arrival of moving pictures in Great Britain' (2005, p. 875). Indeed, sport would feature regularly throughout the early silent period in Britain, including – as well as horse racing – films of water polo, polo, the quintessentially English sport of cricket, and association football. Many of these films were produced by the British Mutoscope & Biograph Company, whose technical manager and cameraman was William K.L. Dickson, director of some of the earliest moving image work for the Edison Manufacturing Company (Brown and Anthony, 1999).

While other sports did feature, there were aesthetic – as well as cultural – reasons why boxing, particularly in American cinema, was the most popular sporting subject in the early days of cinema. The fixed camera position and limited movement in early cinematography meant that trying to film sports in which participants ranged widely on the field of play was difficult and much less successful. Early examples of this challenge include the Edison Manufacturing Company's *Hockey Match on the Ice* (1898) directed by William Heise, in which we only see players competing for the hockey puck when it is directly in front of the camera, and where much of the short film features players waiting for the puck to return after it has gone to the right of the camera's position. This is also the case with Robert Paul's 1896 footage of the Epsom Derby, *The Derby*, where we have again a fixed camera position capturing horses as they canter by at the end of the race before crowds move onto the track. While both these surviving films may well be but extracts of what were originally longer actualities, the limitations on camera movement are clear. However, the boxing ring by its nature limited the movements of the fighters and ensured both energetic and often entertaining moments for the spectators.

Outside the United States, boxing-themed films were made in the formative years of cinema in other countries, including Britain, France and Germany. French pioneers the Lumière brothers produced *A Friendly Boxing Match* (1896) and the comedy boxing short *Boxeurs un tonneaux* in 1898 (Musser, 1994, p. 140). One of German film pioneer Max Skladanowsky's earliest films, *Das boxende Känguruh* (1897), featured a man sparring with a kangaroo while Birt Acres also featured a boxing kangaroo in an early film, *The Boxing Kangaroo* (1896). Given its popularity in Britain throughout the nineteenth century, it is not surprising to find boxing also featuring in these formative years of British filmmaking, including Acre's *Boxing Match; or, Glove Contest* (1896) and *A Prize Fight by Jem Mace and Burke* (1896) and Robert W. Paul's *Pocket Boxers* (1903). However, films of prize fights, and sport in general, were not as popular in other contexts as in the United States. As Dan Streible notes 'Among the Lumière subjects of the 1890s, numbering more than one thousand, only one, Pedlar Palmer v. Donovan, shot in England, was a fight picture; two were fistic burlesques done by clowns' (2008, p. 48). Indeed, although the Lumières sent out camera operators across Europe and as far east as Russia throughout the 1890s, they did not consider one of the most significant sporting events of this period worthy of filming, the revival of the Olympic Games in Athens in 1896.

There was a further distinctiveness to the American experience. Where boxing featured in early German, French and British actualities, these films tended to have generic titles, as indicated above. However, American fight films generally foreground the boxers participating in the contests featured in order to build on their popularity already with the general public (Streible, 2008, pp. 31–32). Indeed, we might see in these early American films a precursor to the star system that would play such a central part in the evolution of Hollywood cinema throughout the next century. Boxer Jim Corbett has been described as the first 'movie star' signing a film contract after his retirement from professional boxing and appearing in a series of shorts as himself before starring in feature films including *The Burglar and the Lady* (1914), *The Other Girl* (1916) and *The Prince from Avenue A* (1920) (Edgington, Erskine and Welsh, 2010, p. viii).

Prize fight films and technological innovations in cinema

Even before the first public projections of film to audiences, the early experiments to capture movement on film in Thomas Edison's laboratories in West Orange, New Jersey, featured athletes and sporting contests. Primarily due to the efforts of William K.L. Dickson, who directed most of the early Edison company films, a rudimentary motor-powered camera called the Kinotograph was invented in late 1890, and the first experimental films were shot the following year in 1891. Among these early films made in 1891 was one short entitled *Men Boxing*, directed by Dickson and William Heise. While this early film featured two Edison employees, the era of filming professional boxers in action began with the film of a boxing exhibition match between Mike Leonard and Jack Cushing (1894), fought in Edison's film production studio, the Black Maria. These early Edison films were viewed via a peep-show-like machine called the Kinetoscope, where viewers could pay to see footage of each round. However, pressures to realise the full potential of boxing on film expedited attempts in the United States to produce the first projector for a general screening. This was eventually developed, initially called the 'Panoptikon', by a company formed by Woodville Latham and his two sons, Otway and Gray, and for their first public demonstration, they got two well-known boxers, Albert 'Young Griffo' Griffiths and 'Battling' Charles Barnett to re-enact a fight they had had in Madison Square Garden on May 4, 1895. The popularity of the *Young Griffo v. Battling Charles Barnett* (1895) film ensured that re-enactments of major fights would continue to be a popular subject of film for the decade that followed. The film, regarded as the first to be screened to a paying audience in the United States, was projected on May 20 at a Broadway storefront theatre by the Latham's renamed 'eidoloscope' and subsequently toured the US. As Dan Streible notes

> in 1895–96, fight pictures emerged as the first genre of moving pictures to be distinguished by special forms of production and presentation … Why did boxing and cinema develop this interrelationship? … The most important determinant … was sociological. In the 1890s, prizefighting and filmmaking shared a milieu: an urban, male community known to its contemporaries as the 'sporting and theatrical' world.
>
> (2008, p. 23)

The Lathams in particular were one of the earliest groups to dedicate themselves entirely to prize fight films. Their dedication would lead to significant advances more generally in film technology. As well as developing the technology to project films, they also acquired a number of Edison's cameras and increased their capacity to film and the quality of the work projected in order to better capture prize fights and exploit their commercial possibilities. In conjunction with former Edison employee Eugene Lauste, as well as director William K.L. Dickson, they made a critical technological breakthrough with the development of the 'Latham Loop', which 'enabled cameras and projectors to handle longer films' (Streible, 2008, p. 45).

It has been claimed that Enoch J. Rector, who worked for some time with the Latham's Kinetoscope Exhibition Company (later called the Lambda Company), had an important role to play in the development of this technology (Ramsaye, 1926, p. 125). He was certainly the first director to make the most extensive and successful use of it when he directed the filming of the world heavyweight championship bout between the then champion 'Gentleman' Jim Corbett and Bob Fitzsimmons on March 17, 1897 (Fig. 2.3). The filming of the fight required the development of cameras capable of capturing each of the fourteen three-minute rounds and the footage, shot on 63 mm film and running in total for 100 minutes, is regarded as the first 'widescreen' and 'feature-length' film. The production of the film would also be significant in terms of editing. Actuality films prior to *The Corbett–Fitzsimmons Fight* tended to be short, consisting of single shots from a fixed camera position. However, at 100 minutes in length, *The Corbett–Fitzsimmons Fight* required significant editing on a scale never before accomplished in film. The fight was shot on three cameras, each of which had to be reloaded after six minutes, and Rector then edited the shots together to give continuous coverage of the fight itself. While these edits are quite crude, consisting of jump cuts as the footage of one camera came to an end and another camera's footage was chosen to follow the continuing fight, they nonetheless mark the beginning of what became a fundamental technique in film.

FIGURE 2.3   Photographic print from the 1897 'Gentleman' Jim Corbett–Bob Fitzsimmons boxing match.

The influence of prize fight films on boxing

The Corbett–Fitzsimmons Fight was the first true box office smash in the United States and internationally with the film reputedly taking a gross of $750,000 with a net profit of over $100,000 (Streible, 2008, p. 73). For the first time a full record of an individual fight was available and it began what is now the customary re-examination of fight footage fuelling disputes and controversies surrounding the fight itself, including the allegation that Corbett was struck by a foul blow from Fitzsimmons in the fourteenth round. These disputes were added to during the early years of cinema by a press keen to benefit from the film's popularity, including some press concerns which had a commercial interest in *The Corbett–Fitzsimmons Fight* film itself (Streible, 2008, pp. 73–74).

The filming of early fights such as that of Corbett and Fitzsimmons would also change forever the nature of boxing. The negotiation of the rights for the fight film, whereby the majority of the royalties was divided between the fight promoter Dan A. Stuart (30 per cent) and the film's director Rector (40 per cent), with the balance divided between the fighters themselves 'marked a turning point in the development of prizefighting' (Streible, 2008, p. 60; Musser, 1994, p. 84). Before the advent of cinema, ticket sales were rarely sufficient to cover the large payments given to boxers – profits depended on theatrical tours and betting. However, with films of the fights, a new source of revenue emerged that would be crucial to the profitability of fights subsequently and film rights would play an increasingly prominent role in fight negotiations in later years (Musser, 1994, p. 84). The presence of cameras and the filming of fights also affected boxing itself and, possibly, the performance of the boxers as the venue, ring, and surrounding auditorium were adapted in order to facilitate the best filming of the event. There were even suggestions that the length of the Corbett–Fitzsimmons championship bout was influenced by prior arrangements with Rector's Veriscope Company in order to ensure adequate footage for projection (Streible, 2008, pp. 60–62).

Prize fight films and the emergence of fiction cinema

One of the challenges in these early years, and concerns for viewers, was whether or not fights were actually legitimate contests or faked for the camera. Indeed, most fight films in the 1890s and early 1900s were actually faked, not just in the occasional re-enactment of famous contests by professional boxers themselves, but due to the limitations of lighting and filming which meant the boxers would have to adjust their position or their actions to suit both. This would also slow the acceptance of such fight pictures by a general public already suspicious of a sport associated with criminality and corruption. The two-month delay in exhibiting the film of the Corbett–Fitzsimmons fight, for example, first screened on May 22, 1897 at the New York Academy of Music, led to a large number of re-enactments being filmed and distributed, some of which claimed to be an 'exact reproduction of the encounter' (Streible, 2008, p. 67). However, these 'faked' films might be regarded as among the first to feature 'actors', particularly those in which the German entrepreneur Siegmund Lubin, one of the major producers of prize fight films in the 1890s, specialised in which actors (anticipating the direction cinema in general would increasingly take) were hired to recreate the moves of famous boxing matches for the camera. With his 1899 *Re-enactment of Sharkey–McCoy Fight*, Lubin developed this genre still further by re-enacting a fight for which there was no film available (Streible, 2008, p. 136). This also applied where the quality of the film of actual prize fights was quite poor, which was often the case in these formative years of the cinema. Lubin's work in particular became increasingly sophisticated as the 1890s developed, including ever more numbers of extras to represent supporters at the fight and images of people betting on fights.

We can see in these early re-enactments and their popularity the beginnings of the popular fictional narrative film that would dominate cinema from the second decade of the twentieth century. Indeed, this playing with fact and fiction demonstrates a feature more generally of early cinema which, as Tom Gunning has noted, comprised a combination of fact and fiction from its very beginnings (1989, pp. 3–4). While fake fight films were often frowned upon and heavily criticised by boxing advocates and those involved in the fight game themselves, they were popular with the public. Up to 1906 'fake' fight films outnumbered actualities in every year and did so 3–1 between 1897 and 1904, with Charles

Musser describing such films as 'the poor man's way to see the fight' (1994, p. 202). Musser's comments could be applied to film as a whole in this period which was frequented primarily by the urban working class (Manchel, 1980, p. 11; Butsch, 2001, pp. 107, 110).

Despite their popularity, fight films would continue to be viewed with suspicion throughout the first decade of the twentieth century, a suspicion that when combined with racist reactions to the emergence of African American Jack Johnson as world heavyweight boxing champion eventually led to their demise. In the five years subsequent to his victory over James J. Jeffries in 1910 to win the world title, films of Johnson's fights were repeatedly censured and banned. Outside of the ring, Johnson led a flamboyant lifestyle and was an outspoken figure challenging the submissive role expected of African Americans in this period, and was subject to repeated arrests and threatened with prison as a result of his relationships with White women and prostitutes. *Jeffries–Johnson World's Championship Boxing Contest, Held at Reno, Nevada, July 4, 1910* (1910) and subsequent films featuring Johnson fights faced censure. Bans were imposed on the screening of the film in cities across the US and Congress eventually banned the movement of prize fight films across state lines in July 1912 under what became known as the Sims Act, a ban that remained in place until 1940 (Orbach, 2010, pp. 270–346). This ban followed Johnson's subsequent title defence in 1912 against Jim Flynn and ensured the commercial failure of the *Jack Johnson vs. Jim Flynn Contest* (1912) film. Congress's ban was added to when the Supreme Court affirmed film censorship twice in cases in 1915, upholding a federal statute that banned Johnson's later films (Streible, 2008, pp. 195–196). The decision to ban the films of Johnson's fights and disrupt the fight film business was clearly, as the debate in Congress at the time indicated, motivated by race issues and indeed by racist attitudes to the continuing success of Johnson (Streible, 2008, pp. 244–245). However, it ensured the demise of the prize fight film as a popular form.

The arrival of the Hollywood sports films

Coincidentally, precisely at the time that cities, states and Congress were busy censoring and banning prize fight films, the film industry itself was moving from the East coast of the United States to the West. By 1911, Hollywood California was already a major base for some of the United States' largest production companies and by 1915, most American films were being made in the Los Angeles area (Koszarski, 1994, p. 99). This period also witnessed an evolving style in film production, not just in the United States but internationally and the consolidation of narrative fiction films as the dominant form. While the form of films was evolving, the places where films were screened also became more distinguished and the *picturepalace* or *cinema* became a popular venue in cities and towns across the Western World.

Interestingly, given the controversy surrounding boxing, some of the most successful sports fiction films of the silent period chose a comedic approach to the subject including the Charlie Chaplin films *The Knockout* (1914)[2] and *The Champion* (1915). These films exploited Chaplin's lightweight frame, placing him in the ring with fighters many times his size to hilarious results. This would also be a feature of later boxing-themed films featuring comic actors, including Buster Keaton in *Battling Butler* (1926), a film in which he plays a delicate boy from a wealthy home who pretends to be the world championship contender – with whom he shares a name – in order to prove his masculinity to the girl he loves. With the arrival of sound, comic actor Harold Lloyd would also enter the ring in *The Milky Way* (1936), as milkman Burleigh Sullivan who boxes to earn money to save his ill horse Agnes, refusing to remove his glasses even when he fights. All of these films exploited the comic possibilities of pitting an ordinary character of slight frame (a character most viewers could readily identify with) against a formidable opponent in the ring while affirming the underdog myth that would become such a prominent trope of the sports film in subsequent decades.

These comic films were partly responding to, and satirising, the role sport played more generally in American society, particularly with regard to the rehabilitation of the American male in the rapidly changing consumer culture of the early twentieth century. A government study, *Defects Found in Drafted Men*, undertaken at the end of World War I, found that approximately one-third of all draftees to military service were found to be physically unfit (Tucker, 1922, p. 377). As a consequence, physical fitness became an increasing subject of national focus, evident in the expansion of school athletic programmes and the growing importance of athletics at college level (Manchel, 1980, p. 16). Equally, the growth of consumer culture and the rising demands for women's rights in the early twentieth century were viewed as presenting further threats to masculinity. These concerns would also be reflected in sports films produced in this period. As Aaron Baker observes,

> Several sports films from the teens through the Depression era represent sports as a response to the loss of restraint created by the new consumer ethos. They also show sports as an antidote for the feminization of the culture caused by the loss of traditional forms of physical work and the increasing assertion of women.
>
> (2003, p. 54)

Relevant films here include *The Pinch Hitter* (1917), *Brown of Harvard* (1925) and *The Drop Kick* (1927). These films also share a common setting, college, and reaffirm the importance of sport as a crucial means of encouraging robust masculinity by means of individual achievement. The title of the college football-themed film, *Maker of Men* (1931), is suggestive of a recurring theme found in Hollywood films featuring sport, and above all American football, particularly in the first half of the twentieth century. These films drew on the role football played more generally in American life in the period, especially as it 'fantasized and mythologized the heroic symbol of the varsity athlete' (Umphlett, 1984, p. 27). For Wiley Lee Umphlett,

> movies quickly recognized the fact that accomplishment through athletic action and physical effort has greater appeal to the American imagination than does achievement in scholarship and the arts. Thus, most early films of college life depict athletic heroes who rarely refer to their studies – and, in fact, never seem to have time to go to class.
>
> (1984, p. 27)

Among the most popular American football-themed films of the silent era were those based on Rida Johnson Young's 1906 Broadway play *Brown of Harvard*. Altogether three cinematic adaptations were produced under this name, including in 1911 (directed by Colin Campbell), and 1918 (directed by Harry Beaumont), the latter of which featured the Washington State University football team and its legendary coach, William 'Lone Star' Dietz. However, the most commercially successful adaptation was that directed by Jack Conway and released by Metro-Goldwyn-Mayer in 1926. Tom Brown (played by William Haines, one of the biggest Hollywood stars of the late 1920s) is an obnoxious and spoilt young man from a prosperous family who arrives at Harvard University and immediately falls in with the wrong crowd, primarily interested in drinking and parties. The film also suggests the perceived 'dangers' of homosexuality in such a context, particularly through the character of Jim Doolittle (Jack Pickford), Tom's 'shrimp' roommate and initially his closest college companion. Jim is portrayed as effeminate with little interest in 'manly' college pursuits like sports while also – the film insinuates through physically intimate moments and suggestive glances – being romantically attracted to Tom. Tom's lack of the 'right stuff' on his initial arrival in college is also underlined by his failure to attract the attentions of the girl he fancies, Mary Abbott (Mary Brian), who is instead interested in the more dedicated sportsman Bob MacAndrews (Ralph Bushman). When Tom underperforms with the crew team due to a hangover, he is on the verge of leaving college but his father encourages him not to give up and 'go back and fight for' the girl he loves. Tom eventually wins the affections of Mary, but not before his companion Jim dies from pneumonia, after racing in the rain while ill to tell Tom the coach wants him to play on the football team. Jim's death thereby removes one of the main distractions to Tom realising his true masculinity, affirmed in the final big game where Tom carries the ball 90 yards and provides the final heroic pass for MacAndrews' winning touchdown. As Aaron Baker summarises,

> He therefore wins Mary's affection by no longer lying about with other men drinking and singing, but instead by embodying the right kind of disciplined, competitive, and heterosexual masculinity.
>
> (2003, p. 56)

Of the team sports featured in American college films, American football is by far the most popular, reflecting its popularity in American educational institutions since the late nineteenth century (Conklin, 2008, p. 9). The vast majority of these films, of which there are over 200, were released before 1954 by which time television provided the main access to football coverage for audiences. The 1920s and 1930s in particular are regarded as the Golden Age of American sports, a period when college football teams began to attract ever-increasing numbers of supporters, many of whom had never been to college themselves but were attracted by the increasing presence of football in the growing radio and print networks of the American mass media (Andrews, 2000, p. 35). While the advent of television contributed hugely to the growth and commercialisation of professional football from the 1950s onwards, the popularity of college football in films prior to this period was important in educating the general public on the rules of the game and preparing the ground for the expansion and huge popularity that television brought to the professional game subsequently.

The relationship between masculinity and sportsmanship also provided fruitful material for the great comic geniuses of the silent era. The success of films such as Harold Lloyd's *The Freshman* (1925) and Buster Keaton's *College* (1927) depended on the familiarity of audiences with the prominence of sport in college life, particularly as 'makers of men'. The popularity and influence of the college film is foregrounded from early in *The Freshman* when the impressionable Harold Lamb (Harold Lloyd) admires a poster pinned to his bedroom door from a fictitious film called *The College Hero* (Fig. 2.4). Harold takes from this film's hero his nickname 'Speedy', as well as the little jig he does throughout the film on first meeting people.[3]

In both *The Freshman* (1925) and *College* (1927) the theme of the unlikely triumph of the underdog became established as a central trope for American sports films in subsequent decades. *The Freshman* in particular was one of the most commercially successful films of 1925, the third highest grossing film at the US box office that year (Koszarski, 1994, p. 33), and was very influential for the form and development of later sports films. The film was co-directed by former professional baseball player Fred C. Newmeyer who also directed the further sports films *The Quarterback* (1926), *The Fighting Gentleman* (1932) and *The Big Race* (1934).

Harold Lamb believes absolutely in the American Dream and arrives at college sure of his place within it. He also views sport as a crucial means of achieving this ambition of success and popularity, despite the major financial and physical challenges he faces along the way. From the beginning of *The Freshman*, sport is highlighted as the primary concern of college students who, as the opening intertitle tells us, would rather be 'Right Tackle than President'. Harold is obsessed with becoming the college sporting hero at Tate College, described in the film as 'a large football stadium with a college attached'. Excited in his bedroom while preparing to leave home, dressed in the college colours,

FIGURE 2.4 Harold Lloyd as Harold Lamb in *The Freshman* (1925) (Pathé/The Kobal Collection)

Harold imagines he will become the most popular man on campus and football captain while flicking through the Tate College Yearbook of 1924. However, on arriving at Tate he realises that, despite earning a name for himself for his generosity by buying ice cream for all, he will never be as popular as the football team captain Chet Trask (James Anderson).

The exaggerated masculinity associated with football in this period is highlighted at Harold's first football practice, where we are told 'men are men and necks are nothing' and the head coach (Pat Harmon) is 'so tough he shaves with a blow torch'. The coach's first words, relayed through the intertitle, are concerned with making men out of the boys. Chet, the team captain, coach avers, is 'the only man on your team with the real Tate spirit!' In his continuing speech, believing he is referring to Chet but with Harold standing next to him, the coach outlines the positive attributes sought for men in this period, 'a regular go-getter – a red-blooded fighter – the kind of man that Tate is proud of!' However, with the slight figure of Harold Lamb standing to his right, dressed comically in his football gear with his jock strap and cup around his head and covering his nose while still wearing his glasses, Lloyd cleverly satirises the coaches' words and the hypermasculinity that characterised American sport in this period, including its representation in film. Furthermore, Harold soon proves to be a poor footballer, and is used instead as a 'dummy' for tackling practice. After receiving considerable abuse in this role, the coach eventually recognises Harold's spirit and gives him a job as the team's waterboy, while pretending he's among the substitutes though with little possibility of ever playing.

Harold does nonetheless eventually get his opportunity to play in the obligatory 'big game' that provides the film's climax. When many of the Tate players are injured against the Union State team, 'Speedy' is the only substitute left on the bench. He is not long in the game however before he too is stretchered off, but he quickly recovers and returns to the play. Despite taking several further hard tackles, mistaking a gentleman's hat for the ball, and other misadventures, through creative use of the strings of the ball Harold manages to carry it over the line for the winning touch down. Chaired from the field by his fellow players at the end as the hero of the game, by the film's close, Harold receives a note from his sweetheart Peggy (Jobyna Ralston) declaring her love, while the coach is teaching 'Speedy's' introductory jig to other students in the college.

The Freshman is a film that, in line with of many subsequent sports films, contains contradictory messages regarding sport. While it pokes fun at the role of sport in college life and familiar tropes of the college film, particularly the heroics on the sporting field and exaggerated masculinity, it nonetheless affirms the importance of sport for the assertion of character and proving one's masculinity in the film's climax. Furthermore, in a trope that would recur throughout sports films subsequently, the film ultimately confirms the central message of the American Dream that regardless of one's position in life or disadvantage, the opportunity still exists to be successful through effort and hard work, even for such an unlikely underdog as Harold 'Speedy' Lamb.

A similar message is also apparent in a film released two years later by another comic genius of the silent era, Buster Keaton. Inspired by the success of Lloyd's film, Keaton would also choose a college setting for his 1927 production *College* (1927). Possibly as a result of the box office failure of his previous film, *The General* (1926), Keaton chose more tried and trusted material already with a popular following for *College*. This applied not just to the choice of familiar sports – baseball, and track and field – that Keaton engages with in the film but also the clichéd central plot which the film also shares with *The Freshman* of a central protagonist who sees sport as the only means of winning the affections of the woman he loves. In common with *The Freshman*, *College* contains contradictory messages regarding sport. While at first the film appears to critique sport's role in school and college life, towards its close, sporting ability becomes crucial to the rescue of the central protagonist's sweetheart.

A critique of sport comprises much of the opening scene of the film when the lead protagonist Ronald (Buster Keaton) lectures his fellow high school students at their graduation in his valedictory address entitled 'The curse of athletics', after been awarded the medal for most brilliant scholar. Keaton's inclusion of this speech is not accidental; in 1926, the American Association of University Professors published a report criticising American football in particular 'for its hysteria, drinking, betting, overpaid coaches, and professional temptations' (Manchel, 1980, p. 20). In the same year, influential British philosopher and social critic Bertrand Russell in his acclaimed study *On Education* observed that 'the belief that a young man's athletic record is a test of his worth is a symptom of our general failure to grasp the need of knowledge and thought in mastering the complex modern world' (Russell, 1926, p. 88). Similarly for Ronald in *College*, 'Future generations depend upon brains and not upon jumping the discus or hurling the javelin'. His success as a student at high school is contrasted in this scene with the school's star athlete, Jeff Brown (Harold Goodwin), who took seven years to graduate because he 'believed so much in exercise'.

However, immediately after his address, Ronald runs into Mary Haines (Anne Cornwall), 'winner of every popularity contest in which the boys were allowed to vote' who gives out to him for his 'ridiculous speech'. 'Anyone prefers an athlete to a weak-kneed teacher's pet' she tells Ronald and, out of love for Mary, he decides he'll have to become an athlete to win her heart. He enrolls at Clayton college, where Mary and Jeff are both students and going out together by the time of Ronald's arrival with a suitcase containing only sporting items, including baseball and football gear, and instructions on how to play baseball, football and how to sprint. He quickly throws himself into college sports, beginning with baseball, before turning to track and field events, including discus and javelin throwing and hurdling. Ronald's attempts at these sports results in repeated failure and sometimes hilarious moments, including being overtaken by two young children while hurdling.

However, in the film's climax, Ronald suddenly reveals startling sporting abilities when he learns Mary is locked in her room against her will by Jeff and in need of rescue. In his attempt to reach her, he demonstrates great skill in all the sports he earlier seemed to fail miserably at from sprinting to the high jump, hurdles and long jump, eventually pole vaulting through a window to reach her. Once in Mary's room, Ronald continues to display his athletic skills by throwing, shot-put-like and discus-like, various objects at Jeff and in fending off Jeff's attacks before grabbing him and bringing him to the ground in an American football tackle. He then chases Jeff out the window, throwing a lamp stand, javelin-like, after him. When Ronald and Mary are discovered together in her room, they declare they are going to be married and run to a church. However, Keaton rather mischievously disrupts the romantic and upbeat ending here by including shots at the film's close of a married Ronald and Mary sitting surrounded by their children, growing old together and finally their gravestones. While he may have wished in these final moments to undermine the familiar and utopian trajectory that preceded them, they nonetheless provide a contradictory and unconvincing close to a film that affirms sporting ability as a means to success.

Conclusion

From its earliest days, cinema drew heavily on the popularity of sport for its continuing appeal once exhibitors could no longer depend on the novelty of the new invention to attract audiences. Indeed, efforts to film boxing in the United States in particular expedited the development of various aspects of cinema including projection, the ability to film longer sequences, editing and the emergence of film stars. As narrative fiction films became the dominant form in film production, sport would continue to feature prominently. Both *The Freshman* and *College* reflected the increasing role of sport in American life, and its association with the growing college scene. The 1920s were a period of optimism and growing prosperity as well as increased free time for many Americans, much of which was spent in following sport, particularly American football. The media played a crucial role in popularising sport, including radio and the print media while film responded to an audience increasingly engaged with sporting teams and contests. While *The Freshman* and *College* appear at first to satirise the role of sport in college life and its association with 'masculine' values of strength, courage and individualism, they also ultimately contain contradictory messages regarding sport itself, seeming to confirm its role as a means to success by each film's close. Indeed, these films had a crucial role in popularising a recurring theme throughout the mainstream sports film genre examined in the next chapter: sport as a means for all, regardless of their station or position in life, to realise the American Dream of success.

3

THE SPORTS FILM GENRE

Genre has played a crucial role in the history of film. It is, however, a classification mechanism associated first and foremost with mainstream films and particularly those emanating from Hollywood, and it as such that this chapter will consider the emergence and characteristics of the sports film genre. This is not to say that these characteristics are not found in films emerging from other societies; indeed, the influence of Hollywood cinema has been so significant that non-Hollywood sports films, as will be considered in Chapter 6, often exhibit similar characteristics to films associated with Hollywood. The commercial popularity internationally of Hollywood film is such that its influence in various forms, including in sports films, is hardly surprising. As noted by Scott Robert Olson, 'Worldwide, audiences are 100 times more likely to see a Hollywood film than see a European film ... Hollywood satisfies 70% of international demand for television narrative and 80% of demand for feature films' (1999, p. 23).

A genre emerges, according to Rick Altman, when a previously adjectival term, such as western in 'western chase' film evolves to function as a noun with the ability to 'commandeer entire texts and demonstrate a clear ability to pilot them independently' (1999, p. 51). Genre became a key component within the industrial and vertically integrated Hollywood model of filmmaking, distribution and exhibition developed by the major studios in the first half of the twentieth century. Indeed, as Steve Neale summarises:

> the routines and formulas of genre complemented the routines and formulas of factory production. They enabled the studios to plan, to produce and to market their films in predictable ways and to dovetail their output with the expertise of their production staff
>
> (2000, p. 233).

Studios, however, did not define genres alone but rather their emergence also depended significantly on their classification and recognition by filmmakers, distributors, marketers, critics and audiences. Steve Neale has described these elements collectively, drawing on the work of Gregory Lukow and Steve Ricci (1984), as the 'inter-textual relay' or 'the discourses of publicity, promotion and reception that surround Hollywood's film' (2000, p. 2). Therefore, genres are not fixed in form or style but rather are constantly evolving, responding to the various elements in the relay Neale delineates. Nonetheless, they have provided filmmakers and studios with an important means of reducing the significant financial risk involved in making a film by adapting a previously successful model with an already proven audience. Over time, genres became a useful means through which to organise films and for filmmakers and audiences to more easily identify their own preferences in the cinema.

Sport may appear at first to be an attractive cultural practice for the evolution of a film genre. Indeed, film theorists have repeatedly alluded to sport in their descriptions of the functioning of film genres. In describing the process through which genres operate, Robert Altman defined genres as 'a game that we play with moves and players borrowed from the real world' (1999, p. 157) while Thomas Schatz found strong parallels between the 'genre experience' and that experienced in games:

> Genre experience, like all human experience, is organized according to certain fundamental perceptual processes. As we repeatedly undergo the same type of experience we develop expectations which, as they are continually reinforced, tend to harden into 'rules'. The clearest example of this process in any culture is in its games. A game is a system of immutable rules (three strikes in baseball) and components determining the nature of play. Yet no two games in a sport are alike, and a theoretically infinite number of variations can be played within the 'arena' that the rules provide.
>
> (1991, pp. 691–692)

Furthermore for Altman, sport has considerable similarities not just with genres but also with the star system, in that all three constitute 'alternative public spheres in response to the rise of recording and broadcasting' (1999, p. 192). As with film genres, Altman recognised what he describes as constellated communities

> existing without physical interaction among fans of the same sport or team. It is hardly surprising to discover that the rise of spectator sports takes place virtually simultaneously with the development of film genres
>
> (1999, p. 192)

Despite these parallels between sport and film genres, the sports film genre has nonetheless had an uneven and uncertain development, particularly when compared with genres such as the comedy, musical or horror. This is not to say that the sports film genre is by any means a recent development; indeed, by the arrival of synchronised dialogue in cinema in 1927 with the release of *The Jazz Singer*, sports-themed films were already well established in American cinema, such that they could inspire satires on the theme, evident (as considered in Chapter 2) in *The Freshman* and *College*, satires whose success depended at least partly on audience recognition of the characters and themes of previous sports films.

The introduction of sound

While Lloyd and Keaton set a pattern for many sport, college, and comedy films to follow, the advent of synchronised sound would have far-reaching repercussions for cinema. Its arrival also coincided with what has been called the 'Golden Age' of American sports between the 1920s and 1930s (Noverr and Ziewacz, 1983; Swanson and Spears, 1995). Filmmakers responded to sport's growing popularity and importance in American life and in the 1930s alone over 160 films with sport as a central theme were made (Pearson, Curtis, Haney and Zhang, 2003, p. 153). As in subsequent decades, boxing featured in most of these sports films, though American football, horseracing and baseball also figured heavily.

The addition of sound added an exciting new dimension to these films and directors exploited this aspect with varying degrees of success in subsequent decades. This was most evident in the popularity of the musical in the 1930s and 1940s and sports would also feature in some of these films beginning in 1929 with the college-set films *The Forward Pass* (1929), *So This Is College* (1929), and *Sweetie* (1929). As Wiley Lee Umphlett notes 'the underlying significance of these films is that each one is built around a basic plot ingredient that would recur in all the college-life musicals to follow: the big game convention, the triangular plot, the big show scheme, and the college inheritance theme' (1984, p. 48). While Busby Berkeley's *Take Me Out to the Ball Game* (1949), a major box office draw (Howard Reid, 2006, p. 33), marked a commercial high point for the sports-themed musical, one of the most successful sports films of the 1930s also exploited aspects of the musical as well as the college-themed film genre. The Marx Brothers' *Horse Feathers* (1932), like Lloyd's and Keaton's previous sports-themed films, shamelessly satirised the institution of college and the role of American football within it. The Marx Brothers would exploit sport repeatedly for comic purposes throughout the 1930s and 1940s including baseball in *A Night at the Opera* (1935) and horseracing in *A Day at the Races* (1937), taking advantage of the popularity of these sports in this period to realise hilarious, if farcical, scenarios. All of these films evince the Marx Brothers' gift for satirising the elitist pretensions associated with the institutions depicted, an achievement assisted through their depiction of sport, most famously in their transformation of the opera *Il Trovatore* into a baseball game in *A Night at the Opera*. A further comic team from this period to exploit sport (in particular horse-racing) for comic results was Abbot and Costello in one of their most commercially successful films, *It Ain't Hay* (1943).

Sports films: A distinct genre or box office poison?

As *Horse Feathers* indicates, sports themed films were as likely to be described in terms of other genres in this era – the musical or comedy for example – as instances of a distinct sports film genre. This was not unique to films featuring sport; Rick Altman has observed

> Hollywood's classical era tendency to imply the simultaneous presence of enough different genres to assure a film's appeal to the three recognized audience sectors: male viewers, female spectators and the *tertium quid* audience with interests lying outside of traditional male and female domains.
>
> (1999, p. 128)

Nonetheless, the sports genre in fiction film has rarely achieved the recognition of other genres; it is rare, for example, that video libraries will have a fiction film section headed 'sports film', with such films often found catalogued under other genres.[1] Indeed, Altman himself makes almost no reference to the sports film genre (apart from a very brief mention of boxing films (1999, p. 140)) within his lengthy study of film genre. The emergence of certain formulaic presentations, often climaxing with the Big Game, Fight, or Race, from very early in the development of sports films may have influenced the often negative view of these films and delayed the recognition of the sports film genre (Wallenfeldt, 1989, p. iv). As Lewis H. Carlson observes, referring in particular to baseball-themed work in comments relevant to sports films as a whole, these films were characterised 'by trite plots, maudlin characters, and actors who clearly could neither bat, field, nor throw,' such that 'early baseball films appeared artificial and hackneyed' (1998, p. 361). Already evident in early sports films was the frequent, recurring, and predictable pattern where sport was employed to affirm the Horatio Alger myth of rags to riches, though often in an 'obviously contrived' manner, as one reviewer noted (Crowther, 1948). This predictability may have contributed to the perception of sports films historically as 'box office poison' (Carlson, 1998, p. 361; Jones, 2005, p. 30) or less critically significant with C. Richard King and David J. Leonard arguing that even where films 'about athletes or those set in sporting worlds may prove popular and even profitable … they do not rise to the level of critical significance, much less art' (2006, p. 1). In a 1969 *Sports Illustrated* article entitled 'Sport Was Box-office Poison', Robert Cantwell observed that by the late 1940s sports films

> began to form their own record in Hollywood annals – one of fiscal catastrophe. So many bad sport movies were made that they virtually died out as a popular art form. The culmination of it all was probably *The Babe Ruth Story*. It was so awful – and such a staggering box-office failure – that most of the big movie companies shuddered at the very sight of ball and bat.
>
> (1969)

By the time of the production of Billy Wilder's classic *Sunset Boulevard* (1950), the sports film was already considered a cliché-ridden and inferior production. Early on in the film, the lead character, out of work screenwriter Joseph C. Gillis (William Holden), attempts to restart his career by selling a script for a baseball film entitled 'Bases Loaded' only for it to be dismissed by Betty Shaefer (Nancy Olson), the assistant of Paramount Pictures producer Sheldrake (Fred Clark), as 'flat and banal' and 'Just a rehash of something that wasn't very good to begin with'. For Cantwell, as it would seem for Shaefer, sports films lacked substance and credibility. While sport may work in a comic, or melodramatic context, sports films were, Cantwell argued, 'disasters when they were tragic or sentimental. The movie colony was simply too knowing about sports to shed an honest tear over a horse race or a football game' (1969). Indeed, reviews of *The Babe Ruth Story* (1948) highlighted above by Cantwell raised precisely this issue. As the *New York Times* reviewer remarked at the time of the film's release,

> Ruth was a great one with the kid fans, but it smacks of sheer artifice to show his bulbous counterfeit in this movie maundering over pathos-coated tots. It is down-right childish to put forth that a $5,000 fine was given him and a suspension from the Yankees for missing a major game because he was preoccupied in taking an injured dog to a hospital.
>
> It is also a little incongruous to see a picture about a baseball star containing no more than a minimum of action on a playing field – and most of that studio action which is patently phony and absurd. Regardless of advertised coaching, Mr. Bendix still swings like a rusty gate, and the atmosphere of a big-league ball park is as remote from this picture as that of a church.
>
> (Crowther, 1948)

It is this question of credibility that has been a recurring challenge for producers of sports films, an issue related to the challenge of instilling presence to the cinema itself, as discussed in Chapter 1, as audiences became increasingly removed physically, and in terms of subject matter, from the topics of individual films. While genre film developed as a means to address this lack of presence in the narrative film form, sport in films is a constant reminder of precisely this absence.

In the earliest days of film, viewers were likely to see local people they knew, or indeed themselves, in actuality films produced by early filmmakers and exhibited for local audiences in an attempt to instil a sense of presence to the new form. However, with the arrival of mass fiction cinema in the first and second decades of the twentieth century, this became increasingly difficult. The development of genre provided a means of restoring this presence to the cinema as

> increasingly, [the cinema-goer] would be comforted by an atmosphere that he found familiar. Instead of puzzling out ever novel situations, he

would know from the opening scenes what to expect. The remainder of each film – whether comedy, melodrama, or Western – would thus remind him not of home but of his new affective 'home' located in previous film-viewing experiences … Not only did genres prove particularly adept at replacing the experience of presence, but the knowledge that others found pleasure in the same genre even made it possible for genres to stand in for an absent community.

(Altman, 1999, p. 187)

However, filmmakers face a particular challenge in attempting to instil this 'experience of presence' in their films while also representing sport. By its nature, sport engages primarily its immediate participants and audience and sports films face a daunting challenge in trying to recreate this immediacy. Indeed, as Matthew Syed has noted, the notion of a 'sporting movie' is 'a contradiction in terms'. For Syed,

Sport is an exercise in unpredictability, an unscripted battle in which the viewer is absorbed in the plot precisely because he does not know how it will end. A movie is necessarily the reverse: scripted, plotted and directed; a confection in which the drama is choreographed in advance.

(2010)

American film critic Andrew Sarris summarised this position succinctly when he contended that 'Sports are now. Movies are then. Sports are news. Movies are fables' (1980, p. 50). Film makers too have remarked on this drawback of cinema with Ken Loach observing that 'the real enjoyment of football is to be there' while for the screenwriter Paul Laverty, 'A film can never match the excitement of football. Unfortunately we can normally guess in 95% of cases how a film is going to end but the beauty of football is that you just never quite know' (*United We Stand*, 2009). Today, if people seek a representation of the sporting event (apart from attending the event itself), film cannot hope to match the immediacy and versatility of live television, and hence television is by far the most popular form through which the general public engages with sport.

The sports film – particularly the American variety – has attempted to respond to this challenge by seeking to emulate aspects of the televisual presentation of sport, including the ubiquity of the sports commentator in sports films. However, there are limitations to this and films that have tried too hard to emulate television have usually failed in the process, as Ronald Bergan has observed of the American football-themed *Number One* (1969):

One of the problems of Tom Gries' direction is that it tries too hard to compete with TV and fails. TV techniques create the immediacy of the spectacle, moving rapidly from inside the huddle to the sidelines to instant replay. A movie which tries to use the same techniques will suffer by comparison, lacking the spontaneity and excitement of the real thing. Film is a more analytical medium and should add a dimension to a sporting event that television cannot hope to do. It can penetrate the physical and psychological preparations necessary for a big game. It can take a closer look behind the scenes and behind the eyes that stare from a helmet.

(1982, p. 50)

Consequently, partly conscious of the limitations of the form, directors of sports films have tended to focus less on the playing field and more on the circumstances that surround those who engage with sport – in this context the sporting context may offer a commentary on the larger issues, predominately of a personal rather than social nature, with which the film is concerned, a subject returned to below and in the next chapter.

Defining the sports film

As noted above, the sports film genre has had an uncertain development. Indeed, the genre was omitted entirely from Gehring's *Handbook of American Film Genres* published in 1988. While subsequent studies have somewhat addressed this omission, including Lopez's *Film By Genre* (1993) and dedicated studies of sports films, including those by Bergan (1982), Wallenfeldt (1989) and Williams (2006), doubts still remain as to the precise definition of the sports genre. According to Rick Altman,

> If spectators are to experience films in terms of their genre, films must leave no doubt as to their generic identity; instant recognizability must be assumed … in order to be recognized as a genre, films must have both a common topic … and a common structure, a common way of configuring the topic.
> (1999, pp. 18, 23)

However, a recurring issue with sport themed films is that they are often found categorised in terms of other genres (comedy, drama, science-fiction, etc.) or by the individual sport featured (for example the boxing film, the baseball film). *The Babe Ruth Story* was described in the *New York Times* review quoted above as a 'film biography' (Crowther, 1948), with no mention made of its place as a sports film. Furthermore, as Wallenfeldt observes, though the sports film is 'among the most engaging the cinema has to offer and one of Hollywood's specialties … it isn't easy to define the difference between a sports film and a film with sports in it' (1989, p. iv). The ubiquitous presence of sport across a wide array of genres (indeed there is hardly a genre that has not featured sport at some point) means that structurally films featuring sport may vary considerably depending on the expectations of the particular larger genre they are found within. Mosher, for example, has identified four principle archetypal patterns: comedy, tragedy, romance, and satire (1983, pp. 15–19) in the sports film, each of which respond to quite different audience expectations.

Ellis Cashmore (2000, pp. 132–139) adopted a similar approach to Mosher when he identified a number of prominent 'sub-genres' to the sports film, namely the dramatic/biographical, the comedy/fantasy, and the documentary. In the first category, Cashmore placed many of the most critically and commercially successful sports films, arguing that films 'inspired by real lives have been the most enduringly popular' (2000, p. 133). He also lists most sports featured in sports films in the dramatic/biographical sub-genre including boxing (*Kid Galahad* (1937) to *The Boxer* (1997)), athletics (*The Loneliness of the Long-Distance Runner* (1962) to *Running Brave* (1983)), baseball (*The Pride of St. Louis* (1952) to *The Fan* (1996)), American football (*North Dallas Forty* (1979) to *Against all Odds* (1984)), soccer (*Die Angst des Tormanns beim Elfmeter* (*The Goalkeeper's Fear of the Penalty*) (1972) to *When Saturday Comes* (1996)), cycling (*Breaking Away* (1979) to *American Flyers* (1985)), motor racing (*Winning* (1969) to *Days of Thunder* (1990)), skiing (*Downhill Racer* (1969) to *The Other Side of the Mountain* (1975)), horse-racing (*The Killing* (1956) to *The Grifters* (1990)), kung fu (*The Big Boss* (1971) to *Dragon: The Bruce Lee Story* (1993)), roller derby (*Kansas City Bomber* (1972)), pool (*The Hustler* (1961)) and rugby league (*This Sporting Life* (1963)). For Cashmore, comedy and fantasy 'are essential to the appeal of sports' and he lists a wide range of films within this category also including the 'most seminal sports fantasy' *Here Comes Mr Jordan* (1941). Indeed, the comedy sports film, which is discussed in more detail in the concluding chapter, has enjoyed considerable popularity in recent years, evident in the box office success of films such as *The Waterboy* (1998), *The Longest Yard* (2005), *Talladega Nights: The Ballad of Ricky Bobby* (2006) and *Blades of Glory* (2007).

Adopting Cashmore's approach, one might also identify a science-fiction 'sub-genre' to the sports film which would include films such as *Death Race 2000* (1975 and the 2008 prequel *Death Race*), *The Blood of Heroes* (1989), *Futuresport* (1998), *Rollerball* (both the 1975 and 2002 versions) and *Real Steel* (2011). Indeed, these science fiction films which are characterised by often extreme violence have brought to its logical conclusion a pattern found throughout sports films since the 1970s, the increasing presence and intensity of violence, apparent in films such as *The Longest Yard* (1974), *Slap Shot* (1977), and *Raging Bull* (1980). As noted by Bergan,

> *Rollerball* demonstrates the ultimate in contact sport. The final game has no rules and no time limit. One plays to kill. It is science fiction, but as in all the best science fiction, it is a logical conclusion to trends noticeable in contemporary life.
>
> (1982, p. 10)

Documentary

Cashmore's final category of 'sub-genre', documentary, is somewhat misleadingly described. Though sometimes referred to as such, documentary might more correctly be viewed (in Paul Arthur's terms) as a 'mode of production, a network of funding, filming, postproduction, and exhibition tendencies common to work normally indexed as "documentary"' (2005, p. 20). Sport has been a popular subject of documentary from the emergence of the form in the 1920s. Some of the most influential and innovative documentaries ever produced have featured sport prominently including Dziga Vertov's *Man with a Movie Camera* (1929), Jean Vigo's *Taris, roi de l'eau* (*Jean Taris, Swimming Champion,* 1931), Leni Riefenstahl's *Olympia* (1938) and Kon Ichikawa's *Tokyo Olympiad* (1965). While documentaries, including those featuring sport, have been largely confined for much of their development over the past fifty years to television, since the mid-1990s an increasing number of documentaries have had a theatrical release and have enjoyed both critical and commercial success. Indeed, nine of the top ten grossing documentaries of all time at the box office were released in the past ten years,[2] a period that also saw the release of some of the most commercially successful sport documentary films, including *Dogtown and Z-boys* (2001), *Touching the Void* (2003), *Step into Liquid* (2003), *Riding Giants* (2004), *Murderball* (2005) and *Senna* (2010). Documentary director George Hickenlooper has attributed the rise in popularity of documentary to 'people … clamoring to connect – particularly after 9/11 – with things that are genuine and real and I think documentaries are filling that need' (quoted in Arthur, 2005, p. 19). However, contemporary documentaries also reveal the influence of mainstream fiction film producing what Paul Wells describes as 'a hybrid of forms, often erring towards the cinematic vocabularies of narrative "fiction" to apparently present "fact" in a critical (yet sometimes populist) mode' (1999, p. 230). While initially priding itself on its distinctiveness as a form that captured with integrity aspects of social reality, the documentary film has more and more in its cinematic form come to adopt aesthetics associated with popular fiction film. Though documentary has long being viewed as the form best placed to provide complex engagements and understandings of the social and political contexts of the subjects featured, this is increasingly no longer the case in its contemporary cinematic manifestations. The focus has moved rather to exploiting the dramatic possibilities of found footage or renderings of social reality rather than providing a means of understanding or engaging critically with such footage. The sport documentary film has instead focused, as in fiction film, on individualist tales of overcoming and achievement often configured within the familiar three-act structure of mainstream cinema. As Ian McDonald observes,

> in the post-[Michael] Moore moment, sport documentaries have tended to capitalize on the market that has opened up for documentaries by

> emphasizing the human drama decontextualized from issues of power, and therefore complicit in reinforcing dominant ideologies: here, the ideology of sport as the route to success and the exemplar of character
>
> (2007, p. 221)

This 'ideology of sport' is also at the centre of the mainstream sports fiction film, particularly as it relates to the ideology of the American Dream, and will be considered further below and in the following chapter.

Critical commentary and the sports film

A crucial determinant of genre recognisability is critical commentary regarding individual films; as Altman observes, 'Our terms and our concepts derive not so much from cinema itself, but from those who represent cinema to us ... In short, critics and not studios lie at the origin of most generic language' (1999, pp. 124, 127). However, historically, as indicated above, the sports genre when not described in terms of other popular genres has as often as not been identified by critics in terms of individual sports rather than sport as a whole. Currently, as well as 'sports', the American Film Institute's catalogue of films produced in the United States lists over ninety genres, including 'Automobile Racing', 'Baseball', 'Boxing', 'Football' and 'Horserace' ('The AFI Catalog of Feature Films'). By examining reviews in the entertainment-trade magazine *Variety* between the 1930s and the 2000s, it is possible to see this recurring practice of identifying sports films in terms of individual sports, rather than a larger genre. As noted in the previous chapter, the 'prizefight film' was a staple of the earliest film screenings and this term would continue to be used in descriptions of feature films featuring boxing with the arrival of sound. *Variety*[3] described the 1934 release *Palooka* as a 'comedy ... prizefight film' (6 March, p. 14). In the same year *The Big Race*, was described by *Variety* as a 'racetrack yarn' (6 March, p. 27), while the 1936 Warner Bros. release *Down the Stretch* was considered by *Variety* as 'another racetrack pic' (11 November 1936, p. 14). The year 1934 also saw the release of *The Band Plays On*, described by *Variety* as a 'Football Picture' (25 December, p. 12), while the following year Columbia Pictures released the 'Baseball Picture' (8 May 1935, p. 16) *Swell Head*. The general term of the sports film was apparent in critical commentary in this era, however it was often in association with other generic markers, as evident in the description of the Warner Bros. release *The Payoff* as a 'Sports and newspaper story, garnished with gangsterism and romance' (13 November 1935, p. 16).

The practice of identifying sports films with particular sports would continue into the 1980s. In 1984, *Variety* reviewed the Disney made for TV 'Baseball picture', *Tiger Town* (19 December, p. 19), and the following year the 'baseball pic set to rock music' (30 March 1985, p. 12), *The Slugger's Wife*. Another 'formula football pic' (12 February 1986, p. 22), *Wildcats*, was released in 1986. By this stage, however, some sports films had achieved such recognition that their title could itself be used to denote a sub-genre in and of itself, as evident in *Variety* describing *The Karate Kid* as '"Rocky" for kids' (23 May 1984, p. 12). This practice has continued into the twenty-first century with sports themed films still recognised in terms of individual sports. This is particularly so for boxing films such as *Cinderella Man*, described by *Variety* as exhibiting 'a loving understanding ... of the boxing genre from "Champion" to "Raging Bull"' (19 May 2005, Koehler), and more recently the Oscar winning *The Fighter*, which *Variety* also categorised as a 'boxing drama' (10 November 2010, Debruge).

Despite the inconsistencies charted above, several suggestions have been made as to what the sports film genre might encompass. Wallenfeldt confined his focus to films in which competitive sports 'play a central role' (1989, p. iv). For Williams, a sports movie is 'one with a sporting element that is significant to the progression of the picture via character, event, and/or storyline' (2006, p. x). Williams also agrees with Wallenfeldt's focus on competitive sports, using the dictionary definition of sport as a 'competitive physical exercise' to exclude films that focus on sports examining mental acumen (chess) or non-competitive physical sports (mountain climbing) (2006, p. x). This competitive characteristic is also evident in the definition offered by Pearson, Curtis, Haney and Zhang in their study of the development of sports films between 1930 and 1995 where they define the genre as consisting 'of themes or subjects focusing on a team, a sport saga, or a specific sport participant (i.e. athlete, coach, or agent) in which sporting events engaging the participants in athletics were the primary activity of the film' (2003, p. 149).

While the differing definitions may suggest an uncertainty concerning a precise definition for the sports film genre, it should be noted that this apparent difficulty in defining the characteristics of this genre is not unique to films featuring sport. Indeed, what Altman has described as a 'constant sliding of generic terms from adjective to noun' (1999, p. 52) has been a feature of the development of all film genres with the classification of genres often characterised by considerable change and variation (Neale, 2000, pp. 231–257). This has led commentators to move beyond attempting to define genre according to a limited number of prerequisites with Jim Collins proposing 'genericity' (1993, pp. 242–263) as more appropriate to the reflexivity and textual awareness apparent in recent genre films while Rick Altman has suggested instead the term 'genrification', to reflect the continuing construction and reconstruction of genre in film whereby 'the constitution of *film* cycles and genres is a never-ceasing process, closely tied to the capitalist need for product differentiation' (1999, pp. 62–65). David Rowe has also recognised the changing and evolving nature of the sports genre itself arguing that 'to claim that sports films may constitute a genre (perhaps with a range of subgenres) it would be necessary to establish the existence of some shifting yet patterned relationships within or between subject matter, presentation, narrative, and affect'. Taking this as his starting point, Rowe suggests a

> common basis to nondocumentary or instruction-based sports films as a
> genre (or, more cautiously, as a 'complex of sub genres'), underpinning a

panoply of formal, substantive, and stylistic variations: that all films that deal centrally with sports are at some level allegorical, that they address the question of the dual existence of the social and sporting worlds as problematic, and that they are preoccupied with the extent to which (idealized) sports can transcend or are bound by existing (and corrupting) social relations.

(1998, pp. 351–352)

This study is particularly indebted to Rowe's analysis here of the sports film genre. While the sports film may be defined as a production in which a sport, sporting event, athlete (and their sport), or follower of sport (and the sport they follow) are prominently featured, and which depend on sport to a significant degree for their plot motivation or resolution, sport is ultimately rarely the central concern of such films. Rather, sport performs principally an allegorical role in the sports film genre; in the popular Hollywood variety, this is primarily evident in its attempt to affirm the American Dream, a topic we will return to shortly.

The 'fundamental characteristics' of the sports film genre

It is noticeable that increasingly a sports film genre is being recognised by critics in recent years, including the 2002 baseball-themed film *The Rookie* which *Variety* described as a 'feel-good sports drama' (17 March 2002, Leydon); the 2004 ice hockey film *Miracle* which *Variety* noted abounded 'in sports-pic conventions' (1 February 2004, Leydon); while one of the most successful films of 2009, *The Blind Side*, *Variety* observed, was 'another uplifting and entertaining feel-good, fact-based sports drama' (30 March 2011, Leydon) thereby recognising not just the existence of the genre but its many recent precursors. Arguably one of the most significant recognitions of the sport genre's existence occurred on 17 June 2008, when in a CBS television special, the American Film Institute presented the AFI's 10 Top 10, a listing of the ten greatest American films in ten classic film genres ('AFI's 10 Top 10'). Among the genres chosen was the 'sports' genre, further acknowledging its significance. The AFI defined the genre as involving 'films with protagonists who play athletics or other games of competition' ('America's 10 Greatest Films in 10 Classic Genres') and choose from one to ten, the following films: *Raging Bull* (1980), *Rocky* (1976), *The Pride of the Yankees* (1942), *Hoosiers* (1986), *Bull Durham* (1988), *The Hustler* (1961), *Caddyshack* (1980), *Breaking Away* (1979), *National Velvet* (1944) and *Jerry Maguire* (1996). The sports covered in these films are boxing, baseball, basketball, pool, golf, cycling, horse-racing and American football. This chapter will conclude with an examination of the AFI top ten sports films with regard to the 'fundamental characteristics' that genre films share (1999, p. 24) as identified by Robert Altman to reveal some of the salient characteristics of the sports film genre.

- Constantly *opposing cultural values to counter-cultural* values, genre films regularly depend on dual protagonists and dualistic structures (producing what I have called dual-focus texts).

(Altman, 1999, p. 24)

Sports films frequently manifest both dual protagonists and dualistic structures – indeed the competitive dynamic that is frequently at the centre of sports films, whether they are focused on individual or team sports, necessitates this dualism. Rocky Balboa (*Rocky*), Jake La Motta (*Raging Bull*) and Eddie Felson (*The Hustler*) are all to a considerable degree defined by their opponents, Apollo Creed, Sugar Ray Robinson and Minnesota Fats. Equally, *National Velvet* is, to a significant extent, the story of Mi Taylor (played by Mickey Rooney, a much bigger star at the time of the film's release) as it is of Velvet Brown (Elizabeth Taylor). In terms of dualistic structures or 'dual-focus texts', sports films are usually more concerned with life outside the ring or off the pitch than with the sporting moment itself; as Mathew Syed argues, while sports films may feature athletes and lengthy sequences of sporting events, they are actually often less about sport and more focused on 'a wider trajectory' (2010), what Randy Williams describes as 'the drama between the plays' (2006, p. x). *Jerry Maguire*, for example, is focused more on the development of character of the eponymous central protagonist, than with the sporting exploits – actually a very small percentage of the screen time – of his sole client, Rod Tidwell (Cuba Gooding, Jr.). However, as David Rowe notes above, while sports films frequently 'address the question of the dual existence of the social and sporting worlds', they often view this relationship 'as problematic' (1998, pp. 351–352). In recent years, sports films have tended to depict this relationship more optimistically, seeing in sport a means of transcending challenging social circumstances in films such as *Cinderella Man* (2005), *The Blind Side* (2009) and *The Fighter* (2010). Conversely *Raging Bull*, in line with a recurring feature of earlier boxing-themed films, presents one of the darkest depictions of the relationship between the social and sporting worlds with Jake La Motta's life in the ring paralleled with his psychological and physical decline outside of it, and the disintegration of his relationships with his wife and family. This more pessimistic view of sport, though less common in American film, continues to appear in films such as *The Wrestler* (2008) in which we witness the physical and emotional decline of broken-down professional wrestler Randy 'The Ram' Robinson (Mickey Rourke), a character unable to find a satisfactory existence outside of the ring.

- Both intratextually and intertextually, the genre film uses the same material over and over again.

(Altman, 1999, 25)

Sports films again reveal this characteristic; indeed, they have been criticised for frequently suffering from an excess of clichés and 'nauseating sentimentality'

(Sarris, 1980, p. 50). An obvious example of such repeated material is the big game, race or fight finish found in so many sports films, including most of the films included in the AFI selection. Taking the ten films included in the AFI list, we also find that a further recurring pattern is evident, a pattern repeated in many other sports film; the attempt of a marginalised or 'underdog' individual, or team, to achieve success through sport. As noted by Bergan,

> If outsiders won as much as they do on the screen, most bookies would be bankrupt. It's a sure bet that in any race the underdog (or horse) will win … In this fantasy world, unknown stumblebums like Rocky can fight a draw with the world heavyweight champion, and Dean Paul Martin is in the Wimbledon final against Guilermo Villas in *Players* (Par. 1979).
>
> (1982, p. 11)

Raging Bull charts the attempts of a 'bruiser' from an underprivileged ethnic community in New York to achieve the middleweight boxing crown; *Rocky* maps a very similar territory, though in a much more optimistic manner; *The Pride of the Yankees* also features the rise of an athlete – this time a baseball player – from an immigrant family to success as a baseball player; *Hoosiers* concerns the unexpected success of an unfancied high school team in the state basketball championship; *National Velvet* features the unlikely victory of a twelve-year-old female jockey in the Aintree Grand National; *The Hustler* also concerns the attempts of a young pool player, making a living hustling pool on the margins, to find respect and recognition for his pool playing abilities; Danny Noonan's (Michael O'Keefe) family in *Caddyshack* are too poor to afford the fees required so he can go to college and Danny attempts to raise the money by caddying at the local golf club; *Breaking Away*'s Dave Stoller (Dennis Christopher) similarly comes from a lower working class family looked down upon by those who attend the local university. Dave finally earns respect by achieving an unexpected victory and beating the college students in the Little 500 bike race. While *Jerry Maguire*'s lead protagonist clearly enjoys a privileged lifestyle, the film goes to considerable lengths to affirm the challenging social circumstances – including being abandoned by his father and raised by a single mother – which were overcome through sporting success by his only client, Rod Tidwell; in *Bull Durham* it is age that is the major obstacle for minor-league baseball player Crash Davis (Kevin Costner), who seeks some degree of success or recognition in his sport despite being at the latter end of his career.

• The repetitive nature of genre films tends to diminish the importance of each film's ending, along with the cause-and-effect sequence that leads to that conclusion. Instead, genre films depend on the cumulative effect of the film's often repeated situations, themes and icons.

(Altman, 1999, 25)

The ending to many sports films – whether the final big fight (*Rocky*), the big game or race (*The Hustler, Hoosiers, Caddyshack, Jerry Maguire, National Velvet, Breaking Away*) – has become one of the most familiar and expected aspects of the genre, and therefore arguably less relevant to the success of these films. Rather, within individual films it is the progression of characters and their ability to overcome the various challenges they face through individual effort and hard work – hence the clichéd training montage found in almost all sports films – that provides the real story. While the final game climax to these films undoubtedly provides an emotional highpoint, its success is dependent on the ability of the narrative as a whole to underline the challenges that the protagonist must overcome to get there.

- The repetitive and cumulative nature of genre films makes them also quite predictable.

(Altman, 1999, 25)

This is particularly the case in the sports film where the climactic big game or fight victory for the lead protagonist(s) is one of the most recognisable parts of the genre. Though this has been criticised by some critics – and may account for the description of sports films by some as 'box office poison' due to the over-familiarity of the form – it is significant that this pattern returns and continues to attract audiences. As Altman notes

> The pleasure of genre film spectatorship ... derives more from reaffirmation than from novelty. People go to genre films to participate in events that somehow seem familiar. They may be looking for strong emotions, exciting scenes, novel situations and fresh dialogue, but like those who go to the amusement park in search of adventure, they would rather enjoy their excitement in a controlled environment that they recognize.

(1999, 25)

In other words, genre is a safe way of engaging with issues we may be curious about, and may indeed want to learn more about and witness, but don't necessarily want to have to deal with in our daily lives. Furthermore, genre films usually provide a more straightforward and uncomplicated solution to complex social issues that may emerge or are touched upon within a film's narrative, a solution, as considered in the following chapter, that sport would appear to readily provide.

- genre films make heavy use of intertextual references.

(Altman, 1999, 25)

Sports films again follow this practice, whereby each new entry into the canon is arguably as indebted to previous sports films as to the actual practice of the sport depicted in everyday life. The boxing-themed film, the most popular subject to date of sports films, is one of the most obvious candidates here and part of the success of Martin Scorsese's *Raging Bull* depends on its ability to critique the largely positive portrayal of boxing – and its impact on the central protagonist – found in *Rocky* four years previously. Indeed, *Raging Bull*, in its black-and-white cinematography draws heavily on boxing films from the 1940s and 1950s in particular *Body and Soul* (1947) and *The Set Up* (1949). Baseball films similarly are indebted to earlier films, evident in more recent times in the repeated appearance of Kevin Costner in a range of such films since the 1980s including *Chasing Dreams* (1982), *Field of Dreams* (1989), *For Love of the Game* (1999), *The Upside of Anger* (2005) as well as *Bull Durham* (1988).

- genre films … maintain a strong connection to the culture that produced them. Whereas other films depend heavily on their referential qualities to establish ties to the real world, genre films typically depend on symbolic usage of key images, sounds and situations.

(Altman, 1999, p. 26)

This is certainly the case with the sports film genre – indeed, many of the most successful Hollywood sports films (including from our list *Jerry Maguire*, *The Pride of the Yankees* and *Bull Durham*) feature sports much less popular outside of the United States, such as baseball and American football. Indeed, while American films customarily take the majority of their box office from overseas,[4] many of the most commercially successful American sports films in recent years took the vast majority of their box office from within the United States itself, including *Field of Dreams* (1989) (76.3 per cent), *Any Given Sunday* (1999) (75.4 per cent) and *The Blind Side* (2009) (82.8 per cent).[5] However, beyond the focus of these films on sports less popular internationally, they also play a crucial symbolic role within American society, a role, considered in the following chapter, that builds on the place of sport within that culture as a whole.

- film genres are *functional* for their society.

(Altman, 1999, 26)

Whether as ritual, myth, or symbolic affirmation of prevailing ideology, film genres have a crucial functional role for their society. As Altman contends,

Whereas producers and exhibitors see genre films as 'product', critics increasingly recognize their role in a complex cultural system permitting viewers to consider and resolve (albeit fictively) contradictions that are not fully mastered by the society in which they live.

(1999, p. 26)

It is a tiny minority of individuals in American society – and indeed in societies around the world – who ever manage to enjoy professional success through sport. There are even fewer who manage to overcome underprivileged and challenging circumstances to do so. However, in sports film after sports film, we encounter individuals who manage to achieve both these goals. In these films, poverty, deprivation and marginalisation in American society are often acknowledged; however, there is little attempt in the mainstream sports film to engage with the reasons for, or indeed, realistic means for most people to overcome them. Rather, sports films suggest that through sport and individual effort the American Dream of upward social mobility and success can be achieved. It is a double lie, a lie made all the more convincing through the impressive and seductive medium of film. The next chapter will explore this functional role of the sports film genre with regard to race and social class through an examination of some of the more significant and popular sports films produced to date.

4

'TRUTHS THAT TELL A LIE'

Race, social class and the American Dream in the sports film

> In their formulaic narrative process, genre films celebrate the most fundamental ideological precepts – they examine and affirm 'Americanism' with all its rampant conflicts, contradictions and ambiguities. Not only do genre films establish a sense of continuity between our cultural past and present, but they also attempt to eliminate the distinctions between them. As social ritual, genre films function to stop time, to portray our culture in a stable and invariable ideological position
>
> Thomas Schatz (1981, p. 31)

If we wish to understand the functional role of film genres, it is not enough to identify the fundamental characteristics of a particular genre – as we considered in the previous chapter with regard to sports films – it is also necessary to 'isolate the problems for which the genre provides a symbolic solution' (Altman, 1987, p. 334). To understand the functional role of sports films, it is first necessary to examine the role of sport itself in society. As indicated in the introduction to this study, a central issue here is the utopian sensibility that both sport and film, as popular forms of entertainment, invoke, a sensibility that may ultimately obscure and mislead audiences regarding the issues touched upon within the films themselves, including race and social class. Building on the discussion in Chapter 3, the focus in this chapter will also be primarily on American film and society, as the source of the vast majority of sports themed films. However, sport's utopian possibilities are also relevant to the representation of sport in films emerging from other national contexts, an issue explored in more detail in Chapter 6.

The American Dream and the sports film

In American film in particular, the utopian sensibility is closely allied to a central ideology in American life, the American Dream. This is a dream particularly attractive to the marginalised and underprivileged, and one often powerfully affirmed by sport and in film. Indeed, from the codification of sport in the mid- to late nineteenth century, and its emergence in film in the final decade of that century, its representation had significant appeal for large numbers of recent immigrants to the United States, as well as members of the African American community. The American Dream of prosperity and success, 'of a land' as described by James Truslow Adams in his 1931 book *Epic of America* 'in which life should be better and richer and fuller for every man, with opportunity for each according to ability or achievement' (Cullen, 2004, p. 6), often proved to be less than fully achieved for many, particularly those from humble or deprived circumstances. However, sport provided a means to at least vicariously 'live the dream' through sporting heroes – many of whom like boxers 'Gentleman' Jim Corbett and latterly Jack Johnson came from modest immigrant or African American backgrounds – even if their followers' attempts to achieve success in life were fruitless. Johnson might be viewed as the beginnings of a pattern found repeatedly in American sports films whereby, as Bergan notes, boxers can

> take on the aspirations of a whole race such as Joe Louis, Muhammad Ali, or Jack Johnson as portrayed in *The Great White Hope* (TCF 1970), John Garfield as the Jewish boxer in *Body and Soul* (UA 1947) or Rocky Graziano (Paul Newman) in *Somebody Up There Likes Me* (MGM 1956) who has all the little people from the lower East Side pinning their hopes on him. From slave ship or immigration ship to championship.
>
> (1982, p. 14)

Early prize fight films featuring boxers such as Johnson were among the only representations of powerful African American figures in the cinema at that time and thus proved very popular among Black communities while been viewed with suspicion and sometimes fear 'among a White society that used censorship and segregation to exert social control over black America' (Streible, 2008, p. 9). Boxing was considered by many proponents of the sport as not just a means of countering a perceived feminisation of American culture, but also of maintaining the superiority and cultural hegemony of White America. This was evident both in the 'colour bar' to non-White boxers competing for major championships – maintained until the emergence of Johnson at the end of the first decade of the twentieth century and reinforced after Johnson's loss of the title in 1915 – and the restriction upheld for many years on African Americans participating in major boxing clubs and establishments (Streible, 2008, p. 196). Given their popularity among African American audiences, however, one cannot underestimate the importance of early prize fight films featuring boxers such as Johnson in popularising boxing among African American communities and indeed playing an important role in encouraging increasing numbers of Black Americans to participate in this sport. Furthermore, the early association of such sports films with the American Dream of success anticipated a central theme throughout the genre as it developed in the twentieth century.

The American Dream ideology continues to be an essential belief shared by many Americans, regardless of class, race or gender (Smith, 2009; Nixon, 1984). Indeed, so strong is this abiding ideology that it may function as a form of social control as it is viewed as not just an opportunity, but an obligation of every American and those 'who remain content with their status or achievements are perceived by others as deviant' (Nixon, 1984, p. 17). As such, this dream provides a central point of identification and cohesion for American society and a means of controlling dissent within it; as Howard L. Nixon notes

> The American Dream as an ideology has the capacity to help less successful groups to adjust to the disparity between their objective social circumstances and the dream of success by being a set of beliefs and sentiments that provide such groups with a continuing source of hope, which may be quite unrealistic but still gives their lives meaning *within* the existing value system and structure of their society. In this sense, the ideology of the American Dream is an *argument* for the virtues of the American way of life, and as an ideology, the American Dream performs a social control function.
>
> (1984, pp. 17–18)

Despite the promise of the American Dream, the reality, as Nixon intimates, is that equal opportunity does not exist in the United States. Whether as a result of race, ethnicity, gender or social class, success in the United States is more often inherited than earned (Nixon, 1984, p. 10). Indeed, successive studies (Nixon 1984; Wolff 1995; Black et al. 2006; Johnson 2006; Miller, 2006; Smith 2009; Saez, 2010; Congressional Budget Office 2011) have indicated that far from opportunity and equality increasing in the United States, the opposite is actually the case, while the number living in poverty is now at an all-time high of 15.1 per cent, equivalent to over 46 million Americans (U.S. Census Bureau, 2011a).

Despite these realities, the ideology of the American Dream continues to be a powerful force in American life, an ideology repeatedly affirmed by leading figures in American society, including in two major addresses in 2011, by President Barack Obama.[1] In his speech, entitled 'The Country We Believe In', delivered at The George Washington University in Washington DC on April 13, 2011, Obama referred to the importance of preserving 'the American Dream for future generations' and quoted from a letter he received:

> The other day I received a letter from a man in Florida. He started off by telling me he didn't vote for me and he hasn't always agreed with me. But

even though he's worried about our economy and the state of our politics, he said, 'I still believe. I believe in that great country that my grandfather told me about. I believe that somewhere lost in this quagmire of petty bickering on every news station, the "American Dream" is still alive...'

(Obama, 2011a)

The persistence of this 'meritocracy myth' (McNamee and Miller, 2009), in the face of all the evidence that points to its fallacy owes much to two of the most influential cultural forces in American life: sport and film. Individually, both have contributed greatly to the affirmation of this ideology, a fact underscored when we encounter them together within film. Sport provides one of the most popular and influential cultural practices for the affirmation and potential achievement of the American Dream. As noted by Howard Nixon, 'Sport is an appropriate vehicle for testing the ideology of the American Dream because the legitimizing beliefs of the sports institution mirror basic tenets of the American Dream' (1984, p. 25). These beliefs were summarised by Harry Edwards in his influential study *The Sociology of Sport* (1973). Through a survey of references to sport in American magazines, newspapers and a major athletic journal, Edwards identified a 'dominant American sports creed'. Similar to those beliefs that underscore the American Dream, Edwards saw this creed as encompassing a series of beliefs concerned with affirming the advantages and benefits of participating in organised sports including its contribution to building character, instilling discipline, developing competitive instincts, improving physical and mental fitness, and encouraging religious and patriotic sensibilities. Though published in 1973, as will become apparent below and in the following chapters, the beliefs outlined by Edwards continue to be evident within the American sports film genre. However, as with the American Dream, Edwards found limited evidence to support these beliefs in his analysis of sport in American life. Nonetheless, for the marginalised and underprivileged in particular across the United States, sport is frequently viewed as a principle means to overcome their challenging and marginalised circumstances and realise the American Dream.

This is particularly the case for African Americans. As noted by Earl Smith 'African American Civil Society aspires toward the American dream, the ability to pursue success, through sport, or what might be called the "athletic division" of American society' (2009, p. 7). This is reflected in the huge over-representation of African Americans in collegiate and professional sports in the US, when compared with their percentage of the American population (Smith, 2009, pp. 119–120). According to one study, 'African Americans comprise approximately 79% of NBA rosters, 65% of NFL line ups, and 18% of MLB teams (about 18% of MLB players are Hispanic)' (Leonard, 1997, p. 424). However, African Americans only account, according to the latest U.S. census figures, for 12.6 per cent of the population of the United States (U.S. Census Bureau, 2011b). While the over-representation of African Americans may suggest that the American Dream is possible to achieve through sport, the fact is that the likelihood of such success is very slim. Indeed, as the African American writer Henry Louis Gates has observed

> Too many of our children have come to believe that it's easier to become a black professional athlete than a doctor or a lawyer. Reality check: according to the 2000 census, there were more than 31,000 black physicists and surgeons, 33,000 black lawyers and 5,000 black dentists. Guess how many black athletes are playing professional basketball, football and baseball combined, about 1,400. In fact, there are more board-certified black cardiologists than there are black professional basketball players.
>
> (2004)

Furthermore, the focus on sport for success has resulted in many African Americans failing to get the education necessary to achieve these more likely positions in society listed by Gates. Many African American athletes fail to graduate from high school at all, and there are also very high drop-out and failure rates for African Americans engaged in college sports (Smith, 2009, pp. 98–101). Drawing on the work of Erik O. Wright (1998) regarding the exploitation of human capital, Earl Smith has argued that

> Once he or she has used up his or her eligibility or is injured, the athlete is discarded, his or her scholarship rescinded, and with it the opportunity to complete his or her education and graduate, appropriately credentialed, and poised to seek success in the professional labor market. Once exploited, the athletes return, in the case of many African American men, to the ghetto or to rural poverty, virtual wastelands as far as the market economy is concerned. The promise of an education, of a credential, remains unfulfilled. And, like the "coolie" the offer of the "American Dream" is hollow.
>
> (2009, p. 116)

Sports films play a crucial role in sustaining and affirming the myth of achieving the American Dream through sport, despite the rarity of its achievement. Indeed, many of these films continue to promote the myth found in an early baseball film *Headin' Home* (1920) (discussed in Chapter 2) where a marginalised individual transcends his challenging social environment through sport. It is true that films critical of this trajectory have also emerged; boxing-themed films in particular have a long history of depicting individuals whose hopes (and bodies) are cruelly dashed and punished including *Body and Soul* (1947), *The Set Up* (1949) and *Champion* (1949), films discussed later in this chapter. However, significantly those films which have enjoyed greatest commercial success, and would appear to have made the greatest cultural impact particularly on American society, are those which view sport as a crucial, and positive, force in the realisation of the American Dream.

African Americans and the sports film

> As long as White Americans create and sustain images and perceptions of and for African Americans that their surest way to the 'American Dream' is through athletics, they will remain cordoned off in an area where very few make it and most will not. And, African Americans will not try to compete alongside Whites for the money and power that is available in business, the professions, and politics
>
> Earl Smith (2009, p. 224)

In Chapter 1 it was noted that a central feature of Hollywood cinema, and in particular genre films, is their attempt to resolve contradictions and overcome dichotomies evident within individual texts, contradictions that often reflect larger tensions within American society and the ideology that underpins it. As Barry Keith Grant has observed,

> Comparable to myths, genre movies may be understood as secular stories that seek to address and sometimes seemingly resolve our problems and dilemmas, some specifically historical and others more deeply rooted in our collective psyches.
>
> (2006, p. 29)

A recurring feature of sports films featuring African American characters is the inclusion of contradictory elements that the film's narrative trajectory ultimately attempts to resolve and contain. While these films may acknowledge the existence of racism and inequality within American society, and sometimes contain critiques of it, they do so within the context of films that may also contain regressive messages regarding the role and position of non-White individuals in the United States. Indeed, the inclusions of references to racism are present arguably to make the subtly racist message all the more convincing. As noted by Ed Guerrero, drawing on the work of Louis Althusser,

> ideology is a process or relation that must always be modified in response to ever-changing social pressures and realities. Instead of being 'a false consciousness' rigidly imposed from above on a dominated people, ideology permeates all strata of society and is a people's 'imaginary' relation to their real conditions. Because ideology is constantly negotiated, Hollywood cannot construct a permanent, seamless image of white superiority on the screen, any more than the film industry can completely control or eradicate the oppositional or emergent ideological impulses of African Americans or make black people vanish from the historical scene.
>
> (1993, p. 6)

An unsettling development in recent American sports films featuring African Americans is the re-emergence, and indeed popular success, of films that feature regressive stereotypes of African Americans as 'infantile, lazy, and subservient', as well as threatening sexual predators, stereotypes Ed Guerrero has identified from the earliest American films (1993, p. 12). Repeatedly throughout the early development of the sports film, African Americans were found in subservient positions. While *Gentleman Jim* (1942) ignores the issue of the 'colour-bar' so assiduously followed by boxer James Corbett in his refusal to fight one of the major contenders for his title, Peter Jackson, African Americans are almost entirely absent from the film itself, featuring principally (and briefly) as servants in the background of the Olympic Club where Corbett fights. By *The Hustler* (1961), African Americans had not changed their position markedly, as evidenced in the limping cleaner depicted in the background of New York's Ames Billiard Hall in the film's opening and closing sequences. As Bergan has noted of horse racing themed films in the early twentieth century, African Americans featured similarly:

> Twentieth Century Fox's lushly photographed Technicolor racing story *Kentucky* (1938) created a mini-genre. The white porticoed plantation house, the paddock, the track, horses streaming across wild fields, the faithful negro retainers, the black mammy, the young couple keen on horses, and the temperamental thoroughbred breaking his heart to win.
>
> (1982, p. 71)

Among those African Americans who featured as such 'faithful negro retainers' was Louis Armstrong who plays a trumpet-playing groom to a wild horse named Jeepers Creepers in *Kentucky* who can only be soothed by the playing of Armstrong and his band who follow his races in a car.

The Jackie Robinson Story (1950)

It was rare that African Americans featured in other than minor roles in sports films for much of the first half of the twentieth century. However, in the aftermath of World War II and particularly after the successes of the African American Civil Rights Movement in the 1960s, Black Americans began to feature more prominently. As indicated earlier, sport is particularly attractive to members of the African American community as a perceived means of achieving the American Dream and in most American sports films that depict Black athletes prominently, this trajectory is apparent. A pertinent and influential early example is the 1950 film *The Jackie Robinson Story*, featuring the legendary baseball player himself in the lead role. Directed by Alfred E. Green, the film was shot in Motion Pictures Center Studios in Hollywood in February 1950. Significantly, it was a low-budget production produced by B-movie specialist Eagle-Lion Films at a time when Hollywood majors were still hesitant to feature strong African Americans in lead roles. Indeed, the project was turned down by two studios because its promoters refused to depict Robinson being taught how to play baseball by a White man (Bogle, 2001, p. 184). *The Jackie Robinson Story*, nonetheless, in common with previous and subsequent sports films featuring African Americans, uses the figure of Robinson and his individualistic success as an athlete to ultimately affirm the American Dream and what it represents, despite the film's references to instances of racism within American society.

Robinson, as well as been one of the greatest baseball players of his generation, was also the first African American in the modern era to play Major League baseball in the United States, successfully crossing the baseball 'colour line' when he lined out for the first time for the Brooklyn Dodgers in 1947. At a time when much of the United States continued to be segregated, both in sport and in public life, Robinson became a crucial symbol for African Americans wishing to end segregation and discrimination in their country. The existence of racial segregation and discrimination in the United States represented a challenge to the concept of the American Dream itself, which centrally affirms the existence of equal opportunity for all within American society (DeVitis and Rich, 1996, p. 5). Therefore, as apparent in *The Jackie Robinson Story*, Hollywood films that engage with this challenge invariably do so in a manner which ultimately attempts to affirm the Dream. From the opening images of *The Jackie Robinson Story*, this is precisely the message given as the narrator tells us, over images of a young African American boy walking along a dirt road, that 'This is the story of a boy and his dream, but more than that, it is the story of an American boy and a dream that is truly American'. Indeed, from these opening credits onwards, *The Jackie Robinson Story* attempts to control and domesticate the role of Robinson within American culture. It is noteworthy, for example, that a dialogue coach (Ross Hunter) is included among those listed in the credits. Presumably this is not to teach any of the leading actors English but rather to tutor their accents and pronunciation in a manner deemed acceptable for mainstream (White) American audiences.

Baseball has an almost mythological role in American culture, a role affirmed in *The Jackie Robinson Story* (Robson, 2010). The Brooklyn Dodgers General Manager, and the man responsible for signing Robinson, Branch Rickey (Minor Watson) repeatedly refers to baseball in the film as the 'American game' that represents 'democratic principles'.[2] While defending in one scene his signing of Robinson to the International League of Baseball president, Frank Shaughnessy (Harry Shannon), he articulates his belief in the importance of baseball to American life, a belief that reiterates elements contained within the American sports creed summarised above:

> I spent my whole life in baseball and I've always been proud of that because I've always thought that baseball was a fine game, a clean game, I've always thought it had a good influence on the American people, on the kids growing up. I've always thought baseball taught fairplay and sportsmanship.

Indeed, for Rickey, baseball can provide an exemplar for society as a whole, where 'a box score is really democratic ... it doesn't say how big you are or how your father voted in the last election or what church you attend. It just tells you what kind of a ball player you were that day'. In a later scene, Rickey again defends his decision to pick Robinson for the Dodgers team after some players on the team sign a petition refusing to play with the African American. In challenging one of the players of Italian descent, Rickey remarks:

> Your parents came to this country from Italy and were allowed to work as free people and yet you, a child and beneficiary of that freedom want to deny the same opportunity to an American whose parents and grandparents and great grandparents have been in this country for 200 years.

In scenes such as this, *The Jackie Robinson Story* reaffirms American culture and society while at the same time occluding the realities that lay behind it. No mention is made here, for example, that the arrival of Robinson's ancestors in the United States was not as a result of immigration – as in the case of the Italian parents of his teammate – but rather of capture and enslavement. This is a recurring trope throughout the film. While racism is acknowledged, it is given neither a historical nor a political context. Rather instances of racism appear within the film as aberrant elements within a largely supportive White-American structure.

From the opening scene of the film it is this supportive (and paternalistic) White-American society that is foregrounded as we witness an older White boy give Robinson his first baseball glove, thereby beginning, presumably, the journey that takes him to the Major League. Rather than focus on the reality of Robinson's young life, confined primarily, in the days of segregation, to play baseball with other African Americans, here it is White Americans who facilitate his development as a baseball player. Even Robinson's drafting into the army later in the film is presented as the support of the US government at a time when nobody else would give him a job (no reference is made to the fact that the army at the time, like American society as a whole, was rigidly segregated), while a later threatened attack on Robinson by racist supporters after a game is averted through the intercession of two White team mates. Equally, his attempts to find work after college are assisted by his White team mates on the basketball team, who we learn in one scene are concerned about him possibly quitting college and have been sending letters to high schools on his behalf in an attempt to find him work.

As well as 'equal opportunity', a further principle belief of the American Dream is that 'those who work hard gain success and are rewarded with fame, power, money, and property' (DeVitis and Rich, 1996, p. 5). We witness Robinson, therefore, working hard from an early age from shoe-shine boy, to delivering newspapers, all the time carrying his baseball glove. His efforts are paralleled by his own progress as an athlete – in line with the American sports creed's emphasis on sport building character – and we later witness him preparing to represent his junior college in athletics, eventually breaking his brother Mack's (Joel Fluellen) 'broad jump record'. Robinson is also depicted as working hard to put himself through college at UCLA, considering leaving college early at one point in order to get a 'better, full time job' that will allow him to marry his girlfriend Rae (Ruby Dee).

Yet again, supportive White men enter the narrative to facilitate his progress as an athlete as we witness legendary UCLA coach Bill Spaulding (played by Spaulding himself in the film) support a scholarship for Robinson remarking that

> coloured boys are alright with me if they're the right colour ... I like a good clean American boy with a B average. If that's the kind of a boy you're talking about, his colour's blue and gold [UCLA colours].

This scene is also interesting in that Spaulding's colleague is concerned about giving Robinson a scholarship as he 'heard somebody squawking about giving coloured boys too many athletic scholarships'; in one sentence the film not only further supports the contention that White America went to great lengths to facilitate Robinson, but also that many other 'coloured boys' were benefiting from this generosity.

Throughout *The Jackie Robinson Story*, therefore, White America appears as a paternalistic structure intent on assisting Robinson to realise his dream, rather than the developers and beneficiaries of a racist and unequal society. Indeed, despite being manifest within the film, racism is never mentioned once in the entire work. Opportunities to provide either substance or context for instances of racism are avoided, as when Robinson travels to an away game for the Dodgers farm club the Montreal Royals in a city where, we are told, 'they don't like coloured people'. However, the place or team concerned are never identified, nor specifically the Ku Klux Klan, despite what are presumably members of that organisation been depicted in the stand at the game referring to their 'club with branches all over the country' who 'put them [African Americans] in their place' when they 'get uppidy'.

We are, however, reminded of the limited opportunities available to African Americans, particularly through Robinson's brother Mack who despite having a college education, works as a binman; as he remarks to Robinson while kicking his bin, 'here's one place nobody draws a colour line'. Moments such as this, along with the images of overt racism in the film, undoubtedly unsettle the overall narrative trajectory concerned with affirming the American Dream and likely provided important moments of identification for African Americans in the 1950s suffering under an unjust system. However, ultimately in this scene (as elsewhere) Mack defends the job itself responding to Robinson's dismissive 'great job for a college man' by observing 'It may not be a great job but it's steady'. What we are presented with repeatedly in the film in scenes such as this is an acknowledgement of such problems in American society, but only to ultimately affirm the system that perpetuates these problems. It is significant here that this conversation ends with these words by Mack, which attempt to contain the dissent evident in the scene.

Indeed, containing dissent is a recurring trope of the film as a whole. When Branch Rickey signs Robinson to the Dodgers organisation he warns him that, regardless of what racist abuse he may suffer on the pitch, he cannot 'fight back'. 'I want a ball player' Rickey declares, 'with guts enough not to fight back'. It is only after proving his extraordinary ability on the field of play, that Robinson finally earns, according to Rickey, the right to 'fight back' by addressing the United States House of Representatives in Washington DC, 'about things on your mind, about a threat to peace that's on everybody's mind'. Following the logic of Rickey's argument, and indeed the film as a whole, African Americans are required to attain extraordinary individual achievements – above and beyond that of the vast majority of Americans of any colour, ethnicity or belief – in order to 'earn' the right to express their discontent with a racist and discriminatory system. It is a right, therefore, that is denied to the vast majority of those who suffer under this system.

In the final scene of the film we witness Robinson's address to Congress, in words that acknowledge the challenges faced by minorities such as African Americans but ultimately defend the system in which these inequalities are perpetuated:

> I know that life here in these United States can be mighty tough for people who are a little different from the majority. I'm not fooled because I've had a chance open to very few Negro Americans, but I do know that democracy works for those who are willing to fight for it, and I'm sure it's worth defending. I can't speak for any fifty million people, no one person can. But I am certain that I and other Americans of many races and faiths have too much invested in our country's welfare to throw it away or to let it be taken from us.

In defending American democracy, Robinson ultimately defends a system that enacted and upheld discriminatory legislation within the United States, at the very time that he was addressing Congress. Though his words do refer to challenges, these are neither identified nor clearly articulated and his position as a successful African American arguably further obscures this issue by suggesting that it is possible for African Americans to be successful nonetheless. Indeed, the superimposition of the image of the statue of liberty over a mid-shot of Robinson addressing the House of Representatives, accompanied by the strains of 'America the beautiful' on the soundtrack are highly suggestive (Fig. 4.1).

This scene is reminiscent of the image discussed by Roland Barthes in his seminal essay 'Myth Today' of 'a young Negro in a French uniform ... saluting, with his eyes uplifted, probably fixed on a fold of the tricolour' (1957, p. 116).

FIGURE 4.1 *The Jackie Robinson Story* (Eagle-Lion Films, 1950)

Barthes deconstructed the image and identified dual discourses within it, both the surface meaning indicated above, but also a further signification or *myth*:

> that France is a great Empire, that all her sons, without any colour discrimination, faithfully serve under her flag, and that there is no better answer to the detractors of an alleged colonialism than the zeal shown by this Negro in serving his so-called oppressors.
>
> (1957, p. 116)

Similarly, this evocative image of Jackie Robinson (Fig. 4.1), while appearing to provide a positive depiction of an African American, simultaneously exploits this representation to assimilate it within a hegemonic American order that is itself responsible for perpetuating racist policies, such as segregation and the 'colour bar'. This pattern is repeated in the final words from the narrator over a shot again, as in the film's opening scene, of a young African American boy walking along a dirt road. The claim here by the narrator that Jackie Robinson's story is 'A story, a victory that can only happen in a country that is truly free' is extraordinary given that this lack of 'freedom' for African Americans, whether as athletes, bus passengers, or simply visitors to restaurants, continued to be a feature of a segregated American society for several decades after the release of *The Jackie Robinson Story*.

The Blind Side (2009)

American society has undergone significant changes since the 1950s, including the enactment of The Civil Rights Act of 1964 which outlawed some of the most significant types of discrimination against African Americans apparent in *The Jackie Robinson Story*, among them racial segregation. The sports film has undoubtedly responded to these developments with African Americans now more frequently depicted in prominent roles often working together through sport with Whites and other ethnic minorities to bring success in films such as *Remember the Titans* (2000), *Friday Night Lights* (2004) and *Glory Road* (2006). As Tudor notes, 'Such mixing displays the perceived power of sports to cross racial lines and create happy fantasy formations of equality' (1997, p. 74). However, as discussed in the opening section of this chapter, these films also disguise the fact that American society continues to be characterised by race and class inequality. Sociologist Heather Beth Johnson's remarks below merit lengthy quotation in their capturing of the increasing importance of the American Dream today, now often viewed as an achieved reality as much as an ideal:

> Not unlike the generations of Americans before us, my students and I have been immersed in the culture of a deeply held American Dream. We were told that in this country an individual rises and falls based on personal achievement or lack thereof; that one's background or family origin is neither a significant help nor hindrance in the quest for success; and that each of us earns and deserves our relative social positioning. Many a child has been told these things, and the American Dream has surely evolved in various ways over time, but those of us born since the 1950s have grown up in the wake of social movements, groundbreaking court decisions, and unprecedented cultural shifts that have led to a particularly literal interpretation of the American Dream theme. Equal opportunity has been presented to us not so much as an ideal but as an achieved reality. A level playing field has been held out to us not so much as a goal but as an actual, legitimate explanation for how our system operates. So it is not hard to imagine our surprise when we realize that regardless of all we have been taught, despite all our beliefs, things are not exactly what they seem.
>
> To learn that race and class inequality is still happening systematically, and that in fact an historic cleavage such as the racial wealth gap is getting deeper, is to realize that significant sociostructural problems have yet to be solved, and to suspect that there is something wrong with the *system*.
>
> (2006, p. 2)

Significantly, while the representation of African Americans in the American sports film may have evolved to reflect an increasing belief in improved opportunities for racial minorities in American society, sports films nonetheless continue to feature analogous motifs and a similar trajectory to that found in *The Jackie Robinson Story*. The following section examines one of the most commercially successful American sports films of recent years, *The Blind Side* (2009). This film represents a recurring theme found in sports films that feature African American characters. On the one hand it depicts an African American overcoming difficult and marginalised circumstances through his sporting ability; on the other this success is facilitated by hegemonic White American society. In the process, the serious social issues touched upon in the film are obscured and ultimately explained as the result of either flaws within the African American community itself or the operations of fate, rather than as the result of either historical or social factors. Other films that share this paternalistic, and patronising approach to African Americans, and other non-White groups, include *Cool Runnings* (1993), *The Air Up There* (1994), *Jerry Maguire* (1996), *Hardball* (2001), *Radio* (2003), *Bring It On: All or Nothing* (2006) and *The Love Guru* (2008). In each of these films, a White (usually male) character inspires African Americans and/or other non-White groups to overcome challenging circumstances through sport.

In common with several of these films, including *Cool Runnings* (1993), *Hardball* (2001) and *Radio* (2003), *The Blind Side* is also based on a true story, a fact emphasised repeatedly in the promotion of the film (Fig. 4.2). The foregrounding of this element not only added to the poignancy of the events featured for viewers of the film, it also allowed the producers to justify the production and release of a film that might very well be regarded as racist. As one reviewer noted shortly after the film's release

> *Blind Side* the movie peddles the most insidious kind of racism, one in which whiteys are virtuous saviors, coming to the rescue of African Americans who become superfluous in narratives that are supposed to be about them.
>
> (Anderson, 2009)

Indeed, to add to the 'authenticity' of the portrayal, actual footage of American football games are featured, including in the opening sequence which is composed of television coverage of the horrific tackle that ended the career of quarterback Joe Theismann. The film also includes scenes with the actual Michael Oher, after he was drafted by the Baltimore Ravens, surrounded by the Touhy family portrayed in the film. There are also many cameos by former and present American football coaches playing themselves including Houston Nutt, Ed Orgeron, Franklin 'Pepper' Rodgers, Nick Saban and Tommy Tuberville while well-known television sportscasters and analysts, Lou Holtz, Phillip Fulmer and Tom Lemming, also feature.

The Blind Side was one of the most successful films of 2009, and became the most commercially successful American football-themed film ever released after taking $255,959,475 at the American box office.[3] The film also won a best Actress Academy Award for Sandra Bullock who plays Memphis decorator, mother and Republican Leigh Anne Touhy. The production is based on Michael

FIGURE 4.2 *The Blind Side* (Warner Bros., 2009) (Warner Bros. Pictures/The Kobal Collection)

Lewis's book *The Blind Side: Evolution of a Game* (2006) which detailed the real life story of Michael Oher, an African American child from a neglected and underprivileged background who was adopted by the wealthy Irish-American Touhy family in Memphis. Oher eventually developed into an accomplished NFL player, achieving the American Dream, with some help along the way.

As has become the norm in sports films, television is foregrounded repeatedly in *The Blind Side*. The film opens with television coverage of the tackle by Lawrence Taylor that ended the career of Joe Theismann, the Redskins quarterback, but also elevated the role of the player occupying the left tackle position and his importance in protecting the blind side of the quarterback. This focus on television reflects a feature of the opening of the film as a whole; the manner in which it literally 'domesticates' American football as Leigh Anne Touhy reflects not just on the quarterback as the best paid player on the field but also the left tackle as the next highest, because, as she remarks,

> every housewife knows, the first check you write is for the mortgage but the second is for the insurance. And the left tackle's job is to protect the quarterback from what he can't see coming. To protect his blind side.

In this moment, the film not only provides a rationale for its title, but also brings the sporting elements which will be returned to repeatedly into the context of people's homes. And indeed, it is home, and the family that are at the centre of *The Blind Side*, to the exclusion of any substantial engagement with society, or with society's role in the perpetuation of the problematic issues that the film raises. While the Touhy family adopt Michael Oher (Quinton Aaron), family defines his relationship with his team and with the game of football from then on. In order to help Oher improve his game, Leigh Anne asks him to view his quarterback and team members as members of his family:

> This team is your family, Michael. You have to protect them from those guys. Okay? Listen … Tony here is your quarterback, alright? You protect his blind side. When you look at him, you think of me.

In his first game for his high school team, Oher remembers these words from Leigh Anne and they provide inspiration for him to put in a match winning performance on the field.

As with *The Jackie Robinson Story*, the film appears ostensibly to criticise racist attitudes. This is evident particularly in the reaction of Leigh Anne – 'Shame on you' – to the concerns of her female friends regarding Oher being allowed to stay in her home, including the threat he might pose to her daughter Collins (Lily Collins). As her friend Elaine (Eaddy Mays) asks her over lunch:

> That's awesome for you, but what about Collins? … Aren't you worried, I mean, even just a little? He's a boy, a large, black boy, sleeping under the same roof.

Moments such as these in the film reflect the polysemous nature of much Hollywood film, as identified by Rick Altman and Robert Ray. Ray's remarks on Hollywood cinema are equally applicable to the processes apparent in *The Jackie Robinson Story* and *The Blind Side*:

> Hollywood's thematic conventions rested on an industrywide consensus defining commercially acceptable filmmaking. This consensus's underlying premise dictated the conversion of all political, sociological, and economic dilemmas into personal melodrama … Such displacement turned on Classic Hollywood's basic thematic procedure: repeatedly, these movies raised, and then appeared to solve problems associated with the troubling incompatibility of traditional American myths.
>
> (1985, p. 57)

While appealing to the viewer's anti-racist sympathies, *The Blind Side* ultimately employs this encounter with Leigh Anne's racist friend to disguise its recurring racist depictions of African Americans while simultaneously affirming the

American Dream. Apart from the character of Michael Oher, African Americans are repeatedly depicted as neglectful, depraved, criminal and threatening figures in *The Blind Side*. When Leigh Anne and Oher visit an African American area of the city to buy clothes, a threatening atmosphere is evident: 'I've lived in Memphis my whole life and never been anywhere near here. You're going to take care of me, right?' Leigh Anne remarks to Oher. Oher eventually returns to his home neighbourhood to seek his mother and meets with local drug dealer Alton (Iron E. Singleton) who invites him to his apartment where a group are taking drugs and drinking. Alton proceeds to insult Oher and the White family he stays with, with the film recalling the stereotype of the African American sexual predator in his dialogue:

> She got other kids? She got a daughter? You tap that? Yeah, you tapped that! Yeah, yeah, yeah! Big Mike! Big Mike got his white babes! Hey, Big Mike! You should enjoy 'em, man ... I like me some mommy/daughter action.

When Oher tells Alton to 'shut up', the sexual suggestions turn to violence and the threat to kill:

> Who the hell is you telling to shut up? I will bust and cap your fat ass. And then drive east and pay a visit to your cracker Mom! And her sweet little daughter.

Oher attacks Alton, breaks up the party and leaves, only for Leigh Anne to arrive the next day looking for him, in a scene that not only reaffirms a pejorative view of African Americans but also defends gun ownership in the United States:

> Alton: Tell him, sleep with one eye open. You hear me, bitch?
> Leigh Anne: No, you hear me, bitch! You threaten my son you threaten me. You so much as cross downtown you will be sorry. I'm in a prayer group with the DA, I'm a member of the NRA and I'm always packing.

In one sentence, God, the National Rifle Association, and local government are invoked to defend Leigh Anne's adopted son and affirm the shared authority of each in American life.

Significantly, the one positive African American character in the film, Michael Oher, is portrayed as almost mute and inarticulate, of very low IQ and in need of the support and facilitation of rich White America to progress. However, in order to receive this support, Oher must be prepared to forget. As Leigh Anne's husband Sean (Tim McGraw) remarks at one point, 'Michael's gift is his ability to forget. He's mad at no one and he really didn't care what happened in the past.' This point is reiterated later in the film when Michael remembers the words of his mother to him as a child 'the past is gone, the world is a good place, and it's all gonna be okay'. Such dehistoricisation is seductive particularly given the history of the African American experience of slavery, oppression, discrimination and marginalisation within American society. Furthermore, it also discourages an engagement with the real structural issues that continue to perpetuate such marginalisation. Indeed, African Americans, and other ethnic minorities, suffer much higher levels of poverty than other subgroups within the United States. As noted by the National Poverty Center at the University of Michigan,

> Poverty rates for blacks and Hispanics greatly exceed the national average. In 2009, 25.8% of blacks and 25.3% of Hispanics were poor, compared to 9.4% of non-Hispanic whites and 12.5% of Asians.

In addition, African American males account for well over 40 per cent of the male prison population in the United States with, according to one 2008 report, 'One in nine black men aged 20 to 34 … behind bars' (Aizenman, 2008). While the film acknowledges some of the serious social issues that plague African Americans – including poverty, drug addiction, unemployment, homelessness and parental neglect – rather than providing either a historical or social context for such issues, these problems are instead presented as primarily the result of flaws within the African American community itself.

As well as being depicted as untrustworthy, violent and sexually aggressive, African Americans in *The Blind Side* are also portrayed as neglectful of their own social responsibilities in contrast to members of the dominant White community. Oher we discover early in the film is homeless, abandoned by his neglectful father and unable to stay with his drug-addicted mother. He sleeps at night in the gymnasium of Wingate High school until offered a bed by Leigh Anne. Individuals such as Oher, however, could also be considered at risk of what sociologist Zygmunt Bauman has referred to as 'social homelessness', 'in the context of a national culture that preaches unity and egalitarian opportunism while micro-segmenting demographic groups and intensifying class war' (Negra, 2009, p. 288). As Henry Giroux has also observed, 'entire populations are now considered disposable, an unnecessary burden on state coffers, and consigned to fend for themselves' (2006, p. 10). In the case of the children (such as Michael Oher) of such populations, the solution *The Blind Side* suggests is sporting ability and the generosity of a prosperous White family, rather than structural change or societal engagement. Whether in the form of Oher's neglectful mother and father, or the threatening African American community he comes from, these exist in the film principally as a contrast to the generosity of the Touhy family (and by association White America as a whole), and to further elevate their actions.

However, there is another argument evident in this film regarding the position of African Americans. In seeking support for Oher's admission to the school from the school's board, Coach Cotton (Ray McKinnon) appeals to the Christian ethos of Wingate:

> Look at the wall. Christian. We either take that seriously or we paint over it. You don't admit Michael Oher because of sports, you admit him because it's the right thing to do.

In the next scene we witness Oher staring at the archway leading into the school. In a crane shot, giving at first an almost God-like perspective, that swoops down to the archway, the camera highlights the school motto: 'With Men this is possible, With God all things are possible', a slogan that is underlined in the theme of the film where rather than history or society, it is the operations of fate that dictate people's status and wellbeing. Fate, it would appear, dictates that Michael Oher will be adopted by a rich White family and given opportunities few other African Americans in his position enjoy and Oher stops to ponder the motto before entering under the archway, foregrounding it still more. We as the audience, via the camera, follow Oher through the archway and are reassured, both by the gentle and melodic musical accompaniment and by the non-threatening nature of Oher himself, that all is right with the world. It is religion as hope, but also as consolation, a theme returned to later in the film when Leigh Anne reflects on the death of another promising African American athlete, and neighbour of Oher's as he grew up:

> He'd been killed in a gang fight at Hurt Village. In the last paragraph they talked about his superb athletic skills and how different his life might have been if he hadn't fallen behind and dropped out of school. He was twenty-one years old the day he died. It was his birthday. That could have been anyone. It could have been my son, Michael. But it wasn't. And I suppose I have God to thank for that.

Indeed, Christianity is foregrounded repeatedly in the film, evident, for example, in the crucifix Leigh Anne wears in almost every scene. When Oher sits away from the family in the dining room while other family members watch the thanksgiving American football game on TV, Leigh Anne moves all the family into the dining room to join him, and leads a prayer of thanksgiving before they eat dinner. Here both Christianity and American values are affirmed. However, they are also contrasted with the lack of 'Christianity' shown to Oher by his own African American community. Earlier in the film, 'Big Tony' Hamilton, who had allowed the homeless Oher to sleep on his couch, tries to convince his wife not to throw Oher out; 'I try to be Christian about the son, alright?' However, his wife replies 'Let somebody else be Christian about this kid' emphasising again the neglect of the African American community, particularly when compared with the Christian charity very evident both in the admittance of Oher to Wingate Christian school and his eventual adoption by the Touhy family. This focus on Christian values also affirms one of the core beliefs identified by Harry Edwards within the American sports creed 'relating sports achievement to traditional American Christianity' (1973, p. 69).

Fate is also invoked in the final song of the film which complements shots of Michael being drafted by the Baltimore Ravens. As the lyrics of the song 'Chances' by the group Five For Fighting relate 'Chances are when said and done/Who'll be the lucky ones who make it all the way?' presumably referring to Michael Oher's own trajectory.

Social class and the sports film

The achievement of the American Dream through sport, as Howard Nixon observes, is not just beyond most African American men:

> In American society, race, color, religion, sex, age, occupation, social class, sports background, and physical stature or other physical characteristics have affected opportunities for involvement and achievement in a variety of sports roles and domains. Not only are these various forms of social discrimination inconsistent with the egalitarian ideology of American democracy, they also fail to conform to the emphases on merit and even-handedness that are supposed to characterize the dominant organizational form of modern American society and sport, which is rational-legal bureaucracy.
>
> (1984, p. 16)

Nonetheless, the trajectory apparent in works discussed above featuring African Americans is also evident in films featuring protagonists from marginalised working-class communities. As with African Americans depicted in mainstream sports films, repeatedly in the American sports film working-class characters overcome considerable obstacles through sport to realise at least a part of the American Dream. Where they fail to do so, their challenging circumstances, as with African Americans discussed above, are often attributed principally to their own flaws rather than structural issues or inequalities within society as a whole. In reality, few people can give up their sometimes unsatisfactory jobs, with their families frequently dependent on the income received, to pursue dreams of sporting success. Where workers endure poor circumstances, Unions often have limited power to negotiate for improved conditions particularly as management could move the entire company elsewhere, as is depicted in the ice-hockey themed film *Slap Shot* (1977) where the local mill is due to close with '10,000 mill workers placed on waivers'. Furthermore, as apparent in the case of a film such as *Invincible* (2006) (discussed in the concluding chapter) the efforts of organised labour to improve working conditions compares poorly with the hope and emotional fulfilment that sport appears to provide in the life of workers. In such circumstances, workers may indeed feel powerless to improve their conditions. The temporary escape which sport and sports films offer, and the false hope they give of escaping one's challenging circumstances, are very attractive indeed. They present both a challenge to the system and also the possibility of escape. However, rarely do these films acknowledge the systemic challenges that people face to progress, including financial, personal and educational (Kleinhans, 1985, p. 66).

The boxing film

Boxing in film has provided an ambiguous, yet revelatory, picture of sport in America, often focusing on the dark and corrupt aspects of this sport, but also seeing in it an opportunity for those marginalised and less fortunate to realise the American Dream. In 1996, Leger Grindon could count 'well over 150 feature-length fiction productions since 1930' (1996, p. 54) and this number has increased substantially subsequently with boxing films enjoying huge commercial success (in particular the *Rocky* series) and critical acclaim (notably Martin Scorsese's *Raging Bull* (1980) and most recently David O. Russell's *The Fighter* (2010)). The boxing film has offered a particularly apt site on which to explore what has been a central concern of contemporary genre criticism, recognisable narratives involving 'dramatic conflicts, which are themselves based upon ongoing cultural conflicts' (Schatz, 1981, p. viii). Boxing offers a ready-made arena for the portrayal of such struggles.

Boxing has been a staple of Hollywood cinema since the first emergence of film. As indicated in Chapter 2, among the most important film productions in the earliest years of the cinema was the prize fight film. While the practical limitations of filming technology in the early years gave way to more sophisticated approaches to filming sport, boxing continued to provide a powerful forum through which to present an intense physical and emotional encounter. Indeed, those elements that Hollywood has historically prided itself on providing, drama, conflict and potentially life-threatening situations are all available to audiences within the ring. Furthermore, the boxing film offers a particularly vivid arena for engaging central tensions within American mythology, including that between the individual and the community, and for their containment within a reconciliatory narrative (Ray, 1985, p. 58). In Robert B. Ray's study of classic Hollywood films, he identified boxing films in particular within this pattern:

> Often, the movies' reconciliatory pattern concentrated on a single character magically embodying diametrically opposite traits. A sensitive violinist was also a tough boxer (*Golden Boy*); a boxer was a gentle man who cared for pigeons (*On the Waterfront*) … Such two-sided characters seemed particularly designed to appeal to a collective American imagination steeped in myths of inclusiveness … The movies traded on one opposition in particular, American culture's traditional dichotomy of individual and community that had generated the most significant pair of competing myths: the outlaw hero and the official hero.
>
> (1985, pp. 58–59)

Boxing films also reflect this dichotomy, sometimes personified within individual boxers themselves, torn between the often corrupt (and corrupting) world of boxing and their family and domestic responsibilities. One of the earliest sports films of the sound era, *The Champ* (1931), represents the boxing game as the decadent pursuit of the uneducated central protagonist, Andy 'Champ' Purcell (Wallace Beery), a single father who brings up his son in a one-bedroom apartment above a Greek saloon in Tijuana, Mexico and who attempts to enter the ring one last time to provide for him. An alcoholic and chronic gambler, Purcell regularly brings his son with him for luck on his gambling sprees and usually loses what little he occasionally wins, including on one gambling session the horse he had won previously for his son. Despite the neglect which his son 'Dink' (Jackie Cooper) experiences, the film indicates the strong bond between father and son, though this is a bond in which it appears the son cares as much for the father as the father looks after his son, including undressing his father before bed at night and attempting to sober him up before an interview with potential fight promoters. Through such a portrayal, the film clearly creates the context for the viewer to look disapprovingly on this poor working-class man, and ultimately approvingly on the rich couple, including Dink's mother Linda (Irene Rich) and her wealthy husband Tony (Hale Hamilton), who eventually take custody of Dink after Purcell's death following victory in his final fight.

Drawing on the work of Robert Ray, Aaron Baker has noted the manner in which *The Champ* avoids taking a clear position on ideological debates, suggesting instead that the potential and opportunity for advancement and success in the United States can overcome whatever tensions or contradictions exist within the society (Ray, 1985, pp. 55–69). According to Ray, this avoidance of taking a clear position results in 'a split between the moral center and the interest center of a story' (1985, p. 66). This split is evident in *The Champ* between Linda's husband, the wealthy New York businessman Tony, who represents 'family, traditional morality, and the work ethic' (Baker, 2003, p. 107) and the poor working-class Purcell, who lacks each of these, but is nonetheless the main interest centre in the film. Furthermore, class conflict within the film is also contained and displaced. Its containment is evident in the explanation of Andy's difficult circumstances, clearly represented within the film as the result of his own personal weaknesses and demons rather than the difficult economic conditions facing millions of Americans during the Great Depression. Equally, the film suggests that wealthy Americans – as in *The Blind Side* – will voluntarily provide for those in need, rather than the state intervening, evident in the largely positive representation of Tony. In one sequence, we witness Tony visit the casino where Purcell is gambling through the night to find Dink sleeping on the roulette table. In a powerfully suggestive scene, Tony admonishes Purcell for being a bad father and asks him to give custody at least temporarily to Dink's mother, his wife Linda. When Purcell refuses, Tony turns to the sleeping Andy in an obviously caring moment and turns the light off over the table he sleeps on, as the film prepares us for the highly melodramatic final scene where Tony will indeed take custody of Dink after his father's death and Dink will finally acknowledge his mother, running to embrace her at the film's close.

Class conflict in *The Champ* is also displaced via the depiction of a Mexican as the champion Andy must defeat in his final fight, thereby focusing domestic class anger during the Depression onto a convenient external other. As Baker observes

> *The Champ* not only succeeds in performing this displacement but knocks out two of the inconvenient 'lower' characters with one punch – defeating the Mexican and at the same time enabling Andy to die heroically. The film's last image of Dink in his mother's arms becomes a social Darwinist affirmation of 'progress and right order' achieved through the removal of 'inferior' peoples in favor of those better fit to survive the Depression.
>
> (2003, p. 107)

Boxing would continue to be represented as a corrupt and corrupting sport throughout the 1930s, sometimes apparent in such suggestive titles as *They Made Me a Criminal* (1939). As viewed through mainstream Hollywood film in this period, boxing was a sport controlled by gangsters into which ordinary White working-class men, sometimes talented and gifted as in the case of violinist Joe Bonaparte (William Holden) in Rouben Mamoulian's *Golden Boy* (1939), are forced out of necessity. Many of these films, particularly during and in the aftermath of the Great Depression, touched on the social and economic plight of many Americans. However, as with *The Champ*, this criticism was generally safely contained within narratives that usually offered a hopeful resolution without ultimately upsetting the structures that forced fighters into the ring in the first instance. *Golden Boy* concerns fighter Joe Bonaparte, a young man from an Italian American family who despite having considerable talent as a musician, feels compelled to enter the ring in order to make a living and contribute to his family. There is no indication at any point that Joe enjoys boxing – from the beginning of the film he reveals that he has no love for the sport and has serious doubts about continuing at several points only to be manipulated into returning to the ring by Lorna Moon (Barbara Stanwyck), the lover of his manager, Tom Moody (Adolphe Menjou). As Joe fights on, his music becomes less and less important until, in one scene on lifting up the violin, he finds it impossible to play at all. Though ultimately he wins 'the big fight' in Madison Square Garden, it is at the expense of his African American opponent who dies in the ring. Joe realises that boxing is killing his soul and a reformed Lorna leads him back home to his family and his Italian father.

In the aftermath of the Second World War, the dark side of boxing continued to be a concern in films that also contained occasionally significant, if limited, social critique. One of the most important and influential examples is Robert Rossen's *Body and Soul* (1947), a film which shares many parallels with *Golden Boy*.[4] *Body and Soul* is one of the darkest and most realistic depictions of boxing of the first half of the twentieth century, a film that sees little redeeming features in the sport. As with *Golden Boy*, it features a poor working-class character, Charley Davis (John Garfield), who turns to boxing in order to support his widowed mother, despite his mother's hopes that he will get an education and stay away from the fight game. Among the other tropes it shares with the 1939 film is the corrupt gangster, Mr Roberts (Lloyd Gough), who manipulates the boxer with the aid of the 'evil' woman, in this case Alice (Hazel Brooks), whose only motivation appears to be money. Shot by two-time Oscar winner James Wong Howe, a former professional boxer, Howe signals the corrupting influence of boxing on Charley Davis from the opening shots when he awakes from a nightmare and calls for a member of his training camp Ben Chaplin (Canada Lee). This and subsequent scenes throughout the film are shrouded in dark ominous noirish shadows that suggest the corruption engulfing Davis in the fight game. He is eventually convinced to take a dive for a big payday, but his local roots give him pangs of guilt. A fellow Jewish neighbour calls in to his mother's apartment to let him know that all the Jews in the area are backing him as he represents them at a time when 'Over in Europe, people are killing people like us just because of our religion'. In the end, Davis refuses to take the dive and is rewarded in the film's closing scene with the return of the woman he loves, Peg (Lilli Palmer).

In common with *Golden Boy*, the obligatory happy ending to the film attempts to contain *Body and Soul*'s engagement with the serious social issues which it raises. Nonetheless, the film ends with the real possibility that Charley Davis may well be killed by the gangster Roberts for refusing to take a fall in the final fight. Indeed, *Body and Soul* contained enough dark material critical of American society that its director, scriptwriter (Abraham Polonsky, a member of the Communist Party USA) and John Garfield himself would all eventually be called before the HUAC anti-communist hearings (Bergan, 1982, p. 26), an experience that had catastrophic consequences for the career of each of them. As Aaron Baker notes

> Screenwriter Abraham Polonsky's working-class poetry and historical narrative, as well as the film's visual style, encourage viewers to question the values of middle-class American culture.
>
> (2003, p. 115)

The film has been described by Robert Sklar as 'as close to a work of the left as any produced to that time in Hollywood' (1992, p. 183) and one encounters in *Body and Soul* what James Naremore has called the left's 'proletarian concerns' focused on 'middle-European or Mediterranean immigrants ... dealing with the failure of the American dream in the big industrial centers' (1998, p. 125). Indeed, beyond the fight game itself, there is a larger critique evident in the film of the capitalist culture of America, evident particularly in Polonsky's dialogue. In his dressing room before the final fight, when Davis suggests he might beat the challenger Jack Marlowe, Roberts replies

> What's wrong, Charley? The books are all balanced. The bets are in. You bet your purse against yourself. You gotta be businesslike, Charley … Everything is addition or subtraction, the rest is conversation.

As Thom Andersen has noted, dialogue such as this suggests that 'criminality can be businesslike,' while presenting 'a critique of capitalism in the guise of an expose of crime' (1985, pp. 186–187). In Roberts' ability to be both a corrupt promoter and apparently a successful businessman, the film suggests that these two elements may in fact overlap (Baker, 2003, p. 116).

The black-listing of the creative team behind *Body and Soul* may well have influenced the content of later boxing films, including two films made two years later *The Set Up* and *Champion*. Whatever limited social critique of American society Rossen and Polonsky's work contained was much attenuated in subsequent films that looked principally to personal, rather than societal, causes for a boxer's decline. Furthermore, as noted by Baker, both *The Set Up* and *Champion*

> avoid the big events (the Depression, the Holocaust) and ideological issues (racism, the choice of assimilation and quick money or cultural identity and community values) that structure *Body and Soul*.
>
> (2003, p. 120)

Robert Wise's *The Set-Up* nonetheless continued the excavation of the underside of the boxing world evident in *Body and Soul*. While stylistically the film shares much of the noirish detail of *Body and Soul*, *The Set-Up* has the added element of taking place in real time, adding another layer of tension and realism to the portrayal of the society and fight depicted, including the final climactic knockout. As Matthew Syed has observed 'Sport loses its authenticity – indeed its soul – whenever it is depicted in anything other than real time' (Syed, 2010). Wise addresses this challenge by setting the events of *The Set-Up* in real time thereby adding a unique quality to the film rarely found in feature films featuring sport. Watching the film the viewer is brought into the heart of the appeal, and distastefulness, of boxing as we watch a fight take place in actual ring time. It is this heightened realism, as identified by Martin Scorsese, that accentuates the characteristics associated with the boxing culture and the urban community depicted (Scorsese, 2004). In *The Set Up* there are few redeeming features to the boxing game in which fighters have their bodies brutalised well beyond their prime, as in the case of the lead protagonist, the washed-up 35-year-old Stoker Thompson (Robert Ryan), for the enjoyment of a blood-thirsty crowd populated by unsavoury and corrupt characters. It is a sport clearly marked by the exploitation of the fighter, whether White or Black.

Martin Scorsese in his commentary to the 2004 American DVD release of the film, viewed the boxing ring itself as the 'ring of life', within which people may literally be fighting for their own survival, adopting the various offensive and

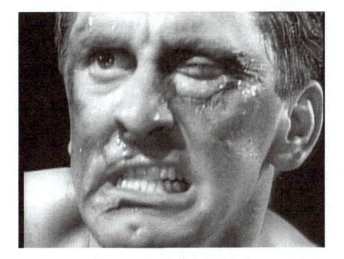

FIGURE 4.3 *Champion* (United Artists, 1949)

defensive strategies they feel will best prolong their survival and hopefully bring victory. Scorsese's comments indicate not just the power of the boxing film to evoke life in general but also its ability to appeal to the disenfranchised working-class man in particular. These films provide an allegory for the individual broken down by a corrupt and corrupting society who nonetheless lives in the hope that they may overcome and realise their dream of success in the end. Indeed, in both *Body and Soul* and *The Set Up*, there are hopeful endings, though endings that do not close out completely the possibility of further suffering ahead for both Charley Davis and Stoker Thompson.

In *Champion*, Kirk Douglas stars as Midge Kelly, a boxer who rises from an impoverished background to become the middleweight champion of the world. While the trajectory might suggest the realisation of the American dream, in reality Kelly's rise to fame is marked by an increasing egotism and brutalisation of himself and everyone close to him in his relentless pursuit of fame and as importantly wealth. By Midge's final fight, his brutalisation and self-destruction are clearly mapped on his face as the match progresses. As the camera lingers in one shot (Fig. 4.3) on his battered and brutalised face, symbolising the corruption of boxing, he rises incredibly from the canvas, seemingly spurred on by the ringside commentator's premature declaration of his opponent as the new champion, to win the fight. However his efforts lead to a brain haemorrhage and death when he reaches the dressing room.

It is ultimately the path of personal destruction rather than a societal critique that *Champion* charts. As Aaron Baker has observed, drawing on the work of Robin Wood (1977),

> By punishing Midge for his greed and violence, *Champion* exemplifies how even many social problem films made in Hollywood conclude with

the naive assumption that America is a place where any injustice can be fixed with only minor reform, offering the 'pretense that the problems the film has raised are now resolved'.

(2003, p. 123)

Films depicting boxing as a corrupt, and indeed dehumanising sport would continue to be produced in subsequent decades including John Huston's *Fat City* (1972) and Martin Scorsese's *Raging Bull* (1980). However, such portrayals were countered by those that portrayed boxing rather as an important opportunity and means for the marginalised and less fortunate to realise the American Dream. An early example was *Gentleman Jim* (1942), which featured Errol Flynn in the central role of boxing legend 'Gentleman' James Corbett. The film provided a template for many subsequent boxing films in its charting of the rise of Corbett from humble Irish immigrant beginnings in San Francisco to wealthy and successful heavyweight champion of the world, along the way bringing respectability to a sport banned when he began following it. In a trope to appear in subsequent films, boxing is also viewed as a means of bringing respectability and assimilating immigrants and their families, such as the Corbetts, into American society. Judge Geary, a member of the Olympic boxing club where Corbett fights expresses his hope at one point of making 'fighters into gentlemen' and while the Corbett family are depicted repeatedly in the film in stereotypical fashion as drunken and fond of fighting, Corbett's success in the ring eventually brings respectability, as he moves his family in one scene, after earning substantial winnings, from a poorer part of the city to the more fashionable area of Nob Hill.

The American Dream was reaffirmed in the 1956 MGM production *Somebody Up there Likes Me*, a biopic directed by Robert Wise featuring the rise from humble Italian immigrant stock on New York's Lower East Side to World Middleweight Champion of Rocky Graziano, played by Paul Newman. As the title of the film suggests, a heavy emphasis is placed on individual fate – with the help of God – in transforming a life from poverty and crime to success. As Rocky says at the film's conclusion, 'You know, I've been lucky. Somebody up there likes me.' Abused and neglected by his father Nick (Harold J. Stone), Rocky turns to a life of crime and is eventually sent to reform school where his ability as a boxer is recognised by a fellow prisoner, Frankie Peppo (Robert Loggia), after Rocky attacks a guard. Peppo encourages Rocky to contact him when he gets out. However, the attack leads to Rocky's incarceration in Riker's Island. On release, he is drafted immediately into the army from which he eventually goes AWOL after attacking a captain, returning to New York City. While trying to track down Peppo, he goes to Stillman's Gym and gets a chance in the ring as sparring partner to a top light heavyweight. After Rocky knocks out the fighter in one round, he is offered further fights and begins to earn a living in the ring. He is eventually found and arrested by the military police, dishonourably discharged and imprisoned in Leavenworth Penitentiary. However, this time his detention further progresses his boxing ability under the guidance of the coordinator of the prison's boxing squad, Sgt. Johnny Hyland (Judson Pratt). Following his release, Rocky pursues a career as a boxer in earnest and with considerable success, eventually developing a sense of self worth, and finding a wife (Norma played by Pier Angeli) as his career progresses.

Repeatedly the film affirms the importance of boxing as a route to success and the damage that can be done to boxers denied this avenue. Rocky's mother (Eileen Heckart) reveals at one point that his father Nick's decline into alcoholism and domestic violence were prompted by his declining self-esteem after she insisted he give up boxing. When Rocky loses his first World Middleweight title fight to Zale, his mother warns Norma not to repeat her 'mistake': 'Did you ever ask him to stop fighting? It's his whole life. Everything he's got. Then it's your whole life too. Don't ever make the mistake of forgetting that, like I did'. Despite hating boxing, Norma nonetheless recognises that it is a crucial part of who Rocky is, replying: 'I didn't marry a man, did I? I married a middleweight'. The night before his second title fight, Rocky, suffering from self-doubt, returns to the Lower East Side. After encountering a former fellow-gang member Romolo (Sal Mineo) trying to avoid arrest from the police, witnessing people sleeping on the street and speaking to his alcoholic father, Rocky realises that his only means of escaping the poverty and life of crime of his community is by winning the championship bout. Indeed, as Ronald Bergan notes, the ending of the film after Rocky's victory where the boxer receives a ticker tape parade on the East Side while looking up to the heavens 'is a spurious celebration of professional boxing as an essential part of the American Dream and a justification of the sermonizing that has preceded it' (1982, p. 34).

Rocky (1976)

The classic and most influential contemporary example of the American Dream trajectory mapped in *Somebody Up There Likes Me* is the 1976 film *Rocky*, one of the most commercially successful sports films of all time, inspiring a franchise that has produced five subsequent films to date and was chosen at number two on the AFI list of best sports films. Indeed, of all the films listed in the AFI's top ten, arguably none has had more influence on subsequent sports films than *Rocky*. In December 2010, Bill Simmons noted the 'astonishing' fact that '[s]ince "Rocky" captured the Academy Award for Best Picture in 1976, Hollywood has churned out an average of one boxing movie per year' (Simmons, 2010). Many of these have mapped similar utopian trajectories, including most recently *The Fighter* (2010) a film discussed below.

Talia Shire, who plays Rocky's love interest Adrian in the film, has described the crucial context that informed the production of *Rocky*:

Sylvester had said something and I think it was very true during 1976, Carter had just been voted in, he was a peanut farmer, and there was a feeling of the mythical America, you know that really all of America was a bunch of people who were discarded and left other places and came in with a dream and this was a country that you could go 15 rounds in, that you were entitled to go the distance. It may not happen but at least you were entitled. The freedom of going the whole way and I think Sylvester really captured that wonderful period of 1976 and Carter coming in with these two funny discarded people ... whoever would have thought that he would become this great fighter and she would become so beloved but that's the American Dream.

(Shire, 2005)

Rocky is one of the most powerful affirmations of this dream in film. For the American sports film, this dream may not always be fully achieved, but athletes are nonetheless given the opportunity to, as Shire says 'go the distance'. Significantly this wish is connected in the film with a realisation of a lack of self worth; as Rocky remarks to Adrian on the eve of the big fight against the heavyweight champion, Apollo Creed (Carl Weathers):

I was nobody ... all I wanna do is go the distance. Nobody's ever gone the distance with Creed. And if I can go that distance and that bell rings and I'm still standin', I'm gonna know for the first time in my life, see, that I weren't just another bum from the neighbourhood.

However, the reality that neither Shire nor Rocky acknowledges is that this opportunity is in reality available to very few, and in most cases, skewed by the inequalities in American life itself outlined earlier in this chapter.

The obstacles faced in life by many marginalised Americans are not absent from *Rocky*, however; it is clear from the opening of the film that Rocky Balboa comes from an underprivileged working-class Italian American background and the challenging circumstances he faces economically as well as physically are apparent in the film. However, rather than placing these challenges within either a social or a historical context, the film focuses instead on individual effort and performance as the means of overcoming such obstacles. Opportunity is affirmed repeatedly in the film including metaphorically in the iconic image (Fig. 4.4) of Rocky with arms aloft after climbing the 72 steps of the Philadelphia Museum of Art while training (a feat repeated in four of the film's sequels), graphically depicting the rise of the underdog. This scene and the accompanying shots of Rocky in training are complemented by emotive music and song on the soundtrack that includes the lyrics: 'Trying hard now/ It's so hard now/ Trying hard now .../Feeling strong now/Won't be long now/Getting strong now/Gonna fly now/Flying high now ...' encapsulating the message of the film as a whole – through hard work and dedication, opportunity is available to all, obscuring the real barriers that exist to many.

FIGURE 4.4 *Rocky* (United Artists, 1976)

This opportunity is affirmed by African American champion Apollo when he decides on his approach to replacing the injured challenger for his title in the 'bicentennial super battle':

> Without a ranked contender, what this fight is gonna need is a novelty. This is the land of opportunity, right? So Apollo Creed on January 1st gives a local underdog fighter an opportunity. A snow-white underdog. And I'm gonna put his face on this poster with me. And I'll tell you why. Because I'm sentimental, like a lot of other people in this country. There's nothing they'd like better than to see Apollo Creed give a local boy a shot at the world title on this country's biggest birthday.

The celebration of American values is clearly flagged here and the 'opportunity' that they offer. The promoter of this fight with Apollo, George Jensens (Thayer David) also affirms this opportunity – with which Rocky agrees – as he attempts to convince Rocky to take the Apollo fight:

[George Jensens]	Rocky, do you believe that America is the land of opportunity?
Rocky:	Yeah.
[Jensens]	Apollo Creed does. And he's gonna prove it to the world by giving an unknown a shot at the title. And that unknown is you.

This could well be a con, and indeed it is set up as such with Rocky himself even disbelieving and hesitant to take the challenge – but the trajectory of the film suggests that such opportunities are real and realisable. Indeed, in the press conference where the fight is announced between Rocky and Apollo, this theme of opportunity is again emphasised and connected to both American history and nationality. As Apollo replies to the press – after declaring his pride in being 'an American' – on being asked why he's fighting a man with virtually no chance to win, 'Look, if history proves one thing … American history proves that everybody's got a chance to win. Didn't you guys ever hear of Valley Forge or Bunker Hill?'

Rocky owes a debt to previous boxing films in its attention to realist detail, though here it is principally in the service of providing a more convincing utopian American Dream trajectory. From the beginning of the film, one is struck by the naturalistic approach to what is essentially a mythological tale. Whether in the opening 'down and dirty' shots of Rocky fighting, or the images of him walking along the street of his local area in Philadelphia, location shooting and natural lighting indicate an attempt to produce a realist aesthetic. This attention to realism is also apparent in references to actual boxers, such as Rocky Marciano and the appearance in the ring before the final fight of former World Heavyweight Champion, Joe Frazier, depicted as a friend of Apollo Creed. However, director John G. Avildsen's attention to realist detail – whether in his exterior shooting in Philadelphia, the interior shooting in Rocky's apartment, or in the fight scenes themselves – some of which were facilitated by the use of Garret Brown's then pioneering steadicam technology – further adds to the obscuring of the unreality which the film itself represents. These are the 'truths that tell the lie' of the American Dream.

Much as we noted above that the American Dream ideology provides both inspiration and an obligation for Americans, an ideology that can be used to criticise those who do not achieve success in life, it is suggested in *Rocky* that the exploitation of individuals by loan-sharks featured in the film is the result not of the inequality in society whereby the underprivileged are forced by lack of opportunity to borrow from such people, but rather it is those who borrow who are themselves admonished for their misguided actions. Rocky in the film's early scenes works as an enforcer for the local loan shark boss Tony Gazzo (Joe Spinell), a figure depicted rather sympathetically in the film, including supporting Rocky financially in his preparation for his fight with Apollo Creed. However, in the only example of Rocky at work for Gazzo, we see him give out to a man who owes $200 that he needs to 'be smart' and three times 'You shoulda planned ahead, you know?'

Furthermore, while the narrative obscures social inequality and the unequal access to opportunity for advancement in American society, it also contains within it an implicitly racist message. While Rocky is depicted as redeeming the marginalised White working class of immigrant origins, his depiction is also a reaction to the dominance of African Americans in sport by the period the film was made, including in boxing. As noted by Ed Guerrero, Apollo Creed

> is both defeated by, and reconciled to, white yearnings for a 'great white hope' and a nostalgic return to a bygone racial order in the first three *Rocky*

films. As an added ideological bonus, Clubber Lang (Mr. T) is brought into the cycle, thus raising the villainy and threat of the 'brute negro' in *Rocky III* (1982).

(1993, p. 116)

The racist reactions to the emergence of Jack Johnson in the early twentieth century were discussed earlier in this chapter, yet such racism is also evident in Rocky, if not as blatantly as previously. As Slavoj Žižek contends, in order for a ruling ideology to function, it 'has to incorporate a series of features in which the exploited majority will be able to recognize its authentic longings' while simultaneously distorting 'the relations of domination and exploitation' (1997, p. 29). From the beginning of *Rocky*, the story of the White man unfairly displaced by the African American is evident. In an early scene, after winning the fight that opens the film, Rocky goes to his gym to find his locker has been emptied and given to another fighter. He confronts the gym manager, Mickey (Burgess Meredith), to discover that the locker has been given to his new hope, Dipper (Stan Shaw), an African American boxer. Indeed, Dipper rubs salt in the wound as a disappointed Rocky, ridiculed and told to retire by Mickey, hears him call after him mockingly as he leaves the gym 'I dig your locker man'.

The issue of race is most clearly invoked in the sequence in which we watch Rocky, Adrian and her brother Paulie watching a press conference in which the fight between Rocky and Apollo is announced. Here the African American shrugs off the race issue when it is raised by the interviewer at the conference. On being asked if it 'is a coincidence that you're fighting a White man on the most celebrated day in US history' Apollo responds, 'I don't know. Is it a coincidence that he's fightin' a black man on the same day?' thereby reducing the racial issue to a mere accident of fate. But more problematically in this sequence, Apollo is depicted as an over-confident and condescending figure – a representation that is developed particularly in the final fight scene – who, the film suggests, needs to be knocked off his pedestal. It is a representation that harks back to the racist depictions of African Americans in the nineteenth century and indeed in the early twentieth century depictions of Jack Johnson discussed in Chapter 2 and earlier in this chapter. It builds on a particularly racist construction of African Americans as representing the worst excesses which the White man should avoid. This is also evident in Apollo's condescending attitude to Rocky's Italian ethnicity – 'If he can't fight, I bet he can cook' – remarks that Rocky clearly resents.

The sense of White paranoia about the African American is most blatantly expressed in the film by the barman in Rocky's local who remarks, while he watches the champion Apollo on TV announce his Bicentennial fight: 'Would you take a look at that guy? Where are the real fighters gonna come from, the pros? All we got today are jig clowns.' The nostalgia for a time of the 'real fighters' is also apparent in Rocky's own respect and admiration for Italian American boxer Rocky Marciano who held the heavyweight crown in the 1950s. The Apollo character was inspired by Muhammad Ali – indeed it has been suggested that the idea for Stallone's screenplay of a working-class White boxer challenging an African American champion was based on the 1975 fight between the largely unknown White boxer 'Chuck' Wepner and Ali, in which Wepner surprisingly went 15 rounds with the then champion (Raskin, 2011).

Though it is not explicitly said, it is strongly suggested that what Rocky's local barman also seeks is a White challenger that can confront the uppity and super confident African American Apollo Creed. While Rocky appears unimpressed by the barman's comments, the trajectory of the film supports this contention – when the final fight happens, Apollo does indeed appear to be a 'jig clown', riding towards the ring in a boat while dressed as George Washington and surrounded by women dressed as the statue of liberty. On entering the ring, Apollo is attired literally in the colours of the American flag and adopts the appearance of Uncle Sam shouting at the crowd in a re-enactment of the famous First World War image 'I want you'. It is an over-the-top entry and performance which undermines any respect the audience may have for the character, and precedes the fight itself in which we discover that much of the confidence Apollo expressed previously was misplaced, with the champion saved by the bell from a likely knockout by Rocky in the final round. Indeed, he is surprised that Rocky puts up as good a fight as he does, remarking 'He doesn't know it's a damn show. He thinks it's a damn fight'. In the film's emotionally charged and uplifting ending, we witness a battered but still standing Rocky call for his partner Adrian while the crowd chant his name; he has had his opportunity, gone the distance and in the process redeemed White working-class masculinity while affirming the American Dream.

'Rocky for this millennium':[5] *The Fighter* (2010)

The commercial success of *Rocky* would lead to the production of not just further sequels but also the release of many subsequent boxing films. While the *Rocky* franchise remains the most commercially successful of all such films produced – earning well over $1.5 billion worldwide to date[6] – the trajectory that *Rocky* mapped has been found many times subsequently in American sports films. Indeed, as will be considered in the concluding chapter, this is particularly evident in sports films made after the events now known as 9/11. Many of these films are also focused centrally on White working-class protagonists, further marginalising the African American representation at a time when African Americans, as noted above, are hugely over-represented in professional sports.

A relevant recent boxing example is the 2010 release *The Fighter*, a film which enjoyed considerable commercial and critical success on release, taking $93,617,009 at the American box office (on a modest budget of $11 million (Lovece, 2010)) and receiving seven Oscar nominations (two of which it won) in 2011. In line with many other sports films released post-9/11, including *The Blind Side*, *The Fighter* is based on the true story of 'Irish' Micky Ward, an Irish American boxer from a working-class neighbourhood in the Massachusetts

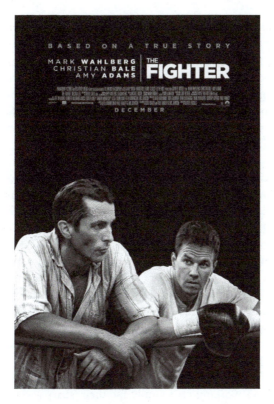

FIGURE 4.5 Poster for *The Fighter* (Paramount Pictures, 2010) (Mandeville Films/ The Kobal Collection)

city of Lowell who rose from humble beginnings to win the World Light Welterweight title. This basis in reality, foregrounded in the opening credit 'Based on a true story' (and on the film's poster (Fig. 4.5)), adds further legitimacy to the American Dream trajectory suggested in the film's tagline 'Every dream deserves a fighting chance' and identified repeatedly in reviews and commentaries following the film's release (see for example Frazier, 2010; Robert, 2011; Marchesani, 2011; Shanahan, 2011; Mediatwin, 2011; Lafalaise, 2011; Heritage, 2011; Smith, 2011; Lopez, 2011).

The Fighter repeatedly affirms its connection with actual people and events, including the appearance of Micky Ward and his half-brother Dicky Eklund during the closing credits, while the film's director David O. Russell went to considerable lengths to bring what one reviewer described as a 'painstaking realism' (Ponto, 2010) to his depiction of Ward's life and boxing career. This includes employing similar betamax video cameras in the film's climactic title fight to those used to film the original title fight for television and also hiring the HBO director and his crew responsible for that fight's TV coverage to recreate the television footage shot-for-shot (Lovece, 2010). Furthermore, the television commentaries heard while the fight takes place, from Larry Merchant, Roy Jones Jr. and Jim

Lampley, are the actual commentaries taken from the 2000 HBO coverage of the fight (Lovece, 2010; Ponto, 2010; Singer, 2011). Indeed, all of the fight footage in the film draws heavily on a televisual aesthetic, including incorporating familiar televisual graphics prior to and during the fights themselves and cutting from long and mid-shots of fighters in action to reaction shots from the crowd.

The film's connection with actual people and events is emphasised from the opening shots where *The Fighter* adopts a documentary style approach under the pretence of a HBO documentary being shot concerning Micky's (Mark Wahlberg) half-brother and trainer Dicky Eklund (Christian Bale). Intercut with home movie footage of a younger Dicky, in line with previous boxing films – particularly *Rocky* with which *The Fighter* was repeatedly compared in reviews following its release (see for example Smith, 2011; Lovece, 2010; Ponto, 2010; Scott, 2010a; Berardinelli, 2010; Ebert, 2010) – these opening documentary shots also foreground the working-class origins of both fighters, as we watch them working on a road crew and moving through a rundown part of Lowell evident in faded shop fronts and dilapidated housing. Indeed, we are repeatedly reminded of Micky's humble working-class roots in shots of his large extended family, composed principally of women, gathered in their home and appearing to drink and smoke constantly.

This engagement with Lowell's working-class community was praised on *The Fighter's* release with Armand White of the *New York Press* contending that the film 'strips away nostalgia about the American Dream' through its 'semirealistic' depiction of Ward's working-class family and their 'sharp accents, bad grammar and worse behavior' (White, 2010). However, the melodramatic approach to this depiction often reduces the characters depicted to mere stereotypes. This is particularly the case with regard to Micky's seven sisters, who rarely feature individually but rather appear in the film principally as a coarse and sometimes violent group dominated by their mother Alice – including in one scene where five of them squeeze with some difficulty onto one couch in their home to verbally attack Micky's girlfriend Charlene (Amy Adams) for being, they claim, an MTV 'skank'. While Ryan Gilbey in *New Statesman* was 'almost certain that there are seven of these sharp-beaked, wrench-faced sisters … it's like trying to count the heads of the Hydra' (Gilbey, 2011). Predictably their dislike for Charlene leads to a physical confrontation on Charlene's porch that Micky has to break up. As noted by A.O. Scott of the depiction of social class in recent American films, including *The Fighter,* these working-class characters 'are variously scary, comical, noble and grotesque, to be pitied, feared and wondered at. But they are consistently exotic, always other' (Scott, 2010b).

While *The Fighter* contains such contradictory elements (evident throughout the sports genre), some of which seem to question the American Dream trajectory, it is ultimately a tale of overcoming and redemption. This is evident particularly in the figure of Dicky. A former professional boxer, Dicky is a local hero in his community at the film's opening. His claim to fame is knocking Sugar Ray Leonard (the legendary boxer, also featured in the film, who won

World titles in five weight divisions) down in the ring in a fight in 1978. However, on leaving the ring Dicky's fortunes have declined substantially and he has developed a drug addiction, spending much of his time in the local crack house. The first hour of the film maps the decline of Dicky in particular and his eventual imprisonment for assaulting a police officer and his deterioration reaches its lowest point when the humiliating HBO documentary *Crack in America*[7] is broadcast. Watched with great discomfort by Dicky with his inmates in prison, and his family at home, the documentary focuses on Dicky's addiction and the damage it has done to his life, family and community.

However, in line with the popular sports film, and in particular the *Rocky* inspired boxing-themed films, the final fifty minutes focus on the redemption of both characters, as Micky returns to training under Sergeant Mickey O'Keefe's (played by Ward's actual trainer in real life) supervision in montage shots that are intercut with Dicky's own training and recovery in prison. Significantly, Micky's redemption narrative is also once again focused on a White boxer, who overcomes a series of African American and foreign boxers in the ring on his way to the top. Indeed, his low point in the film is against an African American boxer, Mike 'Machine Gun' Mungin (Peter Cunninghan), a boxer recently released from prison and 20 pounds heavier than Ward, who gives him a torrid beating in the first fight featured. A central concern of the remainder of the film is Micky's recovery from this loss and eventual achievement of a World title fight which provides the film's climax.

For Dicky, prison is presented as a crucial part of his recuperation, challenging evidence that suggests that prison in the United States has often quite the opposite effect on those incarcerated (see for example Haney, 2003). Dicky does indeed appear to be a reformed character on release, including getting a new set of teeth during his time inside, overcoming his crack addiction, and remarking to Micky: 'Alice says prison might've been the best thing for me. Got me clean. Got me clear. Up here'. While Dicky may represent the inverse of the American Dream trajectory, by the film's close he is transformed into a vital part of the team that leads Micky to boxing glory.

Indeed, Micky's title fight at the film's climax – in a trope evident throughout boxing-themed films – represents in microcosm the trajectory of the American Dream of overcoming adversity to triumph by means of individual endeavour. He begins the fight poorly, evident in the earlier rounds where his opponent Shea Neary (Anthony Molinari) is clearly on top and at one point knocks Ward onto the canvas. However Micky eventually turns the fight in his favour. As we hear Dicky shout on the soundtrack 'don't take the abuse, this is your time Micky', the film goes into slow motion, Ward finds his reach and attacks Neary, throwing punch after punch while coming forward, eventually knocking his opponent down, and winning the fight. It is this final fight which provides the most powerful and seductive affirmation of the American Dream trajectory – that no matter how tough things are, one can overcome through individual effort and belief to achieve success.

Conclusion

This chapter has contended that the sports film genre performs a crucial functional role, affirming, with rare exceptions, the American Dream against all the evidence that points to its fallacy, particularly for those disadvantaged as a result of race or social class. In common with Hollywood cinema more generally, these films may contain elements that challenge or contradict this trajectory. However, such contradictory elements exist principally to accentuate the ultimate affirmation of the American Dream trajectory, through characters that overcome formidable challenges by way of individual sporting achievement. Indeed, where social problems are depicted or alluded to, they are rarely given a historical or social context and are attributed principally to personal flaws or the fate of protagonists and their communities with their resolution lying in individual achievement, often in the sports film genre via sporting success facilitated by hegemonic White American society. However, as this chapter's discussion suggests, this is an achievement associated principally with men; women have largely functioned in peripheral roles within the sports film genre until recent years. For much of its history the sports film has been principally a male preserve, a feature examined in the next chapter.

5

GENDER AND THE SPORTS FILM

Girls are what you sleep with after the game, not what you coach during it
Coach Jimmy Dugan (Tom Hanks), *A League of Their Own* (1992)

The previous chapter examined the engagement of sports films, particularly those emerging from the United States, with the themes of race and social class. In important respects, there are parallels to be found with the representation of gender. Much as the sports film was identified as playing an important cultural role in affirming the American Dream ideology, this ideology has principally been associated with men, an association affirmed within the sports film genre historically. In one of the most influential contributions to gender theory, *Gender Trouble: Feminism and the Subversion of Identity* (1999), Judith Butler criticised the restriction of 'the meaning of gender to received notions of masculinity and femininity' (1999, p. viii). For Butler, rather than being an internal essence, gender is performative and manufactured through a 'sustained set of acts, posited through the gendered stylization of the body' (pp. xv–xvi). This is particularly so for masculine identities; as David Scott has surmised, drawing on the work of Elisabeth Badinter and Monique Schneider, '[w]ithin the western tradition from the Greeks onward, masculine identity seems, much more so than feminine identity, something that had to be *constructed*' (2010, p. 143). Sport is one of the most revealing sites where this construction is evident. Indeed, sport has historically been concerned above all with the glorification of masculinity and the male body. By masculinity, I refer to qualities such as power, strength, height and wealth which men in the United States and elsewhere in the Western World have been encouraged to aspire to. However, hegemonic masculinity has traditionally, in the United States, had further associations, including with race. As noted by Erving Goffman:

In an important sense there is only one complete unblushing male in America: a young, married, *white*, urban, northern, heterosexual, Protestant, father, of college education, fully employed, of good complexion, weight, and height, and a recent record in sports ... Any male who fails to qualify in any one of these ways is likely to view himself – during moments at least – as unworthy, incomplete, and inferior.

(1963, p. 128)

Women may today feature more prominently in professional sports and within the sports film genre and such representations may suggest that a considerable degree of gender equality has been achieved. However, successive studies have indicated that gender inequality in terms of 'material resources, power, and status' (Ridgeway, 2011, p. 4) continues to be a major issue in the modern world, including in the United States and in the world of sport. Indeed, the institution of sport continues to be a principle site for the 'inculcation, expression, and perpetuation of masculine habits, identities, behavior, and ideals, including a belief in patriarchal supremacy over women' (Smith, 2009, p. 160; see also Dunning, 1986). Elite sport in particular and its representation is overwhelmingly associated with men who provide the standard for performance. For McDonald and Andrews,

dominant constructions of athletic masculinity help to construct sport as a male preserve, a site where, regardless of their backgrounds, men are encouraged to (mis)identify the physicality of male athletes as a sign of male social superiority

(McDonald and Andrews, 2001, p. 28; drawing on Messner, 1988)

It is not surprising, therefore, that the sports film, as the examination of the genre to this point indicates, is overwhelmingly focused on male athletes and protagonists. While this chapter will consider the historical legacy of this focus, its chief concern will be the role of women in the mainstream sports film.

Ideal masculinity and the sports film

Film has had an important role to play in affirming the prominence of men in sport, with male physicality a prominent feature in many films, including for example the increasing movement of the camera into locker rooms – in films such as *Jerry Maguire* (1996) and *Any Given Sunday* (1999) – to reveal the impressively toned bodies of male athletes. Indeed, the American sports film has played an important role in the promotion of a particular version of ideal masculinity indelibly associated with the American Dream and defined by Aaron Baker as the 'heroic individual' who 'overcomes obstacles and achieves success through determination, self-reliance, and hard work' (2003, p. 49). In this context, women's roles are 'relative to the male athlete-hero' (Tudor, 1997, p. 79), and in the public sphere they appear principally as entertainers and/or sexualised figures – whether singing the American national anthem before the Super Bowl, titillating a mainly male audience between rounds at boxing matches, or supporting their team as cheerleaders at team sports such as basketball and American football. Furthermore, what may ostensibly appear to be more progressive representations of women athletes in recent sports films may actually disguise a conservative ideology concerned ultimately with the maintenance of White patriarchy.

The focus on masculinity in sport was evident from the codification of sport and the emergence of film in the late nineteenth century. Sport in the United States in this period, in a pattern also reflected in Britain, France and elsewhere in the Western world, was a primarily male domain (Holt, 1990, pp. 117–134). As such, it provided an important forum for demonstrating male (and White) superiority. As noted in Chapter 2, a prominent concern within the British public school system in the nineteenth century was the building of 'character', of which 'manliness' was a central feature, through sport. Similar concerns were also apparent in the United States, particularly the belief in the ability of sport to produce men of action. Boxing above all was viewed by many in American society in the late nineteenth century as an activity that partly responded to the perceived feminisation of urban life (Reiss, 1991, pp. 16–22) while the growing participation in, and spectatorship of, sport in this period reflected a general reaffirmation of masculinity (Gorn and Goldstein, 1993, p. 145). In this context, the presence of women in sport or public life was viewed with suspicion as the 'public sphere was gendered from the start', marked as 'an arena of civic action for the "public man"' (Hansen, 1994, p. 10).

However, this 'reassertion of masculinity' was itself a response to the growing presence of women in public life in the United States and elsewhere in the Western World. From the latter half of the nineteenth century, women had increasingly sought greater equality and by the turn of the twentieth century, opportunities for White middle-class women in education, particularly with the advent of women's colleges, and professional life were considerably greater than before, with women accounting for almost half of high school graduates in the United States and '80% of the colleges, universities and professional schools in the nation admit[ting] women' (Rudnick, 1991, p. 70). Film would eventually comment on the increasing independence of women and indeed sport would occasionally be used to explore this issue, evident in the early G.W. Bitzer directed film *The Athletic Girl and the Burglar* (1905) in which a woman is depicted exercising with weights in her home. When a burglar confronts her, rather than seeking assistance, she tackles him herself, hitting him on the head and knocking him out with a barbell she is exercising with. This film was somewhat unusual, however, in that film tended in general during the silent era to rely on stereotypical conceptions of gender roles, including in films featuring sport (Parrish, 1992, p. 138).

David Scott has contended that boxing was an important forum for the construction of masculine identities in the Western World from the late nineteenth century (2010, pp. 143–165). As noted in Chapter 2, the boxing film was one of the most popular early forms of cinema, and while there is evidence that it attracted some female viewers (Streible, 2008, pp. 7–9), these films appealed primarily to a male audience while focusing exclusively on male boxers and emphasising such masculine virtues as strength, physical superiority and individual valour. Indeed, where female boxers did feature, they did so primarily for the comic possibilities of the depiction to audiences expected to view the encounter as absurd, as in the Edison Manufacturing Company films *Comedy Set-To* (1898) and *The Gordon Sisters Boxing* (1901).

Chapter 2 considered the importance of sports films in the silent and early sound period as a crucial means of encouraging robust masculinity by means of individual achievement, evident in the films *The Pinch Hitter* (1917), *Brown of Harvard* (1926) and *The Drop Kick* (1927). Indeed masculinity and the extolling of the 'manly' virtues were such a pervasive aspect of sport and the sports film in this period that they provided ripe material for comedy. Whether in the work of Charlie Chaplin, Harold Lloyd or Buster Keaton the machismo and physicality associated with sport offered great subject matter for humour in films such as *The Freshman* (1925), *College* (1927) and *City Lights* (1931). Often these films find comedy in the sometimes perverse and surprising ways in which seemingly less physically impressive and talented individuals manage to nonetheless defeat apparently far superior opponents, from Chaplin's placing of a horse shoe in his glove in *The Champion* (1915) (a trick he repeated in *City Lights* 16 years later) to Keaton and Lloyd's antics in the ring in *Battling Butler* (1926) and *The Milky Way* (1936) respectively.

The popularity of the boxing film was contributed to by the frequent employment of prominent boxers in early film, a practice already discussed in Chapter 2. As will also be considered in the next chapter, athletes would feature increasingly in films in subsequent decades, including the infallible masculinity of Olympic gold medallist swimmer Johnny Weissmuller in the title role in the very popular *Tarzan* series produced by MGM in the 1930s and 1940s, particularly in contrast to the unambiguous femininity of Maureen O'Sullivan in the role of Jane (Warren, 1979, p. 57). Indeed, athletes have repeatedly featured in the role of the King of the Jungle including American footballers Jim Pierce (*Tarzan and the Golden Lion* (1927) and Mike Henry (*Tarzan and the Valley of Gold* (1966), *Tarzan and the Great River* (1967) and *Tarzan and the Jungle Boy* (1968)).

Significantly, opportunities for female athletes to make this transition were almost non-existent in the early twentieth century. When they did, they performed in roles evincing traditional feminine qualities, such as grace, balance, and beauty, and in sports that had little or no physical contact between competitors. Examples include Norwegian ice-skater Sonja Henie who specialised in musicals set on ice and managed to make the transition from sport to film with some success, and Esther Williams, who began as a successful competitive swimmer before being signed by MGM in the early 1940s. Following her victory at the 1936 Winter Olympics, Henie was signed by Darryl F. Zanuck of Twentieth Century Fox for a fee of $75,000 to star in *One in a Million* (1936) and she starred in seven further films for the studio, becoming one of their greatest attractions (Hirschhorn, 1981, p. 129). Williams enjoyed great success in the late 1940s and the early 1950s in a string of films, some of which had sporting themes, in particular *Take me out to the Ballgame* (1949) and *Million Dollar Mermaid* (1952), a biographical musical concerning legendary Australian swimmer and film star Annette Kellerman. Kellerman had also made the transition from swimmer to actress with some success during the silent era, starring in a series of aquatic-themed films including *The Mermaid* (1911), *Queen of the Sea* (1918) and *Venus of the South Seas* (1924).

Women in the sports film: Inspirational muse or femme fatale

As the twentieth century developed, the representation of women in the mainstream sports film largely followed from the dominant representations found in Hollywood cinema. Drawing on psychoanalysis, Laura Mulvey in her seminal article 'Visual Pleasure and Narrative Cinema' (1975), viewed the structuring of mainstream film form as a reflection of the unconscious of patriarchal society. Historically, Mulvey argues, woman has been the object of the male gaze where the 'woman displayed has functioned on two levels: as erotic object for the characters within the screen story, and as erotic object for the spectator within the auditorium' (1975, p. 838). In this context, in opposition to the active/male figures in these films, the passive/female presence tends to 'freeze the flow of action in moments of erotic contemplation' (1975, p. 837). While it is true that men have also been objectified in mainstream film, significantly this is principally within scenes of action, most popularly in the boxing film (Creed, 1998, p. 78). Richard Dyer has also noted this pattern in terms of the history of the pin-up 'where time and again the image of the man is one caught in the middle of an action, or associated, through images in the picture, with activity' (1996, p. 270).

For Mulvey woman presents a particular threat, her sexual difference (absence of a penis), that is engaged by mainstream cinema in two principle ways:

> The male unconscious has two avenues of escape from this castration anxiety: preoccupation with the re-enactment of the original trauma (investigating the woman, demystifying her mystery), counterbalanced by the devaluation, punishment or saving of the guilty object (an avenue typified by the concerns of the film noir); or else complete disavowal of castration by the substitution of a fetish object or turning the represented figure itself into a fetish so that it becomes reassuring rather than dangerous (hence over-valuation, the cult of the female star).
>
> (1975, p. 840)

The pattern Mulvey delineates recurs throughout the history of the sports film. Women have featured principally in the genre as either beautiful, inspirational, and often sexualised, figures for male protagonists or untrustworthy and exploitative femme fatales. Early examples include the sports films listed earlier from Chaplin, Lloyd and Keaton, each of which depends on the central protagonist drawing inspiration from a female muse. In Keaton's *Battling Butler* and *College*, for instance, concern for the women they love transforms the central male protagonists in each film from poor athletes into formidable sportsmen. In *Battling Butler*, despite been presented for much of the film as a puny spoilt young man from a wealthy home with little ability as a boxer, Alfred Butler (Keaton) is transformed into an impressive fighter at the close when he notices the woman he loves watching him been attacked by the professional fighter he has pretended to be. In *College*, Ronald (Keaton) breaks every athletic record – from sprinting, to long jumping and pole vaulting – in his rush to save the woman he loves, despite failing miserably as an athlete throughout the film. This trope is apparent particularly in boxing-themed films including *The Prizefighter and the Lady* (1933), where boxer Steve Morgan (Max Baer) recovers in the final big fight when he realises that the woman he loves still loves him; James Cagney (as boxer Danny O'Hara) finds similar female inspiration from Olivia de Havilland (as Lucille Jackson), to knock out his opponent in *The Irish in Us* (1935).

A recurring trope found in many sports films is the wife or partner who is transformed over the duration of the film from being critical of their partner's involvement in sport to inspiring them to sporting success. In *The Winning Team* (1952) (based on the true story of baseball legend Grover Cleveland Alexander) the film suggests the inspiration behind Grover's (Ronald Reagan) success was his wife Aimee (Doris Day), who helps him to overcome a visual disability after being hit by a baseball and return to a 'winning team', despite her initial concerns and disapproval of her husband's involvement in baseball. Aimee's importance is particularly apparent in the final climactic big game of the World Series at Yankee Stadium when she arrives just in time to inspire Grover and the St Louis Cardinals to victory. As Grover remarks to her before the final game: 'I've been stealing strength from you all season – every game, every pitch. Without you there, I couldn't have done any of it'. The following game depicts Grover looking repeatedly to his wife's seat for inspiration, only throwing the match-winning ball to strike out the Yankees when he sees her finally arrive and take her seat. A more recent example of this trope is found in *Rocky II* (1979) in which Rocky's wife Adrian Pennino (Talia Shire) is initially critical of Rocky's return to the ring before eventually becoming a vital inspiration for him; as Adrian remarks from her hospital bed before Rocky's rematch with World Heavyweight champ Apollo Creed, 'There's one thing I want you to do for me … Win', which Rocky duly does.

When not a figure of inspiration, the unfaithful and untrustworthy woman is also a recurring character in sports films. As Bergan notes, women often 'foul up relationships. They come between a boxer and his manager in *Kid Galahad* (1937 and 1962), between a man and his horse in *Maryland* (1940), and between a man and his car in *Grand Prix* (MGM 1966)' (1982, p. 9). One of the earliest boxing films of the sound era, *Iron Man* (1931) features a boxer, Kid Mason (Lew Ayres), who ignores his manager Robert Armstrong's (George Regan) advice and takes on a fight, which he subsequently loses, in an effort to earn money for his gold-digging wife Rose (played by the 'laughing vamp' Jean Harlow). When Mason loses, Rose quickly disappears, only to return when her husband begins to enjoy some success in the ring again under Armstrong's management. Three years later, in *Palooka* (1934), Lupe Vélez played the opportunistic cabaret dancer and singer Nina Madero who exchanges one champion for another, only interested in exploiting the boxers for their celebrity and money. In *Golden Boy* (1939) the reluctant boxer Joe Bonaparte (William Holden) is manipulated into returning to the ring by Lorna Moon (Barbara Stanwyck), the lover of his manager, Tom Moody (Adolphe Menjou). Robert Rossen's *Body and Soul* (1947) features a similar narrative where the corrupt gangster, Mr Roberts, manipulates boxer Charley Davis to fight for him with the aid of the deceitful Alice (Hazel Brooks), who 'exemplifies the seduction that lures ... Davis into corruption' (McCann, 2007, p. 118). A comparable character features in *Champion* in the person of Grace Diamond (Marilyn Maxwell) who is employed by boxing impresario Jerome Harris (Luis Van Rooten) to seduce fighter Midge Kelly away from his manager and eventually contributes to his corruption. *Flesh and Fury* (1951) also includes a manipulative and untrustworthy woman, Sonya Bartow (Jan Sterling), who seduces the deaf mute fighter Paul Callan (Tony Curtis) in order to make as much money as possible for herself, convincing Callan to take on dangerous and crooked opponents for her financial gain. A further example is the sinister character of Harriet Bird (Barbara Hershey) in *The Natural* (1984) who seduces Roy Hobbs (Robert Redford), after witnessing his skill as a baseball player, only to shoot him after luring him back to her hotel room. Later in the film, when Roy achieves success with the New York Knights he is distracted again by another deceitful woman, Memo Paris (Kim Basinger) who is employed by the club's part owner 'The Judge' (Robert Prosky) and gambler Gus Sands (Darren McGavin) to distract Hobbs and thereby cause the Knights to lose the pennant so that 'The Judge' can become the sole owner of the club.

Sometimes the two aspects of the dominant representations of women in the sports film are found within the same film. In *Body and Soul* Alice is contrasted with Charley's real love Peg (Lilli Palmer) who reminds the boxer by the end of the film of more important values than those of exploitation and personal greed surrounding the fight game. The devious woman also appears in *The Spirit of Youth* (1938), where boxer Joe Thomas (Joe Louis) is seduced by cabaret singer Flora Bailey, played by Mae Turner who was famous for playing femme fatale characters in Black cinema in the 1930s. Bailey is involved with gambler Duke Emerald (Jewel Smith) who persuades her to distract Thomas from his training by encouraging his drinking and nightlife so that he can bet successfully against him. Though Thomas's career begins to decline, he is eventually reunited with his childhood sweetheart Mary Bowdin (Edna Mae Harris) who inspires him to victory in the film's climactic fight. The return of a childhood sweetheart, Iris Gaines (Glenn Close), also inspires a return to form for Roy Hobbs in *The*

Natural, and offers a contrast with the deceitful temptresses Harriet Bird and Memo Paris elsewhere in the film.

Throughout much of its history, the sports film has followed this pattern, notwithstanding the increased visibility of strong women in prominent roles in recent years in films such as the Oscar-winning *Million Dollar Baby* (2004) and *Whip it* (2009). As suggested by the 2008 AFI selection of Top 10 best sports films considered in Chapter 3 – *Raging Bull* (1980), *Rocky* (1976), *The Pride of the Yankees* (1942), *Hoosiers* (1986), *Bull Durham* (1988), *The Hustler* (1961), *Caddyshack* (1980), *Breaking Away* (1979), *National Velvet* (1944) and *Jerry Maguire* (1996) – the sports film has overwhelmingly been focused on male protagonists, with only one in the AFI list, *National Velvet*, featuring a female lead. Though a significant text in terms of the representation of gender, *National Velvet* nonetheless reflected what has been a continuing feature of sports films featuring female lead protagonists: the maintenance of patriarchy.

Representations of women since World War II

The MGM production *National Velvet* was released in 1944 during World War II. This context had a more than significant impact on the film. Apart from the many women involved with the medical services in the war, women played a crucial role on the home front in the work place producing munitions and taking the place more generally of men who went to war, leading to what Mary Ann Abate has described as 'a paradigm shift' in American society (Abate, 2008, pp. 145; see also Chafe, 1991, p. 121). In its depiction of a female jockey winning the Aintree Grand National against the odds (and the rules), *National Velvet* reflected this paradigm shift. However, it would be wrong to overstress the film's progressiveness; Velvet Brown (Elizabeth Taylor), in a pattern that continues to feature in sports films featuring female lead protagonists, is prepared and guided in her efforts to achieve Grand National success by the more experienced male jockey, Mi Taylor (Mickey Rooney) (Fig. 5.1). Furthermore, while Pie wins the Grand National, the horse is disqualified as Velvet falls off and fails to make it to the enclosure, a disqualification that is further confirmed when her sex is discovered in the medical facility at the track. Velvet may be celebrated by the media and welcomed warmly by her community after completing the race in the film, yet the question remains: if this film is progressing the representation of women, why does Velvet ultimately win nothing? Indeed, the stereotype of women as 'the weaker sex' is surely confirmed by Velvet's inability to 'stay the course' and remain on her horse.

National Velvet indicated a development in film that became apparent particularly following World War II as a number of significant texts emerged to suggest women's changing roles in society at large. In a further MGM film, *Pat and Mike* (1952), Katherine Hepburn plays Pat Pemberton, a successful tennis player and golfer engaged to a domineering and unsupportive fiancé, Collier Weld (William Ching). She is spotted by sports agent Mike Conovan (Spencer Tracy) who, impressed with her all-round sporting ability, including in

FIGURE 5.1   Velvet Brown (Elizabeth Taylor) is prepared by Mi Taylor (Mickey Rooney) to ride Pie in the Grand National in *National Velvet* (Metro-Goldwyn-Mayer, 1944) (MGM/The Kobal Collection)

target shooting, signs a contract with her and promises to promote her into the 'King of the World! Queen, I mean'. Though the film suggests Pat's ability and independence, ultimately her success is achieved under Conovan's guidance, much as Velvet Brown depends on the direction of Mi Taylor. As Bergan notes,

> By the end of [*Pat and Mike*], she has dumped 'Collier' and married sports promoter Spencer Tracy, although she has to prove she's weaker than him in order to protect his male ego. Another example in a Hollywood movie of struggling feminism, manacled in the end by a patriarchal ideology.
>
> (1982, p. 113)

Partly as a response to the growing woman's movement and to women's increasingly active roles more generally in society, from the 1970s onwards women began to feature more frequently in prominent roles in sports films. Indeed, these women now appeared in roles and possessed qualities perceived historically as masculine, such as authority, strength, aggression, force and intellect. While these films continued to be in the minority, the representations of women found therein often suggests the tensions inherent in placing strong females in contexts that have historically been predominantly the preserve of men. As Deborah Tudor contends,

> Introducing a female character who possesses overt signs of 'feminism' such as independence and subjectivity, introduced problems into films that represent a social institution still conceptualised as a male preserve. Sports is culturally male not only through the fact that male athletes are considered the standard of performance, but also in the mode of address of broadcast sporting events. The primacy of males as the audience of sports remain a factor in their presentation on television, despite audience numbers that reveal increasing numbers of women viewers.
>
> (1997, pp. 80–81)

As a consequence, the threat that such strong women may pose to patriarchy is contained through three principle means in the sports film: through the often negative, or comic, portrayal of women in positions of authority; by positioning leading sporting females clearly under the guidance (and authority) of men; or by the sexual objectification of women for principally male gratification. Such depictions of women may ultimately reflect anxieties regarding masculinity itself and represent an attempt to reassert masculine authority and patriarchy. While King and Leonard have referred to a recurring theme found in many sports films of a 'flawed white masculinity finding solace through sports' (King and Leonard, 2006, p. 9) evident in films such as *Rocky*, *Cinderella Man* and *The Fighter*, sports films also reveal at times a crisis of masculinity that sport only temporarily relieves. Such anxieties were already evident in the immediate post-war period in films such as *Body and Soul, The Set-Up* and *Champion* each of which depicted damaged lead male protagonists grappling with aspects of their own masculinity and their relationships with women. Indeed, it is interesting to note the evolving depictions of such relationships between the 1970s and the twenty-first century. Sports films have revealed sometimes deeply flawed and often paranoid male protagonists who have great difficulties relating to women. These difficulties occasionally erupt in violence, particularly in films of the 1970s and 1980s. As Robin Wood has contended with regard to depictions of violence against women in cinema, such films

> have generally been explained as a historical response to 1960's and 1970's feminism: the male spectator enjoys a sadistic revenge on women who refuse to slot neatly and obligingly into his patriarchal pre-determined view of 'the way things should naturally be'.
>
> (1987, p. 81)

In more recent times, sports cinema has more and more resorted to comedy and sexualisation to disguise what is arguably a continuing anxiety. A further feature evident in several recent prominent sports film is a nostalgia for a time of more traditional gender roles, evident in dramas such as *Space Jam* (1996), *The Rookie* (2002) and *Cinderella Man* (2005), in which the supportive home-maker wife of prominent athletes is confined primarily to the reassuring domestic space.

One of the most unsettling depictions of nostalgia, masculinity in crisis and violence against a woman is found in Martin Scorsese's *Raging Bull* (1980), adapted by Paul Schrader and Mardik Martin from former middleweight boxing champion Jake La Motta's memoir *Raging Bull: My Story*. Influenced by classic boxing films such as *Body and Soul* (discussed in Chapter 4), *Raging Bull* is similarly shot, unusually for a film made in the 1980s, in black and white which contributes to the sense of nostalgia Pam Cook has recognised in the work (1982, p. 39). A further classical Hollywood reference is Columbia Pictures' *On the Waterfront* (1954), and lines from former boxer Terry Malloy (Marlon Brando) in that film provide La Motta's (Robert De Niro) closing words in *Raging Bull*: 'I could've been a contender. I could've been somebody instead of a bum'. Scorsese's film is an unsettling account of one man's rise to (and inevitable fall from) World Middleweight Champion and the personal and social demons that plague him along the way. However, his greatest demon is internal, a deep sense of insecurity which he inflicts on all who are close to him in his life, particularly his wife Vickie (Cathy Moriarity). Despite the success he enjoys in the ring, including becoming world champion, La Motta remains a deeply paranoid and insecure figure threatened by his wife's sexuality and convinced that she is unfaithful; as he remarks to his brother Joey (Joe Pesci) at one point while asking him to watch her while he travels to a fight 'Any woman, given the right circumstances, will do anything'. For La Motta the only possible response to this insecurity is violence; much as success through violence in the ring provides him with a surrogate sense of empowerment, so too does he inflict violence on his wife outside the ring in response to his own personal insecurities. Ultimately, however, boxing for La Motta becomes a form of self-punishment and Scorsese frequently includes shots of him been punched repeatedly and brutally in the head, making little if any attempt to defend himself or protect his face, most disturbingly in the fight against Sugar Ray Robinson (Johnny Barnes) where he loses his world championship title.

Pam Cook has contended that while *Raging Bull* undoubtedly features the brutal decline of a boxer, the film is nonetheless suffused with nostalgia for a strong robust masculinity and traditional patriarchal culture:

> The decline and fall of its hero, Jake La Motta, provides a pretext for the playing out of a number of anxieties about the irrecoverability of the past. His collapse into impotence is the mainspring of a scenario which evokes profound loss: loss of a great classic cinema, of community values, of family life, of individual energy ... A tragic scenario in which the hero's suffering teaches us something about our own life, and how to accept its terms.
>
> (1982, p. 39)

Ultimately, while masculinity is undoubtedly put into crisis, the film does so in order that 'we can mourn its loss' (Cook, 1982, p. 33). Such masculine insecurity (and nostalgia) is also evident in the American football-themed film *The Longest Yard* (1974) which opens with a scene in which disgraced ex-pro Paul Crewe (Burt Reynolds) beats up his rich girlfriend, apparently in protest that she has further undermined his 'unmanly' position since he left the game by supporting him subsequently, buying as she remarks 'those caps on your teeth, and the clothes that you're wearing and the bloody tan that you've got'. It would appear that his girlfriend's economic dominance has further threatened Paul's masculinity and therefore requires punishment. Deborah Tudor also identifies this attitude in a further American football film *North Dallas Forty* (1979)

> where female party guests are routinely humiliated, stripped and insulted. When Phil lodges a mild protest, Seth counters with 'Hell, these girls know what happens at these parties; that's why they come'. The stated critique of sports does not extend to its sexism in either of these films.
>
> (1997, p. 72)

Under suspicion or 'doing it for daddy'

In one of the most commercially successful boxing films of the 1970s,[1] the romantic comedy *The Main Event* (1979), Barbra Streisand plays perfume manufacturer Hillary Kramer who after losing all her money, finds one of her few remaining assets is a boxer's contract. When the boxer concerned, Eddie 'Kid Natural' Scanlon (Ryan O'Neal), indicates he no longer wishes to fight – having instead taken up a career as a driving instructor – she sets about convincing him to return to the ring, which he eventually does. While Kramer occupies a role in the film normally held by men, the film exploits this unexpected position of a woman for mostly comic purposes. Indeed, the film's humour depends on the inversion of established gender roles and the audience's recognition of the 'oddity' of a woman in a role usually associated with men. This includes one scene in which we witness Kramer attempt to convince a promoter to give Eddie a fight by emphasising his sexual appeal to women – 'We'll shorten his shorts, I'll show more leg' – rather than his boxing ability. Eddie's response to Kramer also exploits the film's suggested 'abnormality' of this relationship for comic effect:

> What do you think I am, a piece of meat? One of your perfumes? You treat me like an object! What do you think I am, a girl? No, I am a person! I have feelings! I'm a man!

As viewers, we are not encouraged to take Kramer seriously as either a boxing manager or a strong female protagonist. The film repeatedly undermines both these positions; Kramer throws in the towel in Eddie's final fight to express her love for him even though he is on the verge of winning while the film frequently sexualises her by depicting her in revealing outfits and as the subject of suggestive comments by men.

The Main Event's undermining of the progressive potential of a woman in a prominent role is a recurring feature of the mainstream sports film where women rarely threaten male superiority. Indeed, women involved in sport, particularly in positions of authority, are often viewed with suspicion, an attitude also apparent in *Slap Shot* (1977), *Major League* (1989), *Major League II* (1994) and *Any Given Sunday* (1999). As Deborah Tudor observes, an important aspect of American sports ideology is 'the hostility of males to women who transgress the boundaries and attempt to exert authority in what is one of the last perceived male bastions' (1997, p. 29). When Reggie 'Reg' Dunlop (Paul Newman) learns that widowed female owner Anita McCambridge (Kathryn Walker) has taken over the minor league ice-hockey team he coaches in *Slap Shot*, he is dismayed, particularly when she reveals she has no interest in hockey, objects to the violence in the sport, and is to fold the team as 'a tax loss'. Reg's response is to question the impact McCambridge will have on her son without a strong male figure in the home: 'Your son looks like a fag to me,' he tells McCambridge. 'You'd better get married again, cos he'll have somebody's cock in his mouth before you know it'. In *Major League*, the new female owner of the Cleveland Indians baseball team, Rachel Phelps (Margaret Whitton), a former showgirl who inherited the team after her husband died on their honeymoon, attempts to put together the worst possible team in order to activate an escape clause allowing her to move the franchise to sunny Miami. In *Any Given Sunday*, Christina Pagniacci (Cameron Diaz), the female owner of the American football team The Miami Sharks, is depicted as a selfish, vulgar and domineering figure with little respect for the team's coach, Tony D'Amato (Al Pacino). Such negative portrayals of female owners reflects less on professional sport itself, within which women rarely achieve such positions, than what Susan Faludi has described as 'the backlash against women's rights' which she argues 'charges feminists with all the crimes it perpetrates' (1992, p. 14). As Aaron Baker notes, in films such as these 'female owners vilify feminism through their selfish, controlling behaviour, yet much of what they do is typical of the business of sports when it is run by men' (2003, p. 144).

Despite their more prominent representation in sports films, as Earl Smith has observed, women in revenue-generating sports in the United States still contend with two major challenges, their marginalisation and the sexualisation of female athletes. While men's programmes receive up to 20 times more funding than women's programmes in some institutions,

> as opportunities have opened up for female athletes, the down side is that men now hold over half of the top coaching positions once held by women, mostly in basketball and soccer.
>
> (2009, p. xviii)

Much as men now occupy most of the coaching positions, so too do women in mainstream sports films featuring lead female protagonists often act under the guidance and instruction of men, in a pattern already delineated in sports films such as *National Velvet* and *Pat and Mike* and also evident in one of the most commercially and critically successful sports films of the early twenty-first century. Directed by Clint Eastwood, *Million Dollar Baby* (2004) took over $100 million at the US box office and a further $116,271,443 internationally.[2] The film was also the recipient of 55 major international awards and was nominated for seven Academy awards, four of which it won including in the prestigious categories of Best Director and Best Film. In many respects, *Million Dollar Baby* shares considerable parallels with previous sports and boxing-themed films discussed in this book; at its heart is the familiar trajectory of an underprivileged and marginalised working-class character for whom sport provides one of the few avenues to respect and success. However, in featuring a female in the role of a boxer and in its gritty depiction of the female fight game (including the bloodied and bruised bodies of female boxers), *Million Dollar Baby* appears to depart significantly from a fundamental prerequisite of the genre. Indeed, Margaret 'Maggie' Fitzgerald's (Hilary Swank) toned and muscular body and physical power contest established gender configurations that have long justified limiting women's role in sports. As Joyce Carol Oates famously remarked,

> Raw aggression is thought to be the peculiar province of men, as nurturing is the peculiar province of women. (The female boxer violates this stereotype and cannot be taken seriously – she is parody, she is cartoon, she is monstrous.)
>
> (1987, p. 73)

The perceived 'oddity' of female boxing is commented on within *Million Dollar Baby* with Frankie Dunn (Clint Eastwood), trainer and owner of the dilapidated Los Angeles boxing gym the Hit Pit, describing the sport at one point as the 'latest freak show'. However, in this remark and in Dunn's initial reluctance to train waitress Fitzgerald in her attempts to establish herself as a boxer, the film reveals a strategic amnesia regarding the development of women's boxing. Despite the impression given by the über-masculine environment of the Hit Pit, since the 1970s in the United States women have increasingly been training with men in gyms (Boyle, Millington, and Vertinsky, 2006, p. 101). Furthermore women's boxing has been televised in the US since that decade and has grown to considerable prominence in subsequent years, eventually receiving recognition as an Olympic event.

Dunn's reaction to Fitzgerald reflects more on the sports film genre, and particularly boxing-themed films and the rarity of female boxers therein, than on the actuality of women's boxing itself. However, it nonetheless affirms the mythology of absence and 'freak(ishness)' surrounding women's involvement in boxing and reveals the principally masculine perspective that the film adopts. While Hilary Swank as female boxer Maggie Fitzgerald undoubtedly occupies an unconventional role in a mainstream sports film, her role is nonetheless clearly framed (and contained) by a masculine and patriarchal perspective. It is significant, for example, that *Million Dollar Baby* is narrated by the familiar and reassuring masculine tones of Morgan Freeman – as Dunn's friend and employee, Eddie 'Scrap-Iron' Dupris – who foregrounds the significance of Fitzgerald's story for Frankie Dunn (Tasker, 2011, p. 89).

Indeed, *Million Dollar Baby* is principally the story of Frankie Dunn; as noted by Hamilton Carroll, 'while the plot ... describes Maggie's rise and fall, the principle affective investment of its story is, unsurprisingly, in Eastwood's character' (2011, p. 133). Dunn is estranged from his daughter to whom he nonetheless writes weekly letters, all of which are returned unopened. Though we learn little about her, Dunn's family problems and paternal responsibility are nevertheless a prominent concern throughout a film that, as Carroll continues, is more 'than anything ... about the sacrifices and redemptions of Frankie Dunn' (2011, p. 133). In this respect, Maggie Fitzgerald becomes a surrogate daughter for Dunn with whom he tries to establish and deepen the relationship he had failed to maintain with his biological daughter. However, this father–daughter trope (evoked in the iconic shot and publicity still that provides the cover for this book) within the film is the most prominent aspect of a more general pattern whereby it is men – Dunn and Dupris – who provide Fitzgerald with guidance and support. Other women, whether within Fitzgerald's family or her opponents in the ring, are depicted as irresponsible, exploitative and cheats.

This paternal aspect of the film unsurprisingly has consequences for its representation of gender. In an influential essay published in 1995, bell hooks[3] used the phrase 'doing it for daddy' to illustrate how

> black males and white females ... are bombarded by mass-media images within the pedagogy of popular culture that consistently remind them that their chances of receiving rewards from the patriarchal mainstream and their hopes of salvation within the existing social structure are greatly enhanced when they learn how to 'do it for daddy'.
>
> (1995, p. 84)

hooks identifies in this essay a recurring feature of both Hollywood films and popular publications whereby Black or female characters are depicted in subordinated roles 'always eager to please' their White 'daddies' (1995, p. 88). This includes the arena of boxing where hooks discerns in magazine depictions of White female and African American boxers the suggestion that both are engaged in a tussle for 'white patriarchal power and pleasure' (1995, p. 89).

As such, the relationship that *Million Dollar Baby* constructs between Dunn and Fitzgerald follows from an established, and prominent, pattern found in popular culture that enables the film to contain and diffuse the transgressive femininity – or 'female masculinity' (Boyle, Millington, and Vertinsky, 2006, p. 107) – that Fitzgerald represents. Both characters work through their own familial traumas – Dunn's with his daughter, Fitzgerald with her lost biological father – via their developing relationship such that Fitzgerald can eventually remark to Dunn 'You remind me of my daddy'. However, what may appear to be an innocent and touching remark reflects the general infantilising trajectory which the film adopts towards the boxer.

From the moment Dunn agrees to train Fitzgerald, the power relations within the film are made explicit as he remarks,

> If I take you on, you don't say anything. You don't question me. You don't ask why, you don't say anything except maybe, 'Yes, Frankie', and I'm going to try to forget the fact that you're a girl.

In these remarks, Dunn not only emphasises the hierarchical structure under which Fitzgerald will be required to submit but also the 'problem' that her sex presents to her involvement in the fight game, and the necessity that it be negated or overlooked. Indeed, Dunn's choice of 'girl' (Fitzgerald after all is 31 years old, a fact that Dunn raises in initially refusing to train her) rather than 'woman' is a significant pointer here, further contributing to her positioning in a subordinated role within the narrative.

The most controversial aspect of *Million Dollar Baby* on release was the unsettling and highly emotionally charged (and manipulative) final part of the film. Fitzgerald initially enjoys considerable success in the ring under Dunn's management and finally gets a chance to fight for the World Welterweight Championship. However in the fight itself against the reigning champion Billie 'The Blue Bear' (Lucia Rijker) she is seriously injured by an illegal blow from her opponent that leaves her with an acute spinal cord injury and little hope of full recovery. Unable to live with the severely restricted mobility she is likely to endure for the remainder of her life, Fitzgerald begs Dunn to end her life which he eventually, if reluctantly, does.

While these final scenes are among the most emotionally charged in the film, the decision to end Fitzgerald's life was heavily criticised by disability groups after the film's release (Davis, 2005). For groups such as the American National Spinal Cord Injury Association, the film appeared to 'uncritically [advocate] euthanasia for quadriplegics' (Davis, 2005). As Lennard J. Davis observed in an article in the *Chicago Tribune*,

> There are no scenes in which anyone at the hospital tries to deal with Maggie's depression or offers her counselling or at the least an anti-depressant. And the feisty girl who would stop at nothing to fight in the ring, who after the accident musters the energy to tell her hillbilly family to bugger off, strangely changes character and becomes someone

who gives up her ghost rather quickly – even refusing Eastwood's offer of sending her to college (his one attempt to affect her despair).

(2005)

In choosing to depict Fitzgerald opting for euthanasia in response to her serious acquired disability, *Million Dollar Baby* partakes of a long-standing tradition of representing disability in mainstream film. Paul K. Longmore has delineated a pattern in mainstream films featuring disability where 'the severely physically disabled character seeks suicide as a release from the living death of disablement' (2001, p. 6). As a consequence, Longmore argues the non-disabled audience are 'let off the hook' as it is the disabled character who willingly wishes to die despite opposition from non-disabled characters in the film, as evident in the reluctance of Frankie Dunn to end Fitzgerald's life. Ultimately however, non-disabled characters see euthanasia as 'necessary and merciful' (2001, p. 6). Longmore is highly critical of such depictions as its effect is to unburden the mostly non-disabled audience of any guilt or sense of responsibility regarding acquired disability while contributing to the maintenance of an ideology that contends that 'disability makes membership in the community and meaningful life impossible, and death is preferable. Better dead than disabled' (2001, p. 7).

While problematic in terms of depictions of disability, Fitzgerald's disability and final death is also critical to the depiction of gender in the film. As noted above, a recurring feature of *Million Dollar Baby* is the attempt to contain and diffuse the threat that Fitzgerald's transgressive femininity presents to the patriarchal order through her subordination within the 'father–daughter' relationship she develops with Dunn. As such, her eventual disablement and final death removes this threat while placing the focus squarely on the 'father' figure – Frankie Dunn – in the final scene as Freeman recites a letter he is sending to Dunn's daughter asking her 'one more time to forgive him' and indicating his concern that she 'should know what kind of man your father really was'. As Sherrie Inness contends, 'When a woman who is too powerful and tough appears in the American imagination, her life is invariably cut short, reminding the audience of the threat posed by such women' (2004, p. 11). Ultimately, it would appear the physically strong, independent, and capable woman must die to reassure the threatened hegemonic patriarchal order.

Sexualisation of the female athlete

In his study of *Race, Sport and the American Dream*, Earl Smith expressed concern regarding the sexualisation of women in sport in the mainstream media – in a manner not apparent to nearly the same extent in men's sports – and its relationship with the mixed messages it sends to girls to be fit and athletic but also to maintain 'bodies that mimic the waif-thin models they see on "America's Next Top Model"' (2009, pp. xviii–xix). Indeed, in his analysis of media commentary of female athletes, Smith found that women are 'more often praised for their looks, what they are wearing (or not wearing), and their hairstyles than for their performance in competition' (2009, p. xix).

The sexualisation process that Smith identifies is also relevant to the depiction of women in sports cinema. It is revealing, for instance, to contrast the 1974 version of *The Longest Yard* with the remake starring Adam Sandler as Paul Crewe from 2005. While the 2005 remake may lack the more ominous and violent undercurrents, particularly towards women, of the 1974 original, an increasing feature of the remake is the overt sexual objectification of women, from the opening shots of a beautiful bikini-clad woman swimming underwater in a swimming pool, with the camera lingering in particular on the woman's bottom as she rises from the water. While women now occupy increasingly leading roles in sports films, it is questionable how progressive these more active female characters actually are, particularly given the demographics (largely young males) of those who typically go to watch sports films. It could be argued that the increased presence of physically strong and active, though conventionally beautiful, female characters in these films is but a further attraction to the primarily male audience of such films. The fact that the roles of female athletes in sports cinema are customarily played by photogenic actresses such as Kate Bosworth (*Blue Crush* (2002)), Viola Hastings (*She's the Man* (2006)), and Ellen Page (*Whip it* (2009)) arguably contributes to the sexualisation process that Smith delineates above. As Jeffrey Brown has noted of action films with strong female leads, though these female figures may appear as more complex characters challenging traditional gender roles, they may run 'the risk of reinscribing strict gender binaries and of being nothing more than sexist window-dressing' (2004, p. 47).

Even in films which appear to be depicting women concerned with asserting their own right to participate in male-dominated sports, familiar and regressive representations of women remain, including in one of the most commercially successful baseball films ever released, *A League of Their Own* (1992),[4] a fictionalised depiction of the foundations of the All-American Girls Professional Baseball League. Focused in particular on the fortunes of the Rockford Peaches team, the film's ostensibly progressive depiction of women in a male-dominated sport is repeatedly undermined by familiar and regressive portrayals of female characters. As Richard Alleva remarked in a review at the time of the film's release,

> When a particularly homely player finally fulfils herself, is it through her playing, her super-power-hitting? No. It's by getting drunk and wild enough at a roadhouse to attract the attention of a local boy who will later marry her.
>
> (1992)

Indeed, prominent in the representation of women in *A League of Their Own* (1992) are two familiar categories, the domestic homemaker, Dottie Hinson (Geena Davis) who turns down the prospect of a baseball career to raise a family, and the sexually available female 'All the Way' Mae Mordabito, played (appropriately enough) by pop celebrity and global sex symbol Madonna.

The sexualisation process is also apparent in sports films in the manner through which women are featured as tools to recruit top athletes, as in the character of Autumn Haley (Halle Berry) in *The Program* (1993) who is employed by Sam Winters (James Caan) the coach of the ESU Timberwolves, to help convince talented tailback Darnell Jefferson (Omar Epps) to join his team. The promise of available young women for college athletes is also evident in *Blue Chips* (1994). When potential college player Ricky Roe (Matt Nover) tells Western University Dolphins coach Pete Bell (Nick Nolte) that the only reason he wants to go to college is for the girls he might meet, coach Bell assures him that 'we got a lot of girls at Western'. Women feature similarly in *He Got Game* (1998), where they are used by colleges in their attempt to lure talented high-school basketball players such as Jesus Shuttlesworth (Ray Allen), even bribing Shuttlesworth's girlfriend Lala Bonilla (Rosario Dawson) in their attempt to convince him to come to their school. In one scene Shuttlesworth is being shown around a potential college, Tech U, by another player Chick Deagan (Rick Fox), who makes it clear that beautiful women are available to him if he joins the college. During his tour, Chick brings Jesus to a room in which two almost naked White women are waiting for him and with whom he is then depicted having vigorous sex. For Maria Garcia in her *Film Journal International* review of the film,

> Although Lee's portrayals of these bribes are not inaccurate, they're exaggerated somewhat; the amount of screen time devoted to Jesus' sexual encounter at Tech U, and his revolting discussions with their chaperone about the pros and cons of dating white women – they do your laundry – as opposed to black women – they make you work too hard – cheapen an otherwise well-deserved indictment of the handling of young athletes by colleges and professional sports organizations.
>
> (Garcia, n.d.)

Indeed, contemporary high-school and college set sports films are often characterised by the sexist depiction of young women who seem always sexually available to male athletes, including in *Friday Night Lights* (2004) and *Varsity Blues* (1999). The latter follows the fortunes of the fictional small-town high-school American football team of West Canaan, Texas, and their domineering coach Kilmer (Jon Voight) over one turbulent season. In the character of cheerleader Darcy Sears (Ali Larter) the film depicts a sexually available woman whose interests move from one football player, Lance Harbor (Paul Walker), to another, Jonathon 'Mox' Moxon (James Van Der Beek) for whom she dances provocatively in one scene wearing only a 'bikini' made from whipped cream. In another scene the football players discover the attractive sex-ed teacher Miss Davis (Tonie Perensky) moonlighting as (what else?) a stripper. As one reviewer observed, *Varsity Blues* is laden with a sexism the filmmakers seem to revel in, from Larter's ill-defined sexpot to a sex-starved football jock played by Scott Caan, who frequently shouts about needing some 'ass' and sings songs with lyrics like, 'She broke my heart, so I broke her jaw'.

(McKiernan, 2009)

Given its commercial success in the United States where it took $68,379,000 at the box office alone as well as spawning a franchise that has produced a further four films (2004, 2006, 2007, 2009), *Bring it On* (2000) provides a revealing contemporary exemplar on the position of women with regard to sports cinema. The concerns expressed by Laura Mulvey above regarding women being primarily the object of the male gaze are undoubtedly borne out in this sports comedy concerning the competitive world of cheerleading.[5] The film opens with a group of cheerleaders dancing suggestively while declaring:

I'm sexy, I'm cute. I'm popular to boot. I'm bitchin', great hair. The boys all love to stare. I'm wanted, I'm hot, I'm everything you're not. I'm pretty, I'm cool, I dominate this school.

While this opening dream sequence may be viewed as a satire on cheerleading itself, everything that follows challenges this reading. For instance, this opening scene is followed shortly after by a scene in the girl's changing rooms of Rancho Carne High School where young beautiful cheerleaders in various stages of undress discuss possible captains for their team, with the favourite, Courtney (Clare Kramer) distinguished by 'the guys' loving to 'touch her butt'. Later still, cheerleaders from the school dress down to their bikinis and suggestively wash cars to raise money to hire a choreographer for the team. In this scene, the camera follows the eyeline of Cliff Pantone (Jesse Bradford), the love interest of the central protagonist Torrance Shipman (Kirsten Dunst), as he looks admiringly at Torrance in her bikini, clearly sexually objectifying her for the viewer (Fig. 5.2).

In common with the contemporary popular sports film, *Bring it On* also touches upon more serious issues in American society, particularly through its depiction of San Diego's affluent Rancho Carne High School's main competition, East Compton Clovers, a predominantly African American inner-city team. When Shipman is selected as Rancho Carne's new cheerleading captain, she discovers that her team have been stealing their routines from the Clovers, who have never received the recognition or awards of her high school. As Clovers' captain remarks to Torrance after confronting her following one of the Clovers performances,

Everytime we get some, here y'all come, tryin' to steal it, puttin' blond hair on it and calling it something different. We've had the best squad around for years, but no one's been able to see what we can do.

FIGURE 5.2 Cliff (Jesse Bradford) watches Torrance (Kirsten Dunst) at the car wash fundraiser in *Bring It On* (Universal Pictures, 2000)

The film, however, makes little attempt to delve beneath the suggestions of exclusion, marginalisation and exploitation made here and elsewhere by the Clovers team, suggesting ultimately that these issues can be resolved through sport. As A.O. Scott contended in his review of the film,

> A whole movie, rather than just a subplot, might have been devoted to East Compton's struggle for recognition and to the out-of-uniform lives of Isis's squad, played with gusto by the members of the singing group Blaque. As it is, the Clovers are on hand to serve as symbols of a complexity the movie isn't quite able to explore. They're better dancers and better athletes than their white counterparts, and also, for all their gumption and self-sufficiency, the agents of a white girl's moral awakening.
>
> (2000)

In this respect, *Bring It On* includes a familiar aspect of the popular sports film, whereby it touches upon such serious issues only ultimately to reaffirm the hegemonic order responsible for their perpetuation within a film containing familiar and regressive depictions of women.

It could be argued that *Bring It On* (and other recent college-set sports films) reflects the post-feminist moment which views a 'tawdry, tarty, cartoonlike version of female sexuality' as 'empowering' (Levy, 2006, p. 10). This development has certainly become increasingly apparent in popular culture, and Ariel Levy has listed numerous instances of female sexual exhibitionism in the mainstream media, including female Olympic athletes posing provocatively in *Playboy* and *FHM*, contending that being openly and publicly sexual is now a prominent part of contemporary society (2006, p. 10). However, it is questionable whether a sport (or film) that affirms women's role on the sidelines in support of men who provide the main event can offer a progressive representation of women. As if to reaffirm the patriarchal order, *Bring It On* ends as it began with the Rancho team singing suggestively to the camera, this time the lyrics of Toni Basil's hit 'Hey Mickey!', including the suggestive lines 'So c'mon and give it to me anyway you can/Anyway you wanna do it I'll treat you like a man/But please baby please, don't leave me in the damned Mickey'.

Conclusion

If as Judith Butler contends gender is a performative act lacking an internal essence and characterised by 'the repeated stylization of the body' (1999, p. 44), sports films provide a productive site within which to examine such stylisations. Chapter 4 identified the affirmation of the American Dream as a principle function of the sports film. This is a dream that has primarily been associated historically with White males. While African Americans in the post-World War II era have increasingly being encouraged to identify with this ideology in the sports film, as films from *The Jackie Robinson Story* to *The Blind Side* indicate, such depictions are clearly framed within the context of a paternal White society as part of a project concerned ultimately with maintaining White hegemony. A comparable trajectory is also apparent with regard to the representation of women. Much as sport in society has been principally concerned with men and masculinity, a similar focus is evident within the mainstream sports film genre. Whether in the boxing ring, on the ball park, football field or the basketball court, these films have been primarily about the trials and tribulations of male athletes, to whom women featured in the roles of inspirational lovers or femme fatales to be avoided. While the twentieth century began with films that affirmed a robust masculinity, over time male athletes have increasingly been depicted as flawed and insecure figures for whom sport provides an important (if often temporary) means of reasserting their masculinity. This attempt to recuperate masculinity was also in response to the rising prominence of women in public life, including in sport, and the anxieties that this gave rise to. In the aftermath of World War II, film responded slowly to the changes more generally in Western society, with women featuring increasingly in more significant parts, even on occasion crossing the ropes of the boxing ring. However, a recurring feature of such films is the undermining of strong women. While female owners of sporting franchises are viewed with suspicion, female athletes are subordinated to their male coaches while been repeatedly subject to sexualisation, thereby performing principally for male viewing pleasure. Ultimately, though the contemporary mainstream sports film may have contributed to the myth of gender equality, it has simultaneously played an important role in the maintenance of hegemonic White patriarchy.

6

THE SPORTS FILM, NATIONAL CULTURE AND IDENTITY

> The imagined community of millions seem more real as a team of eleven
> Eric Hobsbawm (1992, p. 143)

The previous chapters examined primarily films that emerged from the United States, given the dominance of that country on world film production and distribution and its formative influence on the development of the sports film genre. Yet from Asia to Australia and Africa, Europe to South America, sport has featured prominently throughout world cinema. The Internet Movie Database (IMDb) lists 71 countries other than the United States that have produced sports films, with over 170 United Kingdom productions alone to date. The sports film also has a long history internationally; one of the most commercially successful Chinese silent films of the 1930s was *Ti yu huang hou* (*Queen of Sports*) (1934) which foregrounded a strong female lead protagonist as an athlete at a time when women rarely featured in such roles in the West. Directed by the seminal Chinese filmmaker Sun Yu, the film concerns an aspiring sprinter from a Chinese village, Lin Ying (Li Lili), who goes to Shanghai to study at a women's sports college, eventually achieving recognition as a leading athlete. However, she is tempted by the social pleasures that fame brings, attractions that eventually lead her to neglect her training. As Zhen Zhang has observed,

> Lin learns a big lesson at the National Trials for the Far East Games (*Yuandong yuxuan dahui*): that the true spirit of sports lies in collective effort, not individual glamour. The didactic message about the need to harness the individual body – in particular, the female body – for nation building is not to be missed.
>
> (2005, p. 78)

This focus on the collective, in contrast to the stress on individualism in American cinema already considered in this book, is also a feature of subsequent Chinese sports films including the box office success *Nǚ lán 5 háo* (*Woman Basketball Player No. 5*) (1957), the first film of influential director Jin Xie and the first colour Chinese sports feature. *Woman Basketball Player No. 5* also shares with *Queen of Sports* a female lead protagonist, in line with many Chinese films of the 1950s (Zhou, 2007, p. 95), in Shanghai girls' basketball team player Lin Xiaojie (Cao Qiwei). Lacking in focus and discipline, Xiaojie is dropped from the team despite been the star player after arriving late for a game; as her coach Tian Zhenhua (Liu Qiong) tells her 'I don't think that someone who is undisciplined and does not think of the group can be of any use in a game'. However, guided and inspired by her coach, Xiaojie realises the importance of supporting the team in a film which utilises sport 'as a vehicle of nationalism and the collective spirit' (Zhang, 2004, p. 206).

Sport also featured prominently in the formative years of sub-Saharan African film production; *Lamb* (1963), a film released three years after Senegalese independence by a pioneer of film production in West Africa, Paulin Soumanou Vieyra, concerned traditional wrestling in Senegal and was part of a general pattern in newly emerging independent African states to 'reassert the value of the cultural heritage from the perspective of a search for identity' (Sakbolé et al., 1996, p. 51). The focus on the relationship of the sports film with national culture and identity in this chapter is not to suggest that this does not apply to American film – indeed, as already discussed with regard the American Dream ideology, Hollywood sports films are often centrally concerned with American identity. However, more often than not when we encounter commentary or analysis of national cinema, it is, as Ian Jarvie has observed, 'touted as an alternative to, even a replacement for, American movies' (2000, p. 81). This is one of the tensions examined in this chapter.

Sport and national identity

National identity as we understand it today is a modern creation for which a pre-modern history has been largely rewritten. While nations may have being viewed in the past as timeless phenomena, they are now more commonly seen to comprise, in Benedict Anderson's oft-quoted formulation, 'Imagined Communities' with historical limits after the enlightenment (Anderson, 1991). Therefore, such 'nations' that have emerged have been largely constructed around invented histories and traditions, formulated by movements concerned to construct such nations in their own interests (Hobsbawm and Ranger, 1983; Hobsbawm, 1992).

Central to this process and the promotion of nationalism have been cultural activities; as Ernest Gellner notes 'culture is now the necessary shared medium' (1983, pp. 37–38). Sport is one of the most popular of such cultural activities. Indeed, in emphasising the banality of nationalism as a 'natural' and often unnoticed part of everyday life, Michael Billig has argued that modern sport has a social and political significance that 'extend[s] through the media beyond the player and the spectator' by providing luminous moments of national engagement and national heroes whom citizens can emulate and adore (1995, p. 120). As Billig's remarks suggest, the mass media (including the cinema) has had a crucial role to play in the popularisation of sport and, indeed, in asserting its political significance.

Particularly since the emergence of national sporting teams in the late nineteenth century, film and latterly television have contributed substantially to the promotion of such teams and sports and in enabling supporters to follow their team's progress often over considerable distances – for example, when participating at the FIFA World Cup. More importantly, perhaps, the media have affirmed the role of the nation and supporters' identification with the national team in the mediated representation of such games. For Lincoln Allison,

> National Identity is the most marketable product in sport. An English audience for football which normally has a ceiling of around ten million could leap to 32 million for the England–Brazil World Cup match in 1970. Women compose a small (though increasing) minority of football fans, around 7–12 per cent, but they were 44 per cent of the audience for England's games in the 1990 World Cup.
>
> (2002, p. 346)

While television has been a crucial part of people's engagement internationally with the FIFA World Cup, national cinemas have also commented on its significance. The Iranian film *Zendegi va digar hich* (*And Life Goes on …*) (1992) includes a scene in which the local people of the earthquake-hit region of Koker attempt to put up an antenna so they can watch the Argentina versus Brazil match in the 1990 World Cup despite the devastation that surrounds them. As one local man replies on being asked how people could watch television after such a traumatic event: 'What can we do? The soccer World Cup is once every … four years and the earthquake – every forty. Yes, life goes on'. In the Israeli film *Gmar Gavi'a* (*Cup Final*) (1992), a kidnapped Israeli soldier finds common ground with his Palestinian captors through their mutual interest in soccer and the 1982 World Cup. The Bhutanese film *Phörpa* (*The Cup*) (1999) concerns the creative efforts made by young Tibetan monks to watch the 1998 World Cup, including sneaking out at night to the one local bar showing the games on TV and eventually convincing their superiors to allow them to screen the final at their monastery. The hosting of the 2010 World Cup in South Africa also inspired the narrative of the British/Rwandan co-production *Africa United* (2010) which concerns five children who travel over 3,000 miles, overcoming considerable obstacles along the way, to take part in the opening ceremony of the World Cup in Johannesburg. In each of these films, sport offers hope and a means of affirming the interconnectedness of societies that may be culturally or ɪically far apart, providing an important cultural form through which a ɪ humanity can be recognised and shared, at least temporarily.

Sport, film and national culture

Sport in film can affirm the nation while simultaneously popularising sport. International sporting victories may contribute to a sense of national solidarity and pride in one's country, but filmic depictions of such victories can also add significantly to this process. The recuperation of German identity in the post-World War II era was helped greatly by World Cup victories, particularly in 1954 and 1990. While the 1954 victory was concurrent with the beginning of Germany's economic recovery after the war, the 1990 victory coincided with German unification after the fall of the Berlin wall. However, both moments have been evocatively rendered and affirmed in two of the most commercially successful German films in the post-war era, *Das Wunder von Bern* (*The Miracle of Bern*) (2003) concerning West Germany's unexpected victory in the 1954 World Cup, and *Good Bye Lenin!* (2003) which features a German nation enthralled by West Germany's path to World Cup victory in 1990. A further example is the 2009 film *Invictus* which concerns Nelson Mandela's attempts to bring his divided nation together, after the abolition of apartheid, through South Africa hosting, and eventually winning, the 1995 Rugby Union World Cup.

Film has also engaged with distinctive national and ethnic sporting cultures, events and themes. One of France's most commercially successful and critically acclaimed animated films, *Les Triplettes de Belleville* (*Belleville Rendez-vous*) (2003), concerns the kidnap of a cyclist competing in the annual Tour de France, a race which Barthes viewed as occupying a mythological place in French culture (1979, p. 87). The most popular film ever at the Norwegian box office is the stop motion-animated feature film *Flåklypa Grand Prix* (*Pinchcliffe Grand Prix*) (1975) concerning a motor race and how 'local forces win over the international elite' (Iverson, 1998, p. 134). In its successful evocation of the Norwegian landscape and rendering of a range of idiosyncratic characters created by popular Norwegian cartoonist Kjell Aukrust, *Flåklypa Grand Prix* struck a chord with Norwegian people in particular, though it also attracted large audiences across Scandinavia. The fascinating documentary *Trobriand Cricket* (1975) reveals the way that Trobriand Islanders off the Eastern coast of Papua New Guinea transformed the English sport of cricket – introduced in the early twentieth century by the British Methodist missionary Reverend Gilmour – into their own distinctive sport that has become a conduit for tribal rivalry and simulated combat. The third highest grossing film ever at the Mexican box office is the sports film *Rudo y Cursi* (2008) concerning the fortunes of two brothers from a fictional farming village who both initially rise to successful careers as professional soccer players, before drugs, gambling and corruption bring their playing days to an end and lead to a return to their humble rural roots (Jaafar, 2009). In Ireland, among the most popular and influential productions of the National Film Institute following its establishment in 1945 were short highlights films capturing the annual All-Ireland finals in the indigenous sports of hurling and Gaelic football. These were productions centrally concerned with affirming the still relatively new independent nation in a particularly challenging period in its development (Crosson, 2013).

Contesting hegemonic constructions of the nation

While directors across the world have employed sport in film to foreground and affirm aspects of national culture and identity, as an international and highly commercialised form, film's relationship with the nation is complex and uncertain. As Andrew Higson contends, '[h]istories of national cinema can only really be understood as histories of crisis and conflict, of resistance and negotiation' (1989, p. 37). This relates both to the complexity of the international film industry but also to 'the contingency or instability of the national' both in terms of the 'cultural difference and diversity that invariably marks both the inhabitants of a particular nation-state and the members of more geographically disperse "national" communities' (Higson, 2000, pp. 64–66). While this chapter will consider relevant films in this respect in the case studies below of British, Australian, and Indian cinema, further pertinent productions are the 2005 Québécois film *Maurice Richard* and the award-winning Iranian film *Offside* (2006).

Maurice Richard concerns not only one of the greatest ice-hockey players of the twentieth century but also a man who was the 'the incarnation of Québec nationalism' (Melançon, 2009, p. 2). While star player and eventually captain of the Montreal Canadiens – Québec's only professional ice-hockey team in the NHL – between the 1940s and 1960s, Richard became a major cultural icon for Canadians, and in particular residents of Canada's primarily French-speaking province of Québec. He has been compared to Major League Baseball's Jackie Robinson (discussed in Chapter 4) as both players represented the possibility of success in North America for the respective underprivileged minority groups from which they came (Melançon, 2009, p. 80). Indeed, Richard is regarded as a key figure in what is now known as 'the Quiet Revolution' in modern Québec's history, a period marked by a growing sense of pride in Québécois identity, sometimes expressed in calls for independence from the rest of Canada, and demands for respect for the culture and language of Québec (Linteau et al., 1991, pp. 307–316). Though ostensibly a film about ice-hockey, it is these themes that lie at the heart of *Maurice Richard*. Richard's attacking and robust playing style on the ice, his status as the greatest goal-scorer of his day, and his bravery in taking on and publicly criticising the establishment in the person of NHL president Clarence Campbell – all prominent aspects of the film – inspired French Canadians that they too could challenge the condescension of the majority English-speaking Canada.

While *Maurice Richard* challenges hegemonic constructions of Canadian identity, *Offside* provides a fascinating insight into Iranian culture and society, and particularly the position of women within it, in a work that was almost entirely shot during an actual FIFA World Cup qualifying match between Iran and Bahrain. Its director, Jafar Panahi, achieves the remarkable feat of making a film concerning individuals obsessed with supporting their nation while simultaneously functioning, as Whannel observes, 'to disturb and disrupt some dominant ideological assumptions of the society within which it is set' (2008, p. 196). Indeed, in common with previous films by Panahi, *Offside* was banned in its home country and the director was subsequently imprisoned for six years in 2010, and forbidden to make films for twenty years, for allegedly producing 'propaganda against the Islamic Republic' ('Filmmaker Jafar Panahi', Anonymous 2012; Kamali Dehghan, 2010). *Offside* concerns the efforts of a young female football supporter (Shima Mobarak-Shahi) to attend a crucial World Cup qualifying game for her country. However, in Iran women are forbidden to attend football matches and women who wish to do so must go disguised as men. Despite being dressed as a man, the girl is recognised by a soldier as she attempts to enter the stadium and is detained in a holding pen (Fig. 6.1) just outside the stadium's main stand with other women who have also tried to watch the game. While almost all those featured in the film, from the young women to the soldiers who detain them, are absorbed with the game being played, the game itself barely features and the focus of the film is on revealing the absurdity of the ban, evident in humorous scenes in which we witness soldiers relaying to the women what is happening inside the stadium. In *Offside*, sport provides a metaphor for the marginalisation of women within Iranian society. As one of the girls detained asks 'Why could Japanese women

FIGURE 6.1 Female supporters confined to a holding pen outside Tehran's Azadi stadium beg soldiers to give them an update on the FIFA World Cup qualifying match taking place inside in *Offside* (Jafar Panahi Film Productions, 2006) (Jafar Panahi Film Productions/The Kobal Collection)

watch the Japan–Iran game here?' Apparently, a less than convincing soldier responds, because Iranian women might overhear men cursing and swearing and because a 'man and a woman can't sit together' at a football match.

As Hjort and MacKenzie contend, films

> do not simply represent or express the stable features of a national culture, but are themselves one of the loci of debates about a nation's governing principles, goals, heritage, and history. It follows that critics should be attuned not only to the expressive dimensions of a nation's films, but to what these films and their categorisation as elements of a national cinema may elide or strategically repress.
>
> (2000, p. 4)

Sport's ability to mobilise and sustain a sense of national identity has, at various points, been exploited by filmmakers in differing contexts. However, sport has also on occasion provided a means for filmmakers to contest hegemonic constructions of the nation, particularly in instances where such constructions obscured or elided identities – sporting, cultural, social class, gendered, or otherwise – that may not concur with established understandings of the nation itself. The remainder of this chapter will consider some relevant examples in both these respects from Britain, Australia and India. While conscious that this focus omits a consideration of the many other contexts within which sports films have emerged – an undertaking beyond the scope of a single chapter – it is hoped that these case studies will nonetheless give some sense of the importance and diversity of sport in film internationally.

The British sports film

While a less prominent feature of British film than of American cinema, the sports fiction film has nonetheless had a long history in Britain and some of the most important figures in British film have chosen sport as a subject of their representations, including Alfred Hitchcock.[1] In terms of sports depicted however, despite its prominence and popularity particularly in England and its association above all with English identity, cricket is one of the least represented sports in British film. While it is alluded to and occasionally referenced in a number of films down the years – including films by Hitchcock (*The Lady Vanishes* (1938)) and Carol Reed (*Night Train to Munich* (1940)) – few films have featured cricket centrally within them. Indeed, when the 1953 film *The Final Test*, concerning the final Test match of England player Sam Palmer (Jack Warner), was first released on VHS by Odyssey Classics in June 1990, it was described by the company on the VHS cover as 'The only feature film about cricket!'

As Charles Barr has observed, 'the strong heritage and class associations of cricket have made it an attractive subject, touched on frequently in short scenes or in dialogue; yet it has never formed the central theme of a successful film'

(2003, pp. 630–631). British films that feature cricket often do so to contribute to the creation of an English atmosphere, as evident in Joseph Losey's films *Accident* (1967) and *The Go-Between* (1971), rather than out of a concern with or interest in depicting the sport for its own sake (Bergan, 1982, p. 12). Glen Jones has argued that cricket (in which tests can last from three to five days) is 'arguably too slow a game to provide ample highs and lows of dramatic struggle' (2005, p. 34), central features of the sports film genre. Indeed, it may be that the televisual format, offering the possibilities of regular intervals for commercials and serial depiction, is more appropriate for the depiction of cricket and dramas that depict the sport prominently often began their lives on television, including *P'tang, Yang, Kipperbang* (1982), *Arthur's Hallowed Ground* (1984) and *Playing Away* (1987), as well as the series *Outside Edge* (1994–96) and the Australian series *Bodyline: It's Not Just Cricket* (1984).

As the use of cricket in British film suggests, sport rarely affirms a 'British' identity, but rather identities that the term British includes. While the notion of national cinema in any context is a complex matter often obscuring a myriad of regional differences, this is particularly the case in terms of British cinema where strong identities – English, Scottish, Welsh, Northern Irish – are subsumed within the term, each of which have increasingly sought to promote their own distinctive national cinemas. A further complicating factor, identified by Sarah Street, is the 'domination by Hollywood which meant that British films could never occupy more than 15% of British screentime' (2003, p. 478). However, while conscious of the shortcomings of the term, it is nonetheless useful as a salient aspect of the British sports film is how the notion of 'Britishness' is itself challenged.

The tensions within British identity are never more apparent than when expressed through association football support. Jack Brand, for example, has commented on the importance of the Scottish national football team in the maintenance of Scottish identity and the revival of nationalism. While the passions inflamed among crowds at sporting events tend to reflect, rather than lead political sentiments, for Brand, 'the fact was that football kept the feeling of Scottishness alive' (1978, p. 138). A relevant sports film in this respect is Michael Corrente's *A Shot at Glory* (2001), a work concerned with the exploits of a Scottish association football team. In the film's opening commentary, the narrator asserts the importance and distinctiveness of football in the Scottish context, above all to the national identity of Scottish people themselves:

> Scotland didn't invent football, but we'll take a back seat to no one in our passion for the game. With 40 professional teams in a country of five million, football is as much a part of the national fabric as single malt and bad weather. Some say it's a religion.

While the film ostensibly contests British identity, in common with many other British sports films it nonetheless abides by the principles of the utopian

American sports film as the underrated and unfancied second-tier Scottish football club Kilnockie succeeds in going all the way to the Scottish cup final. Though they fail to win the cup, the threat of the club moving to Dublin because of financial pressures is removed due to the successful cup run and, as the television commentator remarks after the final, 'Kilnockie may have lost today, but they did not fail'.

A further relevant film with respect to Scottish identity – and the utopian narrative – is *The Flying Scotsman* (2006), based on the true story of Scottish racing cyclist Graeme Obree. This is a film that also features the unlikely rise to sporting success of an unconventional outsider with limited funding and support as well as serious personal issues, including coming to terms with a bipolar disorder. Indeed, Obree's unconventional riding style is viewed with suspicion by the cycling authorities who attempt repeatedly to have him banned from competition, including changing the rules to outlaw his approach to the sport. Despite these challenges, Obree nonetheless succeeds in breaking the world one-hour distance record, and subsequently becoming the individual pursuit world champion on a bicycle he largely designed and built himself from spare parts and washing machine components.

The importance of Scottish identity is a recurring feature of the film. Indeed, its focus on a cyclist provides numerous opportunities for the film's director, Scottish-born Douglas MacKinnon, to foreground the distinctive and stunning Scottish landscape while Obree trains. The attempts of Obree's manager, Malky (Billy Boyd), to secure the funding necessary for Obree's record-breaking attempt is assisted considerably by the hope of their eventual sponsor, Rapid Employment, that a Scot would hold the record: 'to think of that record being held by a Scotsman,' the company's owner remarks enthusiastically, 'By God, what a thrill that would be!' Significantly, Obree's main adversary for the one-hour cycling record is English rider Chris Boardman, and the rivalry between the two is evident in references and symbols of their national backgrounds, including Scottish flags at competitive events and references to their respective Scottish and English backgrounds in media commentary. While the TV commentator declares when Boardman breaks the world one-hour record that 'the world one-hour record holder is now an Englishman', Obree responds angrily when called a 'mad Englishman' by the head of the Cycling Federation, Ernst Hagemann (Steven Berkoff) 'You wanna know what mad is, try calling me English again'. Indeed, this rather condescending description which follows Obree's first unsuccessful attempt at the one-hour record, added to by the further patronising comment – 'I'm a Bavarian, I'm very proud to be called German. But I know you Irish Scots are always fighting' – provides important inspiration for Obree to return the following day and break the record.

More often than not, British sports films that touch on relations between the various parts of the islands of Britain and Ireland, suggest the tensions that exist in these associations. A further relevant example is Steve Barron's *Mike Bassett: England Manager* (2001), a mockumentary following the fortunes from qualification to the FIFA World Cup in Mexico of the most unlikely man to hold the position of his country's football manager. In one scene, after arriving in Mexico for the World Cup, the English team meet up with players from Scotland and Ireland and the encounter, which begins with seemingly friendly banter, quickly descends into a physical confrontation between the players from the various nations. Though foregrounding these tensions, *Mike Bassett: England Manager* also features the familiar trajectory of the underdog overcoming considerable obstacles to be successful. Basset is surprisingly appointed as England manager, despite lacking top-level experience as a manager (his previous experience was a manager of second-tier team Norwich City) and manages to lead England all the way to the World Cup semi-final, despite having a clearly limited (and very old-fashioned) management style and being involved in an embarrassing drunken incident during the World Cup campaign.

In terms of the articulation and celebration of a British national identity, a rare and somewhat unusual sports film example is the 1981 production *Chariots of Fire*. This is one of the most acclaimed British films of the past fifty years, winning four Academy awards (including for Best Picture) and taking almost $60 million at the US box office alone. The film was also viewed as the beginning of a revival (largely unrealised) of British cinema with the screenwriter Colin Welland announcing 'the British are coming' at the Academy awards ceremony after he received his Oscar for Best Original Screenplay (Chapman, 2005, p. 270). Indeed, the film was celebrated as achieving success while maintaining one's own national distinctiveness, 'winning on your own terms' (cited in Leach, 2004, p. 23) as the film's producer, David Puttman, remarked at the time. However, in reality *Chariots of Fire* was largely funded not by British backers – who were hesitant to get involved – but by a Hollywood studio, 20th Century Fox who reaped most of the financial benefits of the film's success. As Sandy Lieberson, President of Fox when the film was produced, remarked

> Although *Chariots* was made by the UK arm of 20th Century Fox ... all profits made by Fox films are remitted to the U.S. to avoid paying British taxes. So, no, there would be no direct return of the film's profits to Britain or the British film industry.
>
> (cited in Andrews, Churchill and Blanden, 1982, p. 15)

Indeed, the success of the film in the United States could be attributed at least partly to its successful evocation of the familiar utopian trajectory outlined already in this book and related to the American Dream. This is a trajectory that sees the film's central protagonists each overcome considerable challenges to eventually achieve Olympic glory.

The film concerns the exploits of athletes preparing for, and competing in, the 1924 Paris Summer Olympics, in particular Eric Liddell (Ian Charleson) and Harold Abrahams (Ben Cross). National identity is complicated in the film by the challenges presented by those who do not fit neatly within the parameters of established British (read English) identity. This includes the Jewish athlete Abrahams, who is conscious of (and experiences) the prejudice members of his community have endured, but also his coach Sam Mussabini (Ian Holm) who is ostensibly forbidden from attending the Olympic Games as a professional trainer of athletes, but who is also an outsider, as an Italian of Arab ethnicity. Furthermore, in the devout Scottish missionary Liddell, the film also touches upon the complex nature of British national identity itself, subsuming as it does a range of other regional identities also viewed as national, including through sporting representation.

However, while the film depicts the tensions that lie beneath the notion of Britishness, including class, nationality, and race, it ultimately presents an uplifting and nostalgic portrayal of the period depicted, in which these tensions are transcended through sport. Both Abrahamson and Liddell achieve Olympic glory by winning the 100 metres and 400 metres respectively, with Liddell winning despite changing to the longer distance from his usual 100 metres event as the heats for his preferred distance took place on a Sunday. To have competed on a Sunday would have contravened Liddell's devout Christianity, but he succeeds nonetheless in the longer event. As Alan Tomlinson has argued,

> *Chariots of Fire*, in revealing to the British public a set of social divisions and inner conflicts and then providing a resolution in the form of nationalist integration, offered a metaphor of adaptation and equilibrium … it operated as a nostalgic evocation of traditional values to the British viewer.
>
> (Tomlinson, 1988; cited in Jones, 2005, p. 36)

The film's evocation of this utopian trajectory was all the more convincing given that it was based on a true story.

As *Chariots of Fire* indicates, British films often share strong formal similarities with Hollywood cinema, particularly in productions where sport is a central concern. These films may contest hegemonic constructions of identity – particularly British identity – but they often abide by the formal characteristics of the utopian sports film. Nonetheless, there are distinctive features to the British sports film and its relationship to the popular Hollywood genre. Chapter 3 considered David Rowe's definition of the sports film and the division that Rowe identifies between sport in film as either a transcendent force or one 'bound by existing (and corrupting) social relations' (1998, pp. 351–352) provides a useful, if admittedly loose, distinguishing point between sport as featured in American cinema and in British film, though often as not British films tend to fall somewhere between these two poles, being set in harsh working-class contexts but aspiring to the transcending moments that are so central to American film, evident, for example, in the film *When Saturday Comes* (1996). This is a production that is set in a challenging North of England working-class context where the chief protagonist, Jimmy Muir (Sean Bean), manages, after many set-backs, to move beyond his monotonous job in the local factory to a place in the city's Premier League team. Muir even succeeds in scoring the winning goal against Manchester United (the dominant team in English football over the past 20 years) in the cup semi-final in a film which unconvincingly suggests that challenging social circumstances can be transcended through sport.

As already considered in this book, this utopian trajectory is at the centre of the Hollywood sports film where as David Rowe notes 'all manner of social structural and cultural conflicts and divisions are resolved through the fantastic agency of sports' (1998, p. 355). British film is undoubtedly influenced by Hollywood and these utopian sensibilities, as films such as *A Shot at Glory*, *The Flying Scotsman*, *Mike Bassett: England Manager*, *Chariots of Fire* and *When Saturday Comes* indicate, are also found in a significant number of British films. Other examples include *Yesterday's Hero* (1979), *There is Only One Jimmy Grimble* (2000), *The Match* (1999) and *Bend it Like Beckham* (2002). The final of these, one of the most commercially successful British films of the early twenty-first century, is focused on the attempts of Jesminder 'Jess' Bhamra (Parminder Nagra), the 18-year-old daughter of Punjabi Sikh immigrants living in London, to play for a girls' football team, against the wishes of her conservative parents. A central conflict in the film is between the traditional values of Jess's parents and the more progressive impulses of Jess, more interested in embracing aspects of English popular culture – in particular football – than submitting to the traditions of her parents. While the film depicts facets of Punjabi Sikh culture, including the wedding of Jess's sister, sport functions within the narrative as the means through which Jess finds her own independence separate from her family. By the film's close, Jesminder's parents rather implausibly finally accept her wish to play football, allow her to accept a scholarship to the US and, indeed, as the last scene of the film suggests, to develop a relationship with an Irish 'gora' – outside of the arranged marriage traditions of her family and culture. Ultimately, as Michael D. Giardina contends,

> *Bend It Like Beckham*'s originary narrative erases political and ethical considerations that mark history as a site of struggle, producing what Henry Giroux (1995) has called 'a filmic version of popular culture', one that effaces the everyday hardships and struggles of daily life in favor of a reformulated, faux progressive New Labour vision of race, gender, and class relations.
>
> (2005, p. 45)

However, not all British sports films follow this trajectory. Indeed, a distinctive feature in British film is how such utopian sensibilities are occasionally challenged. Unlike the more utopian impulses of the American sports film, the British sports film is sometimes characterised by a cynicism and pessimism about the benefits of individualist performance and capitalism as a whole, and indeed might be characterised, as in Ken Loach's work, as anti-capitalist in impulse. This partly reflects the influence of the British social realist filmmakers

FIGURE 6.2   *The Loneliness of the Long Distance Runner* (1962) (Woodfall/The Kobal Collection)

of the 1960s, a period in which sport was among the topics considered. Two seminal films of this era were Lindsay Anderson's *This Sporting Life* (1963) and Tony Richardson's *The Loneliness of the Long Distance Runner* (1962) (Fig. 6.2). The gritty social realism that lies at the heart of these productions became a hallmark of a particular brand of British cinema that still persists to this day. Both these films, far from being fora for the resolution of societal problems, might be described as classic examples 'of the neo-Marxist critique of sport' in that, as Martin J. Bowden notes with regard to *The Loneliness of the Long Distance Runner* in particular, 'like the neo-Marxist critics' they condemn 'organized sport as a perversion of the human spirit' and reject 'the Sports Establishment as an institution' (1994, p. 69).

This Sporting Life features a North of England coal-miner, Frank Machin (Richard Harris) who impressed with the level of attention the local rugby league team receives and disillusioned with the drudgery of his working life as a coal-miner, attempts to improve his circumstances by playing for the team. He is signed by the team's owner and local factory boss, Gerald Weaver (Alan Badel), who is particularly impressed by Machin's aggressive style of forward play. Machin's decision to join the team is also influenced by his attempt to impress, and ultimately develop a relationship with, his widowed landlady, Margaret Hammond (Rachel Roberts). However, she is ultimately unable to reciprocate emotionally, viewing Machin as 'a great ape on a football field'. As Phil Wickham has contended, sport is used in *This Sporting Life* 'as a symbol to provide a contrast to Frank's emotional pain – as the team's hard man he takes a pride in inflicting physical pain on his opponents. On the field he has power and is in control; away from the scrum he has none' (n.d.). However, even on the field, Machin is exploited by the team's owner for his physical presence and aggressive tendencies. The depiction given of rugby is among the harshest and most unrelenting portrayals of sport of the period, as the camera takes us right inside the scrum on the muddy field of play where we encounter the raw physicality and brutality of the sport. Here sport provides few moments of transcendence but rather accentuates the sense of exploitation of the working-class protagonist at the narrative's centre.

Based on a short story by Alan Sillitoe, *The Loneliness of the Long Distance Runner* begins with shots of a young runner on a country road accompanied by the voice over 'My family has been running ever since I can remember and what we have usually been running from is the police'. The film features an imprisoned working-class young offender, Colin Smith (Tom Courtney) (Fig. 6.2) who is trained to represent the Borstal against public school boys in the all-England Prize Cup for Long Distance Cross Country Running. However, though well ahead and sure to win the race itself, Smith stops before the line and refuses to cross it in a bold statement of protest against the Borstal's governor and the system of which he is part. The film includes in its critique not just the establishment but also the escalating consumerist culture of the time, particularly in its depiction of Smith's spendthrift mother, who rather wastefully spends the insurance money after his father's death from cancer. In a feature that would be repeated in subsequent British films, including Lindsay Anderson's *If....* (1969) and *Chariots of Fire* (1981), *Loneliness...* features the singing of the patriotic hymn 'Jerusalem' (currently used by Team England as their anthem in Commonwealth sporting events) at a gathering of boys at the Borstal. However, the rendition is suggestively intercut with images of a boy being arrested and brutally imprisoned. In both *This Sporting Life* and *The Loneliness of the Long Distance Runner*, organised sport is depicted as exploitative and a limited reward for the deprivations of working-class life. This questioning of the role of sport in contemporary life and challenging of the more utopian impulses found particularly in American sports cinema is one of the most distinctive features of contemporary British film, evident in the work of Ken Loach.

Loach, a football fan and shareholder in non-league side Bath City FC, emerged among the new wave of social realist British cinema in the 1960s led by Anderson and Richardson and his work has often been compared with these directors, sharing similar concerns for working-class experience in films often critical of contemporary capitalist society. Indeed, Loach's first feature fiction film *Kes* (1969) was produced by Richardson's Woodfall Film Productions which also produced *The Loneliness of the Long Distance Runner*. *Kes* focuses centrally on the experiences of a young schoolboy Billy Casper (David Bradley) from a dysfunctional working-class home. Billy lives with his abusive brother Jud (Freddie Fletcher) and feckless single mother (Lynne Perrie) and endures abuse at both home and school. His one escape is when he finds a young kestrel and proceeds to train it and play with it whenever possible. However, apart from the support of one schoolteacher, Mr Farthing (played by the screenwriter of *Chariots of Fire*, Colin Welland), school is represented as a repressive and inhibiting institution providing little support for a young boy's imagination or hope for his employment prospects beyond the local mine where Jud works. It is within this educational context that football also features when the school PE teacher, Mr Sugden (Brian Glover), leads the schoolboys in a game. However, football is revealed as principally an opportunity for the teacher to impress his skills on the boys, while Billy is subject to ridicule and abuse for his lack of interest and failure as a goalkeeper.

Loach's work represents one of the most distinctive aspects of the British sports film, an unwillingness to transcend complex and challenging social circumstances through the intercession of sport. Indeed, Loach's 2004 feature *Ae Fond Kiss ...* provides a significant contrast to *Bend it like Beckham* in a film that also has a footballing connection evident in a provocative early scene where the sister of the chief protagonist, Casim Khan (Atta Yaqub), stands up in front of her Catholic and Celtic football club loving class mates to reveal she's wearing a despised Rangers football club shirt under her uniform. Unlike *Bend it Like Beckham*, however, in *Ae Fond Kiss ...* the issue of a relationship between a member of a family of Asian origin and an Irish person is not so simplistically resolved. In *Ae Fond Kiss ...* the relationship between a young Muslim from a Pakistani family, Casim, and an Irish Catholic schoolteacher, Roisin Hanlon (Eva Birthistle), leads to a traumatic family breakdown for which there is no clear resolution by the film's close.

However, it would be wrong to assume that Loach is critical of sport *per se*; as already noted, the sport of falconry provides Billy in *Kes* with his one imaginative and creative outlet in what is generally a constraining working-class context. Loach's films reveal in particular the importance of sport for working-class, and above all male, camaraderie. This theme is returned to in a number of subsequent films, including most significantly *My Name is Joe* (1998) and *Looking for Eric* (2009).

British public schools, as already noted in Chapter 2, particularly from the mid-nineteenth century onwards, had a crucial role in the codification of sport and the affirmation of its role in British life. Richard Holt has suggested various reasons for this including centrally 'the redefinition of masculinity and the new concept of "manliness"' (1990, p. 97). Indeed, for Holt, 'the most commonly used adjective in the public schoolmaster's vocabulary was "manly". Sport played a central role in the achievement of the kind of proper manliness that parents and teachers desired' (1990, pp. 89–90). However, as Holt also observes in the same work,

> professional football was about 'maleness' rather than 'manliness'. The
> working class imbued sport with a masculine value-system of their

own which differed markedly from the manly Christian ideal. Football enshrined older forms of toughness and rudeness, which stoutly resisted the 'civilizing process' of fair play and sportsmanship.

(1990, p. 173)

Loach's depiction of association football in his films suggests a keen awareness of the crucial role football plays in male working-class culture. His 1998 film *My Name is Joe* is a dark portrayal of the life of an unemployed recovering alcoholic, Joe Kavanagh (Peter Mullan), who is attempting to get his life together and develop a relationship with a local community health worker, Sarah (Louise Goodall). However, his past criminal life comes back to haunt him as he attempts to help his nephew Liam (David McKay) dispose of debts to a local criminal. Football features in the film as Joe is the coach of a local football team made up of unemployed men, some of whom (in real life) had criminal and drug using pasts.[2] While set in the actual slums of Glasgow and unrelenting in its depiction of poverty and drug abuse, *My Name is Joe* depicts football as one of the few positive outlets for these people, providing both moments of humour and a sense of community for people marginalised from society as a whole. However, unlike the American sports film which frequently uses sport as a means of transcending these challenges, and despite the obvious enjoyment that the players get from the game, these challenges remain and indeed on occasion interfere directly with the sporting events themselves, as when local criminals attack Liam in one scene while he is playing over debts owed.

In some ways, Loach's most recent sport-themed film, *Looking for Eric* is a rather surprising addition to his oeuvre in that it provides an unusually uplifting climax to a story placed in a familiar Loachian working-class milieu. However, it is the crucial role that football plays in forming and affirming community that is a central factor in this departure and at the heart of Loach's appreciation of football's importance in British working-class life. This focus is not unique to Loach but is also at the centre of the 1997 adaptation of Nick Hornby's novel *Fever Pitch*, directed by David Evans. In Evans' film, football provides a central means of male rapport and camaraderie for the Arsenal-obsessed Paul Ashworth (Colin Firth) with both his divorced father (Neil Pearson) and his male friends, including his best friend Steve (Mark Strong). As Ashcroft remarks in voice-over at one point in the film,

> it's not easy to become a football fan – its takes years. But if you put in the hours you're welcomed without question into a new family, except in this family you care about the same people and hope for the same things.

This notion of a football family, this time within the football club itself, is also central to Tom Hooper's *The Damned United* (2009), a fictionalised biopic of Brian Clough's 44 catastrophic days as manager of Leeds United in 1974. Through the film's focus on the interplay between characters, in particular

Brian Clough, his predecessor as Leeds United manager Don Revie, and Clough's managerial partner, Peter Taylor, it explores what Marcus Free has described as 'the common metaphor of football club as family, the impression of managers as quasi-fathers to their players, and the implicit fantasy, in football, of managers "producing" players and teams as a form of asexual male reproduction' (2010, p. 542).

Richard Holt has referred to the development of football in Britain as involving working-class men:

> Bound together with the sense of urban community there was the sheer excitement and beauty of the thing – the perfect pass that suddenly switches play from end to end, the shuffle and swerve that turns a defence and sends a winger away with the time to cross to a centre-forward tearing past his marker, the sudden reflex movement of a goalkeeper twisting and diving full-length to save a fierce shot. In the end these moments are instinctive and aesthetic, beyond social and historical analysis ... Sport was a kind of subtle and ubiquitous male language, a bond between husbands whose wives had their own world of neighbours and relatives.
>
> (1990, pp. 172–173)

It is this quality that is central to Ken Loach's *Looking for Eric*. The film is concerned with the challenges facing postman and football fan Eric Bishop (Steve Evets), a single parent of two difficult teenage stepsons who is dealing with both abandonment by his partner and psychological break down. While Eric seeks advice from his poster of former Manchester United striker, Eric Cantona (Fig. 6.3), he finds support from his workmates, particularly his best friend Meatballs (John Henshaw). In one of the film's most humorous episodes, his friends call round to Eric's house where Meatballs leads a self-help session, including meditation on the person each in the group of friends would like most to emulate, with Eric choosing his hero Eric Cantona. In this scene, Loach affirms the importance of this male camaraderie in one of the most unusual depictions of working-class identity, and one that challenges earlier constructions of masculinity associated with sport.

Eric's identification with the ex-footballer leads to Cantona actually appearing to him in his bedroom, offering advice on how the postman might deal with the various challenges in his life, including resolving his relationship with his first wife, Lily (Stephanie Bishop). Significantly, given Loach's suspicions of capitalism and its role in sport, it is FC United, the local non-league team formed in protest over the takeover of Manchester United by American businessman Malcolm Glazer and his family in 2005, that many of Eric's friends support and from whom most of those involved in the film's climactic scene were taken (Chalmers, 2009). This aspect of the film reflects not just Loach's concern with working-class experience but also the disenchantment of a considerable section of local support with Manchester United after the takeover. This focus on FC

FIGURE 6.3   Eric Bishop (Steve Evets) seeks advice from his poster of footballer Eric Cantona in *Looking for Eric* (Sixteen Films, 2009) (Les Films du Fleuve/The Kobal Collection)

United is developed in the documentary *United We Stand* included among the extras in the DVD release of *Looking for Eric* where the crucial role of camaraderie and community (words used repeatedly within the documentary) to football supporters and the disillusionment of many with the direction Manchester United and football generally has taken are prominent themes. As *Guardian* sports writer David Conn remarks, 'a club means something that people belong to, not something that people own' (*United We Stand*). This disenchantment is also evident in one scene from *Looking for Eric* where FC United fans and supporters continuing to support Manchester United clash in a bar. For the supporters of the smaller club 'the fat bastard chairman' sold the Premier League team for '30 pieces of silver', driving up the ticket prices such that ordinary working-class men can no longer afford to attend games, while more disreputable types such as Zac (Steve Marsh), a dangerous local gangster who threatens Eric and his family, has a corporate box at Old Trafford, Manchester United's stadium.

Eric's biggest challenge in the film, however, involves his son Ryan (Gerard Kearns) who has got involved with Zac and agrees to hide a gun for him in their house, leading to a raid by the police. Afraid to go to the police for help and threatened with severe repercussions by the criminal if he doesn't agree to keep the weapon, it is again Eric's friends, aided by three coach loads of FC United supporters on their way to an away game, who come to his assistance. Wearing a distinctive Eric Cantona disguise, they go to the house of the criminal concerned and film themselves ransacking his home and stripping him, threatening to release the footage to the internet if he ever goes near Eric or his family again. The climax of the film reaffirms the central role of male association and camaraderie in working class life, as facilitated through support for sport.

The Australian sports film

As a former British colony, it is not surprising that sport also plays a crucial role in Australian society and culture and has featured notably in Australian film. In Andrew Pike and Ross Cooper's guide to feature film production up to 1977, sport figures prominently in approximately 10 per cent of the films listed (Pike and Cooper, 1980). Other surveys of Australian film, including by Eric Reade (1970), Peter Beilby (1978) and Scott Murray (1995) have found a similar percentage of films where sport has a significant presence. Indeed, the first Australian film, *The Melbourne Cup* (1896), directed by the French Lumière operator Marius Sestier, captured on film one of the highlights in the Australian sporting calendar each year, the legendary Thoroughbred 'Race That Stops a Nation'. In a manner comparable to the depiction of boxing in early American cinema, horse racing provided a popular and attractive subject for early filmmakers in Australia and developed into a distinct genre of its own – 'the racecourse drama' – with the emergence of fiction film (Tulloch, 1981, p. 212).

The horse occupies an important place in constructions of Australian culture, identity and society (White, 2011, p. 65) and this has contributed to the production and popular success of such horse-themed films as *The Man from Snowy River* (1982) and particularly *Phar Lap: Heart of a Nation* (1983). Melbourne Cup winning thoroughbred racehorse, Phar Lap, has been described as 'first among all the heroic horses beloved by Australians' (Cusack and Digance, 2009, p. 880) and the film concerning the horse's achievements, directed by Australian director Simon Wincer, was a huge box office success in its home country, taking over $9 million at the Australian box office on release in 1983 (White, 2011, p. 73). *Phar Lap* includes the familiar utopian trajectory of the sports film, depicting the rise of the legendary horse from unfancied colt to Melbourne Cup winning thoroughbred, overcoming various challenges along the way. This includes the machinations of Phar Lap's corrupt American owner, David Davis (Ron Leibman), and a cracked right hoof prior to his final race, the Agua Caliente Handicap in Tijuana, Mexico, which the horse wins nonetheless with blood streaming from its split hoof.

While Phar Lap 'lifted the spirits of a nation' (Didinger and Macnow, 2009, p. 139) during the early years of the 1930s Depression, the filmic depiction of the horse's life also provided an important affirmation of Australian national identity in the 1980s, in line with a series of horse-themed films released in that decade (O'Neill and Phillips, 2010, pp. 4–5). As noted by Carole M. Cusack and Justine Digance:

The Australian film industry in the 1980s was mining a rich stream of history to create a national identity for an increasingly fragmented and multicultural society in the wake of 20 years of large-scale immigration; in addition to 'Phar Lap', 1981's 'Gallipoli', 1982's 'The Man from Snowy River' and 1987's 'The Lighthorsemen', all emphasized the vital role of the horse in forging the Australian identity, and linked that image to the courage and tenacity of the soldiers who fought in the First World War, drawing on the Anzac legacy.

(2009, p. 881)

Horse-themed films have continued to feature prominently in Australian cinema, evident most recently in a further Wincer-directed work, *The Cup* (2011), a production also based on the true story of a Melbourne Cup winning thoroughbred, Media Puzzle. *The Cup* includes the familiar and clichéd sports film trajectory, criticised by critics at the time of the film's release (see Buckmaster, 2011, for example), and described by the film's California-based co-production company, Myriad Pictures, as an 'incredible story of inspiration and triumph over adversity'.[3] In the case of *The Cup* this is focused on the experience of Media Puzzle's jockey, Damien Oliver (Stephen Curry), who succeeds in riding the horse to victory despite a series of prior racing defeats and particularly the trauma of losing his brother Jason (Daniel MacPherson) in a tragic racing accident (similar to that in which they lost their father) seven days before the race.

This 'triumph over adversity' trajectory evident in *The Cup* is clearly linked to national, as much as personal, recovery, particularly in the film's rather forced allusions to the Bali bombings of October 2002 in which 202 people were killed, including 88 Australians. Damien Oliver's success in the film is inspired partly by another major Australian sporting figure, North Melbourne Australian rules football player Jason McCartney, who despite having second degree burns on 50 per cent of his body, managed to rescue many others injured in the Bali bombings. McCartney (Rodger Corser) is featured in the film, including a scene in which Damien visits him in hospital, and it provides a further affirmation of the inspirational sports film trajectory. Indeed, the film's production notes make explicit the producer's belief in Oliver's success providing a means for the Australian nation to deal with the trauma of the bombings:

To his countrymen, still in shock from the Bali bombings, his gutsy ride speaks volumes about Australia's mettle. And to his fellow horsemen, hardened competitors who have 'seen it all' his gritty performance in the face of unbelievable pressure is a testament to the one attribute that knows no measure: the human spirit ... 'Australia was looking for a hero – and Damien became that hero.'

(*The Cup* 'Production Notes', 2011, pp. 5, 25)

While films such as *Phar Lap* and *The Cup* indicate the significant influence of American sports cinema on Australian film, there are notable examples that have challenged the more conventional constructions of the form and, indeed, hegemonic constructions of Australian identity itself. A relevant film here is the biopic of Olympic swimming champion Dawn Fraser, *Dawn!* (1979). Fraser won gold medals at the Melbourne (1954), Rome (1960) and Tokyo (1964) Olympics in the 100 metre freestyle event. However, she was a controversial figure who was suspended for ten years by the Australian Swimming Union, after been arrested for stealing an Olympic flag from a flagpole outside Emperor Hirohito's palace during the 1964 Olympics, an incident depicted in the film. Significantly, this incident comprises the longest single scene and is one of the most pertinent examples of Fraser's embodiment of the Australian anti-establishment 'larrikin' national stereotype discussed below.

Dawn! has been compared in style to the austere work of New German cinema in the 1970s, in its slow pacing and its 'flatness of dialogue coupled with intense emotional undercurrents, a tendency to use minimal music and background sound, and naturalistic episodic sequences rather than strongly structured narrative arcs' (Whannel, 2008, p. 196). The film could also be viewed as indebted to the British social realist films of the previous decade (discussed above) in its focus on working-class experience and challenging of the utopian trajectory of the sports film. As Fraser's father (Ron Haddrick) remarks when first approached by swimming trainer Harry Gallagher (Tom Richards) for £25 'a quarter' to train Fraser to be a championship swimmer, 'We're a working-class family, Mr Gallagher, we haven't any money.' The Fraser's rented home lacks an indoor toilet and, as Dawn (Bronwyn Mackay-Payne) laments at one point, 'we haven't even got a decent sort of bathroom, or hot water, or anything other places have … it's so old and shabby you couldn't bring anyone here'. Due to ill health, Fraser's father had to leave his job, and Fraser also has to leave school in order to work and bring money into the household.

While the depiction is generally tempered, and is far from the at times brutal portrayal of alcohol-afflicted working-class life in the more recent Australian sports film *Swimming Upstream* (2003), Fraser's working-class credentials are nonetheless clear and further affirmed in the various jobs we see her working in. This includes as a clothes shop employee, a price-checker for the department store, Myer, and as a petrol pump attendant. Indeed, despite her complaints earlier on, even after her parents' death, Fraser refuses to leave the 'shabby' home telling her swimming coach Gallagher 'I belong here'.

This focus on Fraser's working-class background is also relevant to the film's engagement with a central stereotype within Australian culture, the larrikin, in its portrayal of Fraser as an anti-authoritarian and working-class 'battler' (Phillips and Osmond, 2009, p. 2126). Dating from the nineteenth century, the larrikin has been defined by Clem Gorman as:

almost archly self-conscious, too smart for his or her own good, witty rather than humorous, exceeding limits, bending rules and sailing close to the wind, avoiding rather than evading responsibility, playing up to an audience, mocking pomposity and smugness, taking the piss out of people, cutting down tall poppies ... larger than life, sceptical, iconoclastic, egalitarian yet suffering fools badly, insouciant and, above all, defiant.

(1990, p. x)

As well as its focus on Fraser's working-class background, the larrikin figure is also evident in *Dawn!* in its focus on the swimmer's anti-authoritarian attitude and unconventional behaviour. From the earliest shots of Fraser in the pool mocking visiting championship swimmers, to her challenging of Gallagher's disciplined training regime ('I might as well be back at school'), insistence on smoking ('Nobody tells me what to do ... When my training interferes with my smoking, I'll give up training'), and her arrest for speaking disrespectfully to police officers, we are repeatedly reminded of Fraser's independent spirit and questioning of authority. Fraser is eventually banned from swimming after the 1964 Olympics, following the incident with the Olympic flag, but also ostensibly for marching in the opening ceremony against the wishes of the Australian Swimming Union who had decreed that no one participating in the first three days of the games could march. As Garry Whannel has argued

The film portrays Dawn Fraser (Bronwyn Mackay-Payne) as a swimmer through whom a whole set of tensions about class, gender, sexuality and patriotism are worked. She wins gold but respect is more problematic and she and the institutions of sport and the media never find a comfortable way of relating. It succeeds in asking a whole range of questions that cosier mythologizing of the road to self-improvement in many other sport films never broaches.

(2008, p. 196)

Prominent among these questions are the issues of gender and sexuality. As considered in Chapter 5, the sports film has historically been associated principally with the affirmation of masculinity and masculine values. However *Dawn!* questions gender categories and sexual conventions; not only is Fraser depicted as been anti-authoritarian, she is also critical of conventional gender typing, evident in one scene in which she questions, 'Why is it so terrible for a girl to drink beer ... it's the same all the time that we're on tour, as soon as I'd mention beer everyone would look at me'. At one point, we witness Fraser impressively down a yard of ale in front of the regulars in her local Balmain hotel bar (which Fraser managed for a period) and the film ends significantly with Fraser in this bar drinking beer with the predominantly male regulars as the credits roll.

However, Fraser's rebellious spirit irritates the male-dominated world in which she participates, whether in the form of the exclusively male journalists who report on her achievements and misdemeanours or the stuffy all-male members of the board of the Australian Swimming Union. When at one point Fraser's coach suggests to the Union that she might lead the Australian team in a forthcoming event, the chairman retorts derisively 'You have to be kidding. The kid is a rebel. She cannot control herself, let alone a team'.

Fraser also finds it difficult to fit into expected gender roles during her short-lived marriage to Gary Ware (John Diedrich), continuing to frequent bars, drink pints of beer and play cards and refusing to move from her home town of Balmain with her husband. After their divorce, we witness Fraser in subsequent relationships, in particular a lesbian relationship with Kate Hansford (Gabrielle Hartley) and it is this encounter which is most detailed in the film, based on Fraser's actual relationship with Joy Cavill, scriptwriter and producer of *Dawn!* (Phillips and Osmond, 2009, p. 2134).

Larrikinism, as John Rickard observes, is 'bound up with understandings of masculinity' (1998, p. 82). While this does not exclude women, or female sexuality, Fraser's engagement in a lesbian relationship challenges this national stereotype. As noted by Phillips and Osmond, Fraser's bisexuality is 'inconsistent with dominant masculine interpretations of larrikinism, with normative sexuality, with sport and sexuality and ultimately with Fraser herself' (2009, p. 2139). While no sexual scenes are depicted between the two, there are clear implications of an intimate relationship from the first scene in which we witness Fraser stay overnight in Hansford's apartment, and she affectionately covers Fraser's almost naked body with a blanket as she lies on her couch. Though the director plays with our expectations somewhat by preparing the viewer for a sexual encounter, only for us to witness Fraser getting out of bed with another man, the passionate and intimate nature of conversations between Fraser and Hansford indicate the intensity of the relationship.

The suggestion of such a relationship, if more implied than depicted in the film, was a radical departure at a time when homosexuality was still a criminal offence in Australia. It is significant that little critical commentary in Australia at the time of film's release remarked on this element and even by the time of the Sydney Olympics in 2000, when Fraser participated in the torch-lighting ceremony, little reference was made to her lesbianism (Philips and Osmond, 2009, pp. 2136–2137). It would appear as Barbara Baird has contended that the 'possibility that a lesbian may belong in a domain of Australian national pride was unthinkable and unnameable' (Baird, 2004, 80–81).

Dawn!'s challenging of established conceptions of Australian identity is also reflected in its disruption of the familiar trajectory of the sports film. The film does contain familiar tropes of the genre, including its focus on Fraser's achievement in overcoming the odds, both socially and physically. While she comes from an underprivileged background, she also suffers from pleurisy, leading to her withdrawal from her first competitive race in Melbourne. There are also recognisable montage sequences in the film of Fraser training hard in preparation for swimming competitions. However, ultimately her sporting victories in no way provide a resolution to the challenges she faces in her own life. Indeed, for a sports film *Dawn!*'s sporting sequences lack the forceful and often quite emotionally manipulative climactic sporting moments of the genre; Fraser's gold medal winning Olympic races, for example, are overall quite low-key in depiction. They also occur in the first half of the film with her final Olympic victory depicted after approximately one hour while the remaining 48 minutes focus on the challenges she faced after her career had ended, including the disintegration of her marriage. By the film's close, Fraser reflects on her failures rather than successes, viewing sport as little consolation for what she has lost in time not spent with her family. Speaking of her relationship with her daughter, she remarks

> I've been a pretty part time mother up till now. And I haven't got much to offer, some gold medals and a half-finished scrap book. But at least I can teach her that life isn't just a serious of hundred metre sprints. I've learnt that.

Dawn!'s inclusion of a lesbian lead-protagonist is also a rarity in sports cinema. While exceptions such as *Personal Best* (1982) exist, sports cinema has been concerned principally with affirming heterosexual relationships. As Aaron Baker has observed, while 'movies about sports may show the use of ideal masculinity to overcome barriers resulting from class, race, or gender, they still almost entirely avoid depicting lesbian and especially gay characters using athletics for self-definition' (2003, p. 50).

Though containing a much harsher depiction of working-class life in the 1950s, Russell Mulcahy's *Swimming Upstream* (2003) (in which Dawn Fraser appears briefly) also disrupts the utopian trajectory of the typical sports film in this biopic of swimmer Tony Fingleton (Jesse Spencer) who declined the opportunity to swim for Olympic glory. Like *Dawn!*, *Swimming Upstream* also seems to question the role that sport plays in society; while recognising the possibilities it may offer to individuals from marginalised communities, the film is cognisant of the limitations of sport in this respect and how sport can also be used for exploitative purposes.

Throughout the film, Fingleton's father Harold asserts his belief in traditional masculine values and in instilling them in his sons with sport playing a crucial role in this process. When Tony's older brother Harold Jr. (David Hoflin) beats him, his father encourages Tony to fight back. Harold then leads the boys in a boxing match (Fig. 6.4) and encourages Harold Jr. to beat Tony further, deriding Tony when he starts to cry by calling him a 'cissy'. When their mother Dora breaks up the fight, Harold criticises his wife asking 'Do you want him to grow up to be a fairy? He's got to learn to defend himself.' As Tony remarks in his narration shortly after, 'The way to dad's heart was to be good at sports. And I was no better at football than I was at boxing'. When Tony tries to encourage his father to

FIGURE 6.4 Harold Snr. (Geoffrey Rush) leads Tony (Mitchell Dellevergin) and Harold Jr. (Kain O'Keeffe) in a boxing match in *Swimming Upstream* (Crusader Entertainment, 2003) (Crusader Entertainment LLC/The Kobal Collection)

come and watch him participate in a sport he is good at, swimming, his father's response indicates his initial doubts regarding its 'masculinity': 'Fancy yourself as Esther Williams now, do ya', Harold retorts, referring derisively to the American competitive swimmer and MGM actress of such swimming-themed works as *Million Dollar Mermaid* (1952).[4] However, Harold does attend the swimming pool and is impressed by the speed of both Tony and his brother John (Tim Draxl). He immediately initiates a strict training regime for them from that evening onwards, despite John already having a piano lesson scheduled: 'No you don't, that's enough puffter stuff,' Harold responds.

Harold is revealed to be a violent and self-loathing alcoholic obsessed with realising some degree of self-respect through his sons, particularly John. However, when John fails to fulfil Harold's hopes, Harold descends further into drunkenness and violence. Even Tony's success in winning Australian championships and eventually a silver medal in the 1962 British Empire and Commonwealth Games provides no satisfaction for Harold. Indeed, it is viewed as another failure as Harold had trained John to the exclusion of Tony and encouraged a competitive rivalry between the two brothers that would eventually damage their once close relationship. Harold's failure to acknowledge Tony's success is also of huge significance for Tony himself, for whom sport throughout the film is a means of somehow finally gaining respect from his father, a respect which is only tentatively given in the film's closing moments. Significantly, this is at a point at which Tony has decided against pursuing his swimming career, opting instead to attend University in the United States.

Contrary to many American sports films, education by the film's close is clearly depicted as more important than sport as a means to progress. Tony turns down the opportunity to swim for Australia in the Summer Olympics in 1964; as he remarks to Harold, 'Dad, I had a choice. It was the Olympics or Harvard'. Sport undoubtedly has an important role in the film and the competitive swimming sequences comprise the film's most dynamic moments, with their use of mobile cameras, multiscreen images, splitscreen, and wipes. Furthermore, sport has a crucial role in Tony getting access to Harvard through a full sports scholarship. However, the limitations of sport are nonetheless acknowledged here, as elsewhere in the film. Indeed, the film lacks the familiar climactic sporting moment – Tony's final race is not a victory but a second place – while sport is used by Tony's father to instill a brutal masculinity in his sons and to realise his own self-aggrandising ambitions, to the detriment of his family and the relationships between his children. As Tony responds in the film's final scene when asked at Harvard if he would not like to be at the Olympics and win a medal 'Someone once told me that if you're a nobody without a medal, You're still a nobody with one.' Significantly, this scene takes place in an empty pool, far from competitive racing, where Tony swims for the joy of the sport rather than the respect of a deeply flawed father.

The sports film in India: *Lagaan* (2001)

> Cricket is an Indian game accidentally discovered by the English
>
> Ashis Nandy (2000, p. 1)

As noted earlier in this book, the codification of modern sport is a process associated particularly with the Western World and colonising countries such as the United Kingdom, for which sport played an important role in the formation of the individuals necessary for the maintenance of the structures of imperial rule (Holt, 1990; Stoddart and Sandiford, 1998; Mangan, 1992). Indeed, the British Empire had a crucial role to play in the spread of popular global sports, such as rugby and cricket. The latter of these is today the leading sport in several former British colonies, including Pakistan and India. Given its popularity in the country, where it has been described as India's 'de facto national sport' (Gooptu, 2004, p. 546), it is not surprising that Indian filmmakers have turned to cricket repeatedly as subject matter for their work and over the past ten years, a series of cricket-themed films have been made in that country including *Stumped* (2003), *Iqbal* (2005), *Chain Kulii Ki Main Kulii* (2007), *Say Salaam India* (2007), *Hattrick* (2007), *Meerabai Not Out* (2008), *Victory* (2009), *Dil Bole Hadippa!* (2009) and *Patiala House* (2011). However, the most commercially successful and critically acclaimed film in this sub-genre to date is the 2001 Hindi or Bollywood film *Lagaan*.

Lagaan was a huge box office success in India on release and also attracted large audiences internationally, including taking over €1.4 million in the UK alone on its first month on release (Wright, 2006, p. 161). It also enjoyed considerable critical acclaim, winning eight awards at the 2002 Indian National Film awards, as well as a further 36 at festivals along with an Academy award nomination in the Best Foreign Language Film category. *Lagaan*'s popular success was unexpected, particularly given the box office failure in India of previous cricket-themed films, including *All Rounder* (1984), *The Kabhi Ajnabi* (1985), *The Cricketer* (1985), and *Awwal Number* (1990) (Gooptu, 2004, p. 533). However, cricket has nonetheless been remarked upon by commentators as crucial to the film's popular appeal (Majumdar, 2001, p. 3399; Basu, 2002). For Indian journalist Ziya Us Salam, *Lagaan* successfully combined 'three factors which guide our nation – cricket, patriotism and romance' (Salam, 2001). Sharmistha Gooptu has also attributed the success of *Lagaan* to the popularisation of cricket as spectacle through the contemporary media since the 1990s in India and the film's ability to recreate this spectacle in its depiction of the climactic cricket game (2004, p. 539).

The foregrounding of spectacle in *Lagaan* is also evident in its successful combination of aspects of Bollywood cinema with Hollywood conventions, including those surrounding the sports film to produce a film with wide popular appeal. Characterised by lengthy song and dance interludes and the foregrounding of 'sentimental melodramatic romance' (Mishra, 2002, p. 13), Bollywood is India's most popular commercial cinema and it has gained an increasing global audience in the past two decades, particularly via the Indian diaspora. As Wimal Dissanayake has observed, popular cinemas such as Bollywood generally 'uphold notions of a unified nation' and play a critical role in how a nation tells 'its unifying and legitimizing story about itself to its citizen' (2000, pp. 146, 145). Much as the Hollywood sports film (as discussed earlier in this book) has employed sport as a vehicle for transcending the challenges and divisions within American society, a similar process is also evident within *Lagaan* with regard to Indian society.

Indian film has a long history and one often associated with the articulation of conceptions of Indian nationhood and identity. Indeed, the 'Golden Age' of Indian cinema emerged in the aftermath of Indian independence in 1947 and many subsequent films were directly engaged with the process of nation-building in the nascent state (Gokulsing and Dissanayake, 2004, p. 17–19). Films such as Hemen Gupta's *Anand Math* (1952), B.R. Chopra's *Naya Daur* (1957), and particularly Mehboob Khan's *Mother India* (1957), in both title and subject matter, used cinema to symbolically articulate the notion of a singular Indian state. Following independence, cricket too grew in popularity and became a crucial marker of Indian national (and masculine) identity and independence (Crick, 2007, p. 4). Therefore, there is an important political dimension to the depiction of cricket in Indian film particularly in a period drama such as *Lagaan* concerning a group of Indian villagers in the late nineteenth century who employ the game of their colonisers to challenge and overcome oppression by the local British cantonment. There is also a significant indigenising of this foreign sport evident within the film where not only do the villagers beat the

British at their own game, but they also claim that the sport is just a version of the Indian children's game *Gilli-Danda*. As one of the villagers asks, 'Why're these Whitey buffoons playing a kid's game?'

Set in 1893, a period in which the British Empire's presence in India was at its height, *Lagaan* charts the suffering of villagers from the Western Indian village of Champaner under a prolonged drought, exacerbated by a double lagaan (tax) imposed by Captain Andrew Russell (Paul Blackthorne), the stern commanding officer of the local British cantonment. Despite an appeal for help to the local Raja Puran Singh (Kulbhushan Kharbanda), the villagers are told that they are all (including the Raja) subject to British law and must pay the tax. However, following their visit to the Raja, the villagers witness a game of cricket been played by British officers. When one of the villagers, Bhuvan (Aamir Khan), mocks the game, it leads to a fight with a British officer. Following the altercation, Captain Russell offers to waive the tax for three years if the villagers can defeat his team in a game of cricket in three months' time. If they lose, however, the villager's tax will be increased threefold. Without consulting the other villagers, Bhuvan accepts the wager, arguing that 'This game is for our fields and harvest' and remembering the 'rage in my heart when I pay Lagaan to the Raja … And he gives it to those Whiteys with their dirty grasping hands!'

Despite their initial misgivings, Bhuvan eventually convinces most of the villagers to participate in the game and they begin preparations, assisted by Russell's sister Elizabeth (Rachel Shelley) who is also concerned about the mistreatment of the villagers. A romantic subplot develops as Elizabeth begins to fall for Bhuvan, though a local girl Gauri (Gracy Singh) already has romantic feelings for him and Bhuvan eventually has to reassure her that it is she he really loves. This upsets another man in the village, Lakha (Yashpal Sharma) who also had hopes of developing a relationship with Gauri and in anger he becomes a spy for Russell, joining the local team in order to disrupt their preparations for the game. When the day of the game arrives, the villagers begin poorly, partly due to the unsporting tactics of the British but also to deliberate poor play by Lakha. However, eventually they manage to win the game, after spending the evening before the final day in prayer and benefiting from considerable good luck in the game itself, possibly (the film's trajectory suggests) through Divine intervention. The result leads to the tax being removed and is followed by the return of the rains again and the disbandment of the British cantonment.

As a Bollywood film, *Lagaan* includes features that may at first appear challenging or confusing for Western audiences. Characterisation and shot structure, for instance, are used centrally in the film to represent the conflict between good and evil, evident, for example, in the characters of the heroic Bhuvan (Fig. 6.5) and the arrogant Captain Russell (Wright, 2006, p. 145). This is apparent from the first encounter between the two in which Russell attempts to kill a deer, while Bhuvan endeavours to save it. Indeed, the British generally in the film are depicted rather two-dimensionally clearly as outsiders and alien to the society portrayed. While the opening scenes depict a harmonious village

FIGURE 6.5 Heroic Bhuvan (Aamir Khan) in *Lagaan* (Aamir Khan Productions, 2001) (Aamir Khan Productions/The Kobal Collection/Hardeep Singh Sachdev)

life captured in fluid cinematography that takes us from the village shrine to the temple, the entry of the British soldiers disrupts this idyllic picture. The noble poverty of the villagers is contrasted with the corruption and decadence of the British. Though touched upon in various ways within the film, it is in the scenes of cricket that this anti-colonial perspective becomes most apparent. The British are portrayed as engaging repeatedly in unsporting and dangerous sporting actions, including sledging (verbal intimidation of players) and attempting to physically injure the villagers. As Russell remarks to one of his teammates Yardley (Chris England) at one point when Lakha is batting, 'Knock his bloody head off'.

To Western viewers, the characterisation of Captain Russell and many of the British Cantonment as irredeemably evil, and by contrast, Bhuvan and the villagers as the epitome of goodness may seem unrealistic and unconvincing. Equally, the sudden movement from the spoken dialogue and narrative of the film to lengthy song and dance sequences may also jar with Western audiences. However, the film must be viewed as emerging from a different culture with different expectations regarding their films. As Wright observes, Indian audiences

are more likely to apply criteria of verisimilitude to a film's moral universe. Behaviour contravening *dharma* (norms), especially kinship codes, may be dismissed vocally as incredible. In *Lagaan*, as Bhuvan faces the crucial final ball, he is strengthened by memories of loyal Gauri, and his mother – the archetypal foundation of Indian society.

(2006, p. 146)

However, in its inspirational narrative of the much put-upon villagers overcoming their oppressive colonial masters against the odds, *Lagaan* also has considerable parallels with the popular Western sports film. While the film undoubtedly provides the viewer with a rich and visually impressive depiction of Indian culture, including nineteenth-century village life, aspects of Hinduism, as well as distinctive elements associated with Bollywood film (particularly the lengthy song and dance routines), *Lagaan* is nonetheless heavily influenced by aspects of Hollywood film. It is less episodic than Bollywood films tend to be, with its largely linear narrative arranged according to the familiar cause-and-effect logic associated with Western cinema. Furthermore, the songs in the film are more integrated into the narrative as a whole in a manner comparable to the popular 1950s Hollywood musicals. Equally, the dialogue is more realistic in tone and the film 'is notable for its efforts to show the passage of time in fashion and other aspects of material culture' in a manner unusual in Bollywood films, but more commonly found in the Hollywood tradition (Wright, 2006, p. 160).

Furthermore, again similar to the popular Western sports film, *Lagaan* rather simplistically transcends the deep divisions, particularly of a religious nature, within Indian society via the intercession of sport. As with most Bollywood films, *Lagaan* draws heavily from the religious context of India, evident for example in the prominence of the village temple, dedicated to Krishna and his consort Radha. Rebecca Brown has observed how the relationship between Bhuvan and Guari in the film 'echoes the stories and imagery surrounding the Krishna–Radha narratives as told in various puranas and illustrated in Indian painting' (2004, p. 79). However, the film has been criticised for the prominence of Hinduism within it and the manner through which it reimagines Indian resistance to British colonial rule through the foregrounding of the religion. As noted by Brown, this

> message of resistance rides on the back of other, more problematic assumptions regarding our understanding of the historical colonial relationship – and it does so in order to serve contemporary Indian political realities. Just as architectural, archaeological, and textual history is often rewritten or ignored in order to support the notion of a Hindu India oppressed by Muslim or British outsiders, *Lagaan* presents a colonial past in which resistance to the colonizer 'unifies' the villagers, but only under the banner of Hinduism. From the conservatism of the film's depiction of the village to its token inclusion of Muslims, Sikhs, and untouchables, *Lagaan* unwittingly reasserts the primacy of Hinduism in India, and does so through the two-pronged approach of recasting both Indian history and Hindu gods.
>
> (2004, p. 79)

Given the divisiveness of religion in Indian history and contemporary politics – evident for example in the continuing dispute over the Kashmir region –

the cricket team in *Lagaan* plays an important and symbolic role in bringing competing and conflicting traditions together, including Hindu (the majority of the team), Sikh (Deva Singh Sodhi (Pradeep Singh Rawat)), and Muslim (Ismail, the potter (Raj Zutshi)). The film also engages rather naïvely with caste in Indian society, particularly in the figure of Kachra, the 'untouchable'. Despite been socially and physically disabled, Kachra is found by Bhuvan to be a natural spin bowler and adds an important skill (and weapon) to the team. Though the team initially resists Kachra joining, Bhuvan defends his inclusion in the team in words that combine Hindu mythology with current human rights discourse:

> You brand people untouchable and pollute humanity itself. Chief, why are you choking the very air of our village with this caste division! Is it right to destroy and shatter hearts in the name of skin colour? Then why worship Ram who ate a tribal woman's half-eaten berries? The Lord who ferries us all across this sea of life was himself ferried by a low-caste boatman. You know all this and yet talk of untouchability!

However, the representation of such non-Hindu characters rarely rises above the level of stereotype within the film, with minimal development given to them within the diegesis. While Ismail is depicted in familiar Muslim terms, including his name and his references to Allah, Deva personifies associations of Sikhs with militarism through both his dagger-neck pendant and his announcement that he wants 'to be in every battle against the British'. As Wright contends, '*Lagaan* does not critique, but participates in, the colonialist othering of a religious minority' (2006, p. 155). The representation of Kachra in the film is also problematic, particularly the limited opportunity the film allows for his own expression, depicting him rather as subject to Bhuvan and the team such that, as Sirivayan Anand has noted,

> The subaltern cannot speak. Totally stripped of agency, Kachra (in Hindustani, it also means waste or garbage) has to simply follow caste-Hindu Bhuvan's words. He never exercises a choice. Kachra – someone excluded from every other social-cultural religious aspect of village life – is never asked whether he would like to be included in such a game. It is not clear whether this Dalit, portrayed so pathetically, is even aware of why the game is being played.
>
> (2002, p. 49)

It is a ultimately a majoritarian Hindu perspective that is prioritised in the film, evident particularly in the character of Bhuvan and his repeated association with Hindu religious figures and spaces, including the Hindu temple at the centre of the village where he calms the villagers intent on attacking the traitor Lakha before the second day's play against the British. Overall *Lagaan* combines aspects of Bollywood cinema and the popular Western sports film to produce an idyllic depiction of nineteenth-century Indian village life in which cricket provides the vehicle for overcoming both external oppression and internal division while affirming the Indian nation.

Conclusion

Sport has featured prominently in national cinemas across the world. As a distinguishing aspect of national culture, it has provided filmmakers internationally with a means of articulating more distinctive films. Global sporting events, such as the FIFA World Cup, have also offered filmmakers the opportunity to connect culturally and geographically diverse communities through a shared appreciation of sport. Films featuring sport also often reveal the tensions that national identities may subsume or elide – whether in terms of ethnic identity, social class, religion, gender or sexuality. These films are identifiable by their attempts to either contain or foreground such contradictions. While both approaches frequently reveal the influence of Hollywood cinema, the latter is sometimes characterised by its contestation of the utopian trajectory found therein occasionally combined with a critique of the institution of sport itself, or its use for exploitative purposes. However, there is also a recognition evident of the importance of sport to marginalised groups in society. As Joe Kavanagh remarks in *My Name is Joe* 'I know it's just football, but it's important to us'. While director Ken Loach is reluctant to use sport, as in many American sports films, to transcend the real social problems faced by working-class communities – after all, it's 'just football' – he is nonetheless cognisant of the important role sport plays in British male culture (as in other cultural contexts), providing a crucial space for association and community building.

7

CONCLUSION

9/11 and the contemporary mainstream sports film

Sports films have grown over the twentieth century and into the twenty-first to occupy an important and influential place in popular culture. They have exploited a fundamental quality of both cultural forms: the utopian sensibilities they can evoke. Sport provided a popular and concordant cultural form that complemented the aesthetics of mainstream cinema and featured from the earliest days of film playing a notable role in the popularisation of the new art form. Indeed, the requirements of filming and projecting prize fights in particular in the United States expedited the development of technologies and aesthetics crucial to the advancement of cinema as a popular form, including the ability to film longer scenes, editing and projection. However, the very ubiquity of sport across various cinema genres has made the task of identifying a distinctive sports film genre challenging, while film has also found it difficult to recreate the immediacy and unpredictability of sport resulting in many poorly received sports films. Nonetheless, a sports film genre is increasingly recognised in popular and critical discourse and is characterised by a number of salient features, including the foregrounding of athletes, sporting events or followers of sport in narratives that depend significantly on sport for plot motivation or resolution.

However, drawing on work in genre theory and cultural studies, and particularly Antonio Gramsci's concept of cultural hegemony, this study contends that it is the function that such films play in popular culture that is of most significance. The mainstream sports film has been centrally concerned with affirming the meritocracy myth of the American Dream while maintaining patriarchal hegemony. Even in films where this utopian trajectory is contested, the failure to realise this dream is typically attributed to personal flaws or fate rather than societal inequalities or systemic challenges that people may encounter, be they in terms of race, gender or social class. While both African Americans and women are increasingly depicted in more prominent roles in mainstream sports films, a recurring feature of such films is the attempt to contain whatever threat these figures may present to hegemonic White patriarchy by customarily subordinating such characters to a paternalistic White society.

The acknowledgement of serious social challenges within many mainstream sports films with regard to the realisation of the American Dream undoubtedly has the potential to destabilise the utopian trajectory itself. However, this aspect reflects the sophisticated functioning of hegemonic popular culture itself whereby 'the ruling ideology has to incorporate a series of features in which the exploited majority will be able to recognize its authentic longings … rearticulating them in such a way that they became compatible with the existing relations of domination' (Žižek, 1997, pp. 29–30). Rarely are such elements given a social or historical context in the mainstream sports film which typically promotes individual performance as the means to redemption and success.

Sport has also featured prominently in films emerging from outside the United States. Indeed, national cinemas reveal a significant engagement with distinctive aspects of national sporting culture as well as global sporting events that may connect culturally or geographically removed communities. While the utopian trajectory that characterises Hollywood sports cinema is also found in films produced in other contexts, occasionally these films may contest this trajectory or question the institution of sport itself and its role in society. National sports films have also been characterised by attempts to contain, or highlight, contradictions within hegemonic constructions of national identity, be they in terms of ethnicity, social class, gender, sexuality or religion.

In the past 15 years, the sports films that have been most commercially successful – and would appear to have struck a chord particularly with American audiences – have emerged in principally two forms: the sports comedy or melodramatic accounts of the 'underdog' overcoming considerable challenges. In the category of the sports comedy, films such as *The Waterboy* (1998, $161,491,646 at the American box office), *DodgeBall: A True Underdog Story* (2004, $114,326,736), *The Longest Yard* (2005, $158,119,460), *Talladega Nights: The Ballad of Ricky Bobby* (2006, $148,213,377), *Nacho Libre* (2006, $80,197,993) and *Blades of Glory* (2007, $118,594,548), have all enjoyed considerable box office success in the United States, far beyond that achieved internationally. These films are characterised repeatedly by unlikely characters enjoying varying degrees of success against the odds, where sport provides a means for the disadvantaged or intellectually challenged to overcome their marginalisation. The comic and satiric approach of these films may appear to question or lampoon the trajectory of rags-to-riches that is a recurring theme in the sports film. However, while comedy often provides anarchic and sometimes counter-cultural moments of pleasure for audiences, including in these comedy sports films, in most cases such issues are resolved in the traditional happy ending where the hegemonic order is restored. Comedy offers a safety net for audiences wishing to experience aspects of life beyond the normal rules and restrictions, without having to take such disturbances too seriously (King, 2002, p. 8). As noted by Geoff King 'One quality that most, if not all, comedy has in common, and that helps to explain its widespread appeal, is that it is usually considered to be relatively "safe" and unthreatening' (2002, p. 2). Indeed, comedy by its nature has a tendency to undermine the seriousness of whatever situation it may be engaged with, as the 'laughter emotion', Elder Olson observes, is 'a relaxation … of concern due to a manifest absurdity of the grounds for concern' (1968, p. 16). These comedy sports films therefore, though touching on serious issues such as parental neglect, poverty and marginalisation, ultimately trivialise these issues both through their comic presentation and also by virtue of the extraordinary intercession of sporting achievement.

Two relevant examples are *Blades of Glory* and *Talladega Nights*, films starring comedian Will Ferrell who has featured in four prominent sports films to date. In *Blades of Glory* ice-skating prodigy Jimmy MacElroy (Jon Heder) was, as the TV summariser remarks early in the film, 'plucked from an orphanage at age four by billionaire champion-maker, Darren MacElroy' after seeing Jimmy demonstrate his skills at the orphanage, a scene which provides the film's opening. Similarly, his main competitor on the ice, Chazz Michael Michaels (Will Ferrell), 'escaped a life of running cigarettes and illegal fireworks by becoming a star in Detroit's underground sewer skating scene'. While both MacElroy and Michaels suffer bans for life for fighting during an awards ceremony, they each ultimately overcome the various challenges they encounter (including MacElroy being disowned by his billionaire 'father' and Michaels being reduced to pantomimes and alcoholism) to win the pairs competition together at the World Winter Sport Games.

A similar trajectory is found in *Talladega Nights*. The film concerns NASCAR driver, Ricky Bobby (Will Ferrell), who also comes from an underprivileged background, raised largely by his mother as his alcoholic father was mostly absent. While working on the pit crew for a race team, he volunteers to take over from the team driver, who expresses little interest in winning, and manages to come in third, securing a place for himself as the team driver subsequently. Despite initial successes on the track, Bobby eventually loses his place to French driver, Jean Girard (Sacha Baron Cohen), and subsequently his nerve after a racing accident. His misfortunes are compounded when his wife leaves him to marry his best friend Cal (John C. Reilly). However, he recovers from these obstacles to return to racing again and eventually to beat Girard, if in a race on foot (rather than by car) to the finish line after both drivers' cars are wrecked in the race that closes the film.

This theme of overcoming the odds is also at the centre of a series of sports dramas that have reached large audiences over the past ten years. Indeed, some of the most commercially successful depictions of a range of sports have been released in this period, including boxing (*Million Dollar Baby* (2004, $100,492,203 at the US box office), *Cinderella Man* (2005, $61,649,911), *Rocky Balboa* (2006, $70,270,943), *The Fighter* (2010, $93,617,009)); American football (*Invincible* (2006, $57,806,952), *The Blind Side* (2009, $255,959,475)); basketball (*Coach Carter* (2005, $67,264,877)); baseball (*The Rookie* (2002, $75,600,072)); winter sports (*Miracle* (2004, $64,378,093), *Tooth Fairy* (2010, $60,022,256)); surfing (*Blue Crush* (2002, $40,390,647), *Soul Surfer* (2011, $43,853,424)) and horse-racing (*Seabiscuit* (2003, $120,277,854)).[1] It is tempting to view these films, both comedic and melodramatic – most of which were made and released in the aftermath of the trauma of 9/11 – as a response to the threat that the attack and contemporaneous political and economic challenges represented to the American way of life and the central ideology that underpins it, the American Dream. As well as the threat which the attack presented to national security, other challenges included the controversy over the 2000 presidential election when more Americans voted for the defeated candidate Al Gore than for the elected President, George W. Bush; the scandal surrounding the collapse of energy giant Enron; and the bursting of the dotcom bubble that wiped billions off share prices internationally.

Significantly, as in the case of *The Blind Side* (discussed in Chapter 4), many of the sports films produced were based on 'true stories', an aspect foregrounded repeatedly in the publicity of the films concerned. Indeed, this focus on 'true events' by fiction films has become a prominent feature of contemporary feature film production more generally including four of the 2011 Academy Award nominees for Best Picture, *The Social Network* (2010), *The King's Speech* (2010), the sports film *The Fighter* (2010) and a further film with a sporting connection (canyoneering) *127 Hours* (2010). The growing popularity of the theatrically released documentary, discussed in Chapter 3, also reflects an increasing demand for aspects of the 'real' in popular culture where, as documentary director George Hickenlooper observes 'people are clamoring to connect – particularly after 9/11 – with things that are genuine and real' (cited in Arthur, 2005, p. 19). Sports fiction films are also responding to this demand in emphasising their connection with actual people and events. However, such appeals to the 'real' place the viewer in a particular relationship with the events depicted. There is a tendency to rely on the 'truth' of the events to defend the depiction, particularly when such as depiction – as discussed with regard to *The Blind Side* in Chapter 4 – may have racist undertones. However, events do not exist in isolation from either history or politics; every story has a context though this context may be only partially depicted within an individual film. More problematically, such an appeal to authenticity 'denies the importance of human subjectivity and negates the necessity of critical thought' (Dittmar and Michaud, 1990, p. 10). As Dittmar and Michaud have contended,

> Representation is necessarily interpretative and responds to contemporary agendas. Thus attention to authenticity is at best insufficient and at worst even misguided. Film, like any system of representation, cannot accurately

reproduce historical events. Its simulation … is necessarily mediated by the cinematic apparatus as well as by the perspectives brought to bear on the depicted events by those engaged in a given film's production and reception. In short, at issue is not simply the believability of these films as records of the past, but what these films tell us as artefacts about ourselves, our culture, and our political choices.

(1990, p. 10)

Ultimately films set in the past, and concerning historical events and figures are primarily the product of contemporary concerns; they offer a 'partial truth that accentuates particular versions of reality and marginalizes or omits others'. (Rowe, 1998; cited in Silk, Schultz, and Bracey, 2008, p. 282)

From the moment the first films appeared, cinema has been enmeshed within the broader social context within which it exists. This is evident, for example, in the many war films that emerged from Hollywood during World War II as the United States became embroiled in the conflict. Sports films produced in this period also responded to the war context, including *Knute Rockne All American* (1940) and *National Velvet* (1944), films which affirmed key principles of the American Dream, even where (as in the case of the latter) the film was not set in the United States. *Knute Rockne All American* concerned the legendary coach of Notre Dame American football team between 1918 and 1931 who revolutionised the game and brought great success to his team. A central theme in the film is the dramatisation of the ideology of the American Dream as Rockne rises from a humble Norwegian immigrant background to sporting success and acclamation. The final credit of *National Velvet* (considered in Chapter 5) provided by the War Activities Committee of the Motion Picture Industry reassured 'Families and Friends of Servicemen and Women' that 'Pictures exhibited in this theatre are given to the armed forces for showing in combat areas around the world'. Though concerning the unlikely sporting victory of a twelve-year-old English female jockey, Velvet Brown (Elizabeth Taylor) in the Aintree Grand National, *National Velvet* is above all an affirmation of traditional American small-town values of family, religion and character. Furthermore, the central theme in the film reiterates again, at a time of war, the powerful role of sport in American life and in the realisation of the American Dream of success.

During World War II more than one-quarter of all Hollywood films and 90 per cent of newsreel were 'impromptu propaganda' (Devine, 1999, p. vii). It is not surprising that Hollywood should have responded in this way to the US involvement in the war, particularly when we consider that the studios worked closely in this period with the Office of War Information, a government agency established to gain support for the war among the American public. In a development reminiscent of this relationship during World War II, following the 9/11 attack on the United States, 40 leading Hollywood executives, including representatives of all of the major studios, met with President George W. Bush's

Senior Advisor and Deputy Chief of Staff, Karl Rove to consider how the film industry could assist in gaining support for the US war efforts. As Silk, Schultz and Bracey have observed,

> While the multi-billion dollar interests of the movie industry are not identical to those of the Pentagon, there does seem to be a clear recognition that movie industry profits are bound up with Washington's attempts to seize control of strategic resources in the Middle East and elsewhere. The meeting speaks to the collective affinity between the US Government and Hollywood in having the responsibility to reassure children of their safety and to the somewhat cloaked deployment of propaganda. As Karl Rove said of the meetings, 'the world is full of people who are discerning and we need to recognize that concrete information told with honesty, specificity and integrity is important to the ultimate success of this conflict'.
>
> (2008, p. 283)

Sport has long been one of the most powerful and effective means of affirming national identity. It has also afforded a powerful tool of control, education, and social reform throughout the world, including in the United States and the former USSR. While providing emotive moments for collective engagement, sport is also one of the most familiar popular cultural forms engaged in the construction of an 'other', a process added to considerably by the sport media. However, the focus on and apparent need for heroes, including the sporting heroes represented in many filmic and media depictions of sport, also reflects deep societal needs that are particularly apparent at times of serious threat to society itself. For Deborah Tudor,

> The endurance of this form indicates a widespread attitude toward the hero originating in Western mythology: the perceived need for a hero of some sort, a (superhuman) man who alters events and overcomes threats to society and changes history. The hope or wish for such a person derives from several social and psychological reasons: hopelessness against the inevitability of disasters, belief that 'men make history', an escape from personal and political responsibility for shaping or participating in society.
>
> (1997, p. 4)

While partly reflecting an unwillingness to engage critically with the political and historical context of 9/11 itself, the focus on the possibilities of success through sport that the mainstream sports film represents also disguises the limited opportunities for such success that actually exist. More seriously, perhaps, the mainstream sports film also obscures the real structural inequalities in American society that have perpetuated the systemic challenges people face to progress.

The Walt Disney Company and the sports film

Among those who attended the meeting with Karl Rove in the aftermath of the 9/11 attack was Walt Disney CEO Robert Iger. Disney is today one of the most powerful and influential media conglomerates on the planet. Unlike in the past when major film studios were stand-alone production and distribution entities, today these companies are primarily distributors and are part of giant conglomerates that have not just film interests but also often publishing, television, merchandising and internet concerns and Disney is one of the largest and most successful examples of this development. These connections have allowed for increased revenue-making opportunities while also enabling individual films to make increased income not necessarily directly accruing from theatrical, DVD or broadcast sales. No company has realised this more, or as effectively, as Disney, with its brand associated with a vast array of products from films to theme parks, family restaurants, shops, hotels, as well as significant sporting interests. The National Hockey League professional ice-hockey team the Anaheim Ducks were originally founded in 1993 by the Walt Disney Company as the Mighty Ducks of Anaheim, taking the name from the commercially successful 1992 Disney film *The Mighty Ducks* (1992). Four years later, Disney acquired an 80 per cent share of America's largest cable sports network, The Entertainment Sports Programming Network (ESPN), and the network accounted by 2008 for almost 40 per cent of Disney's income (Santoli, 2008).[2]

Disney has become one of the most established and recognisable brands, and one associated centrally with the American Dream, an ideology repeatedly reiterated within its products. For James E. Combs

> Disney's version of the American Dream is traditional and nostalgic, celebrated in cartoons and feature-length movies. Traditional moral virtues, such as rugged individualism, patriotism, and thrift, are extolled in cartoon form. Disney thought himself to be an example of the Horatio Alger myth, and such cartoons as *The Tortoise and the Hare* suggest that victory in the social race goes to those who persist in their goal … Disney Studios continues to perpetuate a world-view supportive of the 'conservative' version of the Dream.
>
> (1984, p. 115)

The very ubiquity of Disney and particularly its association with children has made it a very effective communicator and populariser of this ideology. Henry Giroux has observed how:

> Popular audiences tend to reject any link between ideology and the prolific entertainment world of Disney … Even more disturbing is the widespread belief that Disney's trademarked innocence renders it unaccountable for the diverse ways in which it shapes the sense of reality it provides for children as

> they take up specific and often sanitized notions of identity, difference, and history in the seemingly apolitical cultural universe of 'the Magic Kingdom'.
> (2002, p. 105)

Disney's influence and apparent apolitical status makes it all the more important to engage critically with the films produced by this company, including those featuring sport. Indeed, sport has provided Disney with a means of producing fairytales that appeal both to adults and children, initially the principle focus of their products. As noted by Bonzel 'The sports films stories … are often also a form of legend, differing from fairytales only in that they are based on "real" people in "real" places in our "real" history' (2011, p. 203). These claims on 'reality' are among the most appealing aspects of sport for production companies such as Disney as they provide seemingly convincing confirmations of the American Dream. Disney is one of the most prominent producers of sports films, with over fifty such films produced since 1963 ('Disney Sports Movies'), almost half of which were released since 9/11. A central theme found throughout these films is the overcoming of considerable odds through individual effort to achieve success and the American Dream.

Among the theatrical films released by the studio since 9/11 are *The Rookie, Miracle* and *Invincible,* all films based on true stories between the 1970s and 1990s, adding to their claims of authenticity while also providing further 'evidence' of the American Dream's relevance and potential in American life. Indeed, claims to authenticity were a prominent feature not just in the assertion of the truthful basis of each film but also in the emphasis placed in promotional materials, including making-of documentaries, on the efforts gone to by those involved in the productions to recreate the actual clothing, décor and playing styles of the periods depicted (Bonzel, 2011, p. 203). Furthermore, building on the emotional engagement of followers of sport with their favourite sports and players, these films attempt to recreate an 'emotional authenticity', thereby drawing 'the audience in and get[ting] them to emotionally invest in the characters and the story' (Bonzel, 2011, p. 204). Through this process, films can more convincingly produce a persuasive, if partial, 'truth' though one which emphasises specific aspects of history while obscuring or excluding others.

A representative example of this process is *Miracle* (Fig. 7.1). As noted above, sport is one of the most powerful expressions of national identity and has been exploited repeatedly to affirm the nation, above all at the Olympic Games. During the Cold War, and particularly from the first participation at the Games of the Soviet Union in 1952, sport was frequently deployed as a discursive 'rhetoric, a narrative, a moral drama propelled by the Manichean myth of apocalyptical struggle between forces of good and evil, between capitalism and communism, between democracy and totalitarianism, rationality and barbarism' (Wang, 2002, p. 48). One of the Disney's most commercially successful post-9/11 sports films, *Miracle* returned to this Cold War era to depict the famous victory of an unfancied US ice hockey team over the favourites from the Soviet Union at the

FIGURE 7.1   Lobby card for *Miracle* (Walt Disney Pictures, 2004) foregrounding the American flag (Walt Disney/The Kobal Collection)

Winter Olympics in 1980. The return to this moment is particularly significant given the challenges that 9/11 presented to the American way of life, and the ideology that underpins it. The film is part of a re-engagement with this moment also evident in Wayne Coffey's book *The Boys of Winter: The Untold Story of a Coach, a Dream, and the 1980 U.S. Olympic Hockey Team* (2005) and the HBO documentary *Do You Believe in Miracles? The Story of the 1980 U.S. Hockey Team* (2001) as well as the repeated description of the victory as among the greatest moments in American sports history, including by the Disney-owned ESPN network (Silk, Schultz and Bracey, 2008, p. 284).

An examination of the film itself is revealing not just for the aspects chosen to represent and elevate in the film, but also for those elements not engaged with. In the tradition of the sports film, the film is centrally concerned with overcoming both personal – particularly in the person of US coach Herb Brooks (Kurt Russell) – and national traumas through sport while promoting principally White masculine camaraderie and working-class values, such as hard work and persistence. In the transformation of the young White men depicted from outsiders to a team capable of overcoming their formidable Soviet opponents, all the efforts and collegiate rivalries along the way, as Silk, Schultz and Bracey observe, 'are subsumed to the greater national cause manifest in the inexorable rise from minnow to Reaganite hard body capable of defeating the all-powerful, all conquering, Soviet Union' (Silk, Schultz and Bracey, 2008, p. 284).

The film appears in its opening scene to at first place the events depicted within their historical context, referring to Nixon's controversial presidency and resignation, the Vietnam war, the Cold War, the Bicentennial celebrations, and the difficulties of President Jimmy Carter's term in office, including the oil crisis. Indeed, a recurring theme of this montage is crisis, and it ends with the words of Carter in a presidential address:

> It is a crisis of confidence. It is a crisis that strikes at the very heart and soul and spirit of our national will. The symptoms of this crisis of the American spirit are all around us.

A further Carter speech is heard over the radio later in the film as Coach Brooks returns home in his car from Christmas celebrations with the team. Again, Carter recognises an 'erosion of our confidence in the future' after the traumas of the 1970s. In a speech concerned centrally with the American Dream, and the fading faith in the future, Carter calls for Americans 'to stop crying and start sweating. Stop talking and start walking. Working together with our common faith. We cannot fail'. However, these words and *Miracle* as a whole are more concerned with the contemporary crises within American society than traumas in the past. The film's engagement with the success of the US ice hockey team at the 1980 Olympic Games provides a moment of national sporting unity and achievement as a response to the contemporary social, economic and political crises. Significantly, the Twin Towers are captured in an iconic moment in the film, accompanied by the singing of 'The Star-Spangled Banner', prior to a pre-tournament game between the US and the Soviet Union. Indeed, to increase its relevance to contemporary rather than historical events, the film repeatedly obscures the social context of the moment being depicted, evident for example in its downplaying of the Cold War background to the Olympics themselves, with few references to communism and a rather reserved depiction of the 'Soviet threat' particularly when compared with earlier sporting films made during the Cold War, such as *Rocky IV* (1985). As Silk, Schultz and Bracey observe,

> by downplaying the significance of the Soviets as political 'enemy' and collapsing the distance between the past and the present, Disney sutures a particular meaning to the event that reduces the Cold War to a commodity onto which contemporary meanings can be mapped ... In this way, film-goers are invited to consider the defeat of a newly defined 'enemy' in a less certain, enduring war on terror. Indeed, this point was not lost on reviewers of the film; as one editorial proffered, 'In these times of international tensions, it's always good to have a genuine patriotic movie'.
>
> (2008, p. 287)

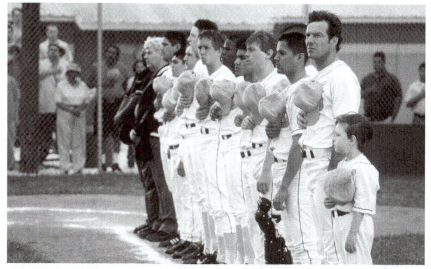

FIGURE 7.2 *The Rookie* (Walt Disney Pictures, 2002) (Disney/The Kobal Collection/ Deana Newcomb)

As President Carter's words quoted earlier suggest, it is working-class principles of hard work and perseverance that are foregrounded repeatedly in the film, evident in the rigorous training regime Brooks initiates for the US ice hockey team on becoming manager. Indeed, the trajectory of the film as a whole promotes, as Leonard has identified, sport as a means of overcoming White class disadvantage, suggesting that

> The 1980 U.S. Olympic hockey team overcame their lack of athletic ability (their whiteness) and the lack of class privilege that was evident in the poor facilities because of their work ethic, intelligence, belief in team, fortitude, self-determination, and heart – because of their whiteness, their masculinity, and their working class identities.
>
> (2008, p. 219)

It is White masculine working-class values that are also at the centre of both *The Rookie* and *Invincible*. *The Rookie* (Fig. 7.2) concerns former Major League Baseball player Jim Morris (Dennis Quaid), who had a short-lived career playing with the Tampa Bay Devil Rays, despite only getting his first game at Major League level at the age of 35. In line with other baseball films, from *Headin' Home* (1920) through *The Jackie Robinson Story* (1950) and *Field of Dreams* (1989), *The Rookie* promotes a similar message that hard work, individual effort and persistence will eventually achieve the American Dream. As Robson observes,

> By playing on notions of Americana and reinforcing assumptions about individuality, the U.S. baseball film reinforces and re-inscribes conservative ideology. At its heart this ideology reflects the dominance of

the capitalist economic system, one in which the triumph of the individual is prioritized above the success of the collective.

(2010)

In the opening sequence of *The Rookie*, this American Dream ideology is given the authority of being 'based on a true story' while simultaneously connected with religion and baseball. *The Rookie* begins with a narrator describing the origins of the town of Big Lake, Texas, linking this origin myth of a man who believed oil existed in the barren location of the town, with religion (through the two nuns that supported him financially), the playing of baseball, and legendary figures in the game Babe Ruth and Lou Gehrig. This opening sequence reiterates a familiar trope found in many baseball films, nostalgia, particularly for the past and the small-town values Big Lake represents, 'a powerful force carefully nurtured by baseball executives since the early 20th Century' (Robson, 2010).

The Rookie's opening scene also begins suggestively with a crane shot that provides a God-like and mythologising perspective on the man stamping the ground beneath his feet in a barren and windswept landscape. With the discovery of oil, following (on the advice of a local priest) the blessing of the site with rose petals and the apparent intercession of Saint Rita, oil workers arrive to the area that would become Big Lake, and baseball (which we witness workers playing) provides, the narrator tells us, a further avenue for success for townspeople. As a worker strikes the ball into the air, the narrator continues that Saint Rita 'decided to bless our little town just one more time', and the ball appears to land in the near-present, caught by the young Jimmy Morris in Groton, Connecticut.

The repeated reference to Saint Rita (evident later in Morris' good luck charm, a Saint Rita prayer medal) reflects the recurring presence of religion in the film, also apparent in the moments of prayer of the high school baseball team before each game. Furthermore, the opening crane shot is repeated towards the end of the film, when Morris enters a Major League baseball stadium for the first time as a player. On entering the gates of Rangers Ballpark in Arlington, Texas, a similar crane shot accentuates the stadium's size and impressiveness, looking down on Morris again (as with Big Lake's founder in the opening shot of the film) from a God-like perspective and emphasising the church-like architecture of the stadium. In each of these moments, baseball and the dreams associated with it are given the significant imprimatur of religious association, a central tenet of both the dominant American sports creed (discussed in Chapter 4) and the mainstream sports film.

The fairytale trajectory that both *Miracle* and *The Rookie* map has significant consequences for the depiction of social class. While each film is a powerful and emotionally charged affirmation of the American Dream, they also marginalise criticisms of this dream, and indeed, alternative responses, such as social protest. In the *Miracle*, Brook's wife expresses doubts about his intense focus on the national hockey team's preparation for the Olympics, to the neglect of his domestic responsibilities, remarking

This. What you're doing. Chasing after something you didn't get, that you may never get. What if it doesn't work out, Herb? Are we gonna do this every four years?

Similarly, in *The Rookie*, both Jimmy Morris's father and his wife express doubts concerning his hopes to realise his dream of playing Major League baseball. As his wife Lori says at one point:

You can't eat dreams, Jimmy. And they don't pay for clothes or shoes or gas or babysitters. Now, I do not want to be the bad guy in this, but somebody around here has got to start being rational.

However, in both films, the wives of Brooks and Morris quickly relent from their critical positions and eventually encourage their husbands to continue to pursue their dreams (in a familiar pattern, discussed in Chapter 5, found in many sports films), while Morris' father in *The Rookie* by the film's close concedes he should have been more supportive of his son's baseball ambitions.

Invincible (Fig. 7.3) is a particularly revealing production with regard to constructions of social class and the American Dream. The film tells a similar tale to *The Rookie*, though in an American football setting. In this case a 30-year-old bartender, Vince Papale (Mark Wahlberg) succeeds in getting selected for the NFL's Philadelphia Eagles despite his advanced years. *Invincible* begins with images of a run-down working-class area, followed by shots of workers protesting, with signs declaring 'No Contract, No Work' as they are being locked out from their place of work. However, such protests, the logic of the developing montage of empty factory floors and 'closed' signs suggests, have little impact. As the film progresses, further mentions of strikes are made, including by Papale's friend Tommy (Kirk Acevedo) in an early scene where they both talk outside the bar where Papale works. However, the ominous threats of strike action are repeatedly juxtaposed in the film with the hope that sport offers, including in this scene where Tommy encourages Papale to go to the try outs and a later scene where a television report contrasts Papale's success in surviving the first round of cuts with the Eagles with threatened strike action:

Union leaders are now calling for a strike against Westinghouse. Two thousand workers could be on the picket as early as tomorrow night. And now over to Wade Chambers and sports. Well, the biggest news today from Eagles training camp is that Philly's own Vince Papale has made it past the first round of cuts.

When Papale learns that he has made the Eagles team, Tommy is the first to hear. Here again this moment of sporting success is contrasted with the ongoing

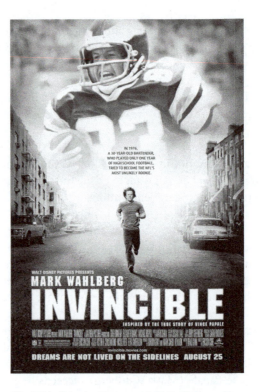

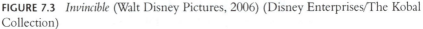

FIGURE 7.3 *Invincible* (Walt Disney Pictures, 2006) (Disney Enterprises/The Kobal Collection)

industrial dispute, and again appears to transcend them for those involved, as the following exchange suggests:

> Papale: Hey, how you doing with the strike and everything? You all right?
> Tommy: I'm good now. I'm good now.

Rather than strike action, sport is presented repeatedly in the film as the principle means towards success and upward social mobility. However, beyond its role in providing Papale with a means of social advancement, sport is also invoked in the film as providing one of the few positive elements in the lives of the characters depicted. While Papale's success lifts the entire community he comes from, his father Frank (Kevin Conway) describes the success of the Eagles as the one thing that got him through the challenges of working-class life and family trauma:

> You know how I used to tell you about Van Buren scoring that touchdown back in '48? … That touchdown got me through 30 years at that factory. Got me through all those times your mother being sick. When I told you not to get your hopes up, it didn't mean that I wasn't.

It is this hope that is at the centre of Coach Vermeil's speech prior to the game against the New York Giants that provides the film's climax. After listing great players from the Eagles' past, including Van Buren, he declares, to the accompaniment of emotive music on the soundtrack:

> They weren't just out here playing for themselves. They played for a city. The people of Philadelphia have suffered. You are what they turn to in times like these. You are what gives them hope. Let's win one for them.

Papale, who now works as a motivational speaker after retiring from football, has described *Invincible* as 'not just my story but it can be anyone's story as well. It's about having a dream and overcoming the odds, adversity, and obstacles that go with making that dream come true' (cited in Bonzel, 2011, p. 201). In these words he affirms both a central tenet of the American Dream ideology and a fundamental message in the mainstream sports film today.

While sport offers one of the most popular metaphors for life, providing as noted in the introduction to this book arguably more idioms to the English language than any other cultural practice, the mainstream sports film is equally a powerful evocation of life itself and the trials and tribulations that attend it. If there is one idiom that more than any other encapsulates the genre, it is 'against all odds' – significantly one of the most used film titles listed on the Internet Movie Database (IMDb) – for it is this theme that repeatedly recurs throughout the history of the sports film. However, the genre's continuing and increasing popularity attests above all to the ongoing challenges that the American Dream ideology faces today; the mainstream sports film is one of popular culture's most enduring and seductive attempts to recuperate this ideology at a point when it is increasingly undermined by the realities of American life.

NOTES

Introduction

1 Louis Althusser has described ideology as 'the system of ideas and representations which dominate the mind of a man or a social group' (1972, p. 158).

1 Reading the sports film

1 Though these narratives are dominant, they are not the only possibilities. Soviet cinema in the 1920s and 1930s for example provided another exemplar where no single character provided the film's protagonist. In films such as Sergei Eisenstein's *Bronenosets Potyomkin* (*Battleship Potemkin*) (1925), the focus is on social, rather than personal forces and the connections that bind people together and serve the greater society.
2 However, it should be pointed out that individual directors within the Soviet film movement had quite differing views on what Soviet montage referred to and how it functioned within their films.

2 Early cinema and the emergence of the sports film

1 Streible, 2006, p. 164.
2 Indeed, the first appearance of Chaplin's legendary tramp persona was in the sport themed film *Kid Auto Races* (1914) concerning a soap-box derby.
3 Incidentally, possibly influenced by the success of Lloyd's film, Columbia produced a film under this title, directed by Walter Lang, two years after the release of *The Freshman*. *The College Hero* (1927) also concerned a freshman who becomes the hero of a college football team, scoring a spectacular touchdown to win the big game at the film's climax.

3   The sports film genre

1 For example, one of the United States largest movie rental chains, Blockbuster LLC, refers to a sports genre on its website [http://www.blockbuster.com/] only in relation to documentaries under the heading 'sports and fitness' and includes recent successful sports themed films *The Fighter* (2010) and *Moneyball* (2011) in its drama category.
2 See Box Office Mojo at http://boxofficemojo.com/genres/chart/?id=documentary. htm for a full list of the top-grossing documentaries of all time.
3 This summary of *Variety* reviews in the 1930s and 1980s draws on Steve Neale's analysis in *Genre and Hollywood* (2000), pp. 231–257.
4 According to one report, almost 70% of the box office for Hollywood films today comes from overseas (Schuker, 2010; see also Holson, 2006, and Goldstein, 2011).
5 Figures available from Box Office Mojo at boxofficemojo.com, viewed 10 February 2011.

4   'Truths that tell a lie'

1 The first speech, 'The Country We Believe In' was delivered on April 13, 2011 to The George Washington University, Washington, DC while the second was given in an address in Dublin during an official visit to Ireland on May 23, 2011. As an African American president, Obama's foregrounding of this ideology is arguably all the more convincing for Americans.
2 Rickey is here echoing the words of Massachusetts state legislator Reverend Roland D. Sawyer, who remarked that 'we encounter a real democracy of spirit' at baseball games (quoted in Bergan, 1982, p. 9).
3 Significantly, and unusually for a Hollywood film, the film took much less at the international box office ($53,248,834) indicating that its appeal was primarily with an American audience. Figures available from Box Office Mojo at http://boxofficemojo.com/movies/?id=blindside.htm
4 Indeed, the play *Golden Boy* on which the film was based was originally written by Clifford Odets with Garfield in mind for the lead role of Joe Bonaparte and Garfield would play the part in a theatrical version of *Golden Boy* on Broadway in 1952. See McGrath (1993, pp. 12 and 222).
5 Smith, Empire, 1 February, 2011.
6 These figures are available at http://www.boxofficemojo.com/
7 This documentary is based on an actual HBO documentary broadcast in 1995 featuring Dicky Eklund and two other crack addicts in Lowell and titled *High on Crack Street: Lost Lives in Lowell.*

5   Gender and the sports film

1 *The Main Event* took $42,800,000 at the American box office and is listed as the third most popular boxing film of the 1970s on Box Office Mojo (http://www.boxofficemojo.com/movies/?id=mainevent.htm).
2 Figures available at http://boxofficemojo.com/movies/?id=milliondollarbaby.htm
3 This reading draws on Boyle, Millington, and Vertinsky's analysis (2006, pp. 99–116) of *Million Dollar Baby* which also employs hooks' essay.
4 Figures available at http://boxofficemojo.com/genres/chart/?id=baseball.htm
5 While the description of cheerleading as a 'sport' may be contentious, *Bring It On*'s distributor Universal studios went to considerable efforts to classify it as such, issuing a 'fact sheet' on the release of the film arguing for such recognition (James Berardinelli, 2011). The film also attempts to justify this classification, including

through its inclusion of a gymnast in the team as there is no gymnastics programme in Rancho Carne High School. As the male commentator for the ESPN2 coverage at the cheerleading nationals in Daytona, Florida (which comprise the climax of the film) remarks, 'let's face it, any sport that combines gymnastics, dance and short skirts is okay by me'.

6   The sports film, national culture and identity

1   Sport features prominently in the films *Downhill* (1927) (rugby), *The Ring* (1927) (boxing) and *Strangers on a Train* (1951) (tennis).
2   This information is available on the website of Peter Mullan's production company, Sixteen Films, http://www.sixteenfilms.com/films/film/23/my_nameis_joe/
3   This description is from The Cup's dedicated page on the Myriad Pictures website at http://www.myriadpictures.com/Library.aspx?projectid=ecd355e1-1708-4230-a12a-34de4f7db7ea
4   This was a film in which Williams played Annette Kellerman, the Australian swimming and diving star who also had a successful acting career in the early twentieth century.

7   Conclusion

1   All these figures are available at boxofficemojo.com
2   Disney is not the only studio with major sporting interests. Time Warner owns not only Warner Bros. but also the Major League Baseball team the Atlanta Braves, the NBA professional basketball team the Atlanta Hawks and the sports magazine *Sports Illustrated* (Bordwell and Thompson, 2010, p. 35). Twentieth Century Fox is part of the third largest media conglomerate, after The Walt Disney Company and Time Warner, News Corporation, owned by Rupert Murdoch. News Corporation also has major sporting interests, including 50 per cent of the National Rugby League in Australia and New Zealand, and controlling interests in a range of sports broadcasters, including Fox Sports, Fox College Sports and the British-based Sky Sports. Major players in the production and distribution of film have therefore become increasingly involved with sport as the twenty-first century has developed, a period in which several of these companies have invested heavily in the production of major sports films.

BIBLIOGRAPHY

Abate, Michelle Ann (2008) *Tomboys: A Literary and Cultural History.* Philadelphia, PA: Temple University Press.

Abe, Ikuo (1988) 'A study of the chronology of the modern usage of "sportsmanship" in English, American and Japanese dictionaries', *International Journal of the History of Sport*, 5 (1): 3–28.

Aizenman, N.C. (2008) 'New high in U.S. prison numbers', *The Washington Post*, 29 February. Accessed 15 June 2011 at <http://www.washingtonpost.com/wpdyn/content/story/2008/02/28/ST2008022803016.html>

Alleva, Richard (1992) 'A league of their own', *Commonweal*, 11 September. Accessed 12 June 2012 at <http://findarticles.com/p/articles/mi_m1252/is_n15_v119/ai_12650245/>

Allison, Lincoln (2002) 'Sport and nationalism'. In Coakley, Jay, and Dunning, Eric, (eds) *Handbook of Sports Studies*. London: Sage Publications..

Althusser, Louis (1972) *Lenin and Philosophy, and Other Essays* trans. Ben Brewster, New York: Monthly Review Press.

Altman, Rick (Spring 1984) 'A semantic/syntactic approach to film genre,' *Cinema Journal*, 23 (3): 6–18.

Altman, Rick (1987) *The American Film Musical.* Bloomington, IN: Indiana University Press.

Altman, Rick (1999) *Film/Genre.* London: BFI Publishing.

Alvarado, Manuel and Boyd-Barrett, Oliver (eds.) (1992) *Media Education: An Introduction*. London: BFI Publishing.

Anand, Sirivayan (2002) 'Eating with our fingers, watching Hindi cinema and consuming cricket', *Himal Southasian* (February): 49.

Andersen, Thom (1985) 'Red Hollywood'. In Ferguson, Suzanne and Groseclose, Barbara (eds.) *Literature and the Visual Arts in Contemporary Society*. Columbus, OH: Ohio State University Press.

Anderson, Benedict, (1991 [1983]) *Imagined Communities: Reflections on the Origin and Spread of Nationalism,* London: Verso.

Anderson, Melissa (2009) 'Saintly white people do the saving in *The Blind Side*', *The Village Voice*, 17 November. Accessed 12 June 2011 at <http://www.villagevoice.com/2009-11-17/film/saintly-white-people-do-the-saving-in-the-blind-side/>

Andrews, David L. (2000) 'Contextualising suburban soccer'. In Finn, Gerry P.T. and Giulianotti, Richard (eds.) *Football Culture: Local Contests, Global Visions*. London: Frank Cass.

Andrews, Nigel, Churchill, David, and Blanden, Michael (1982) 'The hidden spin-off of "Chariots"', *Financial Times*, Section I: Weekend Brief, 3 April, p. 15.

Anonymous (2008) 'America's 10 Greatest Films in 10 Classic Genres' www.afi.com. Accessed 25 April 2011 at <http://www.afi.com/10top10/>

Anonymous (2011) 'The AFI Catalog of Feature Films', www.afi.com. Accessed 24 January 2011 at <http://www.afi.com/members/catalog/about.aspx?s>

Anonymous (2011) 'All-Time Box Office: World-wide', Box Office Mojo. Accessed 11 May 2011 at < http://www.boxofficemojo.com/alltime/world/>

Anonymous (2011) 'AFI's 10 Top 10', www.cbs.com. Accessed 20 January 2011 at <http://www.cbs.com/specials/afi_10_top_10/>

Anonymous (2011) 'Disney Sports Movies', Disney Movies Guide. Accessed 11 May 2011, <http://www.disneymovieslist.com/sports-disney-movies.asp>

Anonymous (2012) 'Filmmaker Jafar Panahi sentenced to six years in prison', *The Green Voice of Freedom*, 27 May. Accessed 12 June 2012 at <http://en.irangreenvoice.com/article/2010/dec/20/2581>

Arthur, Paul (2005) 'Extreme makeover: the changing face of documentary', *Cineaste* 30: 18–23.

Astruc, Alexandre (1948) '*The birth of a new avant-garde: La camera-stylo*'. In Graham, Peter (ed.) (1968) *The New Wave*. London: Secker & Warburg.

Baird, Barbara (2004) 'Contexts for lesbian citizenships across Australian public spheres'. *Social Semiotics* 14 (1): 67–84.

Baker, Aaron (2003) *Contesting Identities: Sports in American Film*. Champaign, IL: University of Illinois Press.

Baker, Aaron and Boyd, Todd (eds.) (1997) *Out of Bounds: Sports, Media, and the Politics of Identity*. Bloomington, IN: Indiana University Press.

Barnes, Simon (2006) *The Meaning of Sport*. London: Short Books.

Barr, Charles (2003) 'Sport'. In MacFarlane, Brian (ed.) *The Encyclopedia of British Film*. London: Methuen/BFI.

Barsam, Richard (2007) *Looking at Movies: An Introduction to Film*. New York: W.W. Norton and Company.

Barthes, Roland (1957 [1993]) *Mythologies*, trans. Annette Lavers. London: Vintage Books.

Barthes, Roland (1977) *Image-Music-Text*. London: Fontana Press.

Barthes, Roland (1979) 'The Tour de France as epic', *The Eiffel Tower and Other Mythologies*, trans. Richard Howard. New York: Hill and Wang.

Barthes, Roland (1981) *Camera Lucida: Reflections on Photography*, trans. Richard Howard, New York: Farrar, Straus and Giroux.

Baseball Films of the Silent Era (2010). Accessed 20 October 2010 at <http://www.silentera.com/PSFL/indexes/baseballFilms.html>

Basu, Srimati (2002) 'Aamir's fables: Lagaan as phenomenon'. Accessed 26 March 2009, at <www.viewsunplugged.com/VU/html/20020404/arts_movies_lagaan_pf.shtml>

Bazin, André (1957 [1985]) 'On the politique des auteurs'. In Hillier, Jim (ed.) *Cahiers du Cinéma, Volume 1: The 1950s*, trans Peter Graham. London: BFI/Routledge & Kegan Paul.

Bazin, André (1960) 'The ontology of the photographic image', trans. Hugh Gray, *Film Quarterly* 13 (4): 4–9.

Beilby, Peter (ed.) (1978) *The Australian Film Producers and Investors Guide.* Melbourne: Cinema Papers.

Bell, E. and Campbell, D. (1999) 'For the love of money'. *The Observer,* 23 May, p. 22.

Berardinelli, James (2010) '*The Fighter* [review]', *reelviews,* 10 December 2010. Accessed 4 January 2012 at <http://www.reelviews.net/php_review_template.php?identifier=2232>

Berardinelli, James (2011) 'Review of *Bring It On*', *reelviews.* Accessed 2 November 2011 at <http://www.reelviews.net/php_review_template.php?identifier=1483>

Bergan, Ronald, (1982) *Sports in the Movies.* New York: Proteus Publishing Company.

Betts, John Rickards (1953) 'The technological revolution and the rise of sports 1850–1900', *The Mississippi Valley Historical Review,* 40 (2): 231–256.

Billig, Michael, (1995) *Banal Nationalism.* London: Sage Publications.

Black, Fred, Korteweg, Anna C. and Woodward, Kerry with Zach Schiller and Imrul Mazid (2006) 'The compassion gap in American poverty policy' *Contexts,* 5 (2): 14–20.

Boggs, C. (1976) *Gramsci's Marxism.* London: Pluto Press.

Bogle, Donald (2001) *Toms, Coons, Mulattoes, Mammies, and Bucks: An Interpretive History of Blacks in American Film.* New York: Continuum.

Bonzel, Katharina (2011) 'Reviving the American dream: The world of sport'. In Bowdoin Van Riper, A. (ed.) *Learning from Mickey, Donald and Walt: Essays on Disney's Edutainment Films.* Jefferson, NC: McFarland.

Bordwell, David and Thompson, Kristin (2010) *Film Art: An Introduction.* 9th edition. New York: McGraw Hill.

Bordwell, David, Staiger, Janet, and Thompson, Kristin (1985) *The Classical Hollywood Cinema: Film Style and Mode of Production to 1960.* London: Routledge.

Bowden, Martyn J. (1994) 'Jerusalem, Dover Beach, and Kings Cross: Imagined places as metaphors of the British class struggle in *Chariots of Fire* and *The Loneliness of the Long-Distance Runner*'. In Aitken, Stuart C. and Zonn, Leo E. (eds.) *Place, Power, Situation and Spectacle: Geography of Film.* Lanham, MD: Rowman & Littlefield.

Boyle, Ellexis, Millington, Brad and Vertinsky, Patricia (2006) 'Representing the female pugilist: Narratives of race, gender, and disability in *Million Dollar Baby*', *Sociology of Sport Journal,* 23: 99–116.

Boyle, R. and Haynes, R. (2000) *Power Play: Sport, Media and Popular Culture.* London: Longman Press.

Brand, Jack (1978) *The National Movement in Scotland.* London: Routledge & Kegan Paul.

Braun, Marta (1992) *Picturing Time: The Work of Etienne-Jules Marey (1830–1904).* Chicago, IL: University of Chicago Press.

Brown, Jeffrey A (2004) 'Gender, sexuality, and toughness: The bad girls of action film and comic books'. In Inness, Sherrie A. (ed.) *Action Chicks: New Images of Tough Women in Popular Culture.* New York: Palgrave Macmillan.

Brown, Rebecca M. (2004) '*Lagaan*: Once upon a time in India (dir. Ashutosh Gowariker, 2001)', *Film & History: An Interdisciplinary Journal of Film and Television Studies* 34 (1): 78–80.

Brown, Richard and Anthony, Barry (1999) *A Victorian Film Enterprise: The History of the British Mutoscope and Biograph Company, 1897–1915.* Trowbridge: Flicks Books.

Buckmaster, Luke (2011) 'The Cup premiere/movie review: slumping over the finishing line', *Crikey,* October 10. Accessed 26 April 2011 at <http://blogs.crikey.com.au/cinetology/2011/10/10/the-cup-premieremovie-review-slumping-over-the-finishing-line/>

Butler, Judith (1999) *Gender Trouble: Feminism and the Subversion of Identity.* London and New York: Routledge.

Butsch, Richard, (2001) 'American movie audiences of the 1930s', *International Labor and Working-Class History,* 59: 106–120.

Cantwell, Robert (1969) 'Sport was box-office poison', *Sports Illustrated,* 16 September. Accessed 3 June 2011 at <http://sportsillustrated.cnn.com/vault/article/magazine/MAG1146656/1/index.htm>

Carlson, Lewis H. (1998) 'Review of *Diamonds in the Dark: America, Baseball, and the Movies', Journal of Sport History,* 25 (2): 360–362.

Carroll, Hamilton (2011) *Affirmative Reaction: New Formations of White Masculinity.* Durham, NC: Duke University Press.

Cashmore, Ellis (2000) *Sports Culture: An A–Z Guide.* London and New York: Routledge.

Chafe, William Henry (1991) *The Paradox of Change: American Women in the 20th Century.* Oxford: Oxford University Press.

Chalmers, Robert (2009) 'The big match: What happened when "good socialist" Ken Loach met Eric Cantona, a legend of one of the world's richest football clubs?', *The Independent,* 19 April. Accessed 20 June 2010 at <http://www.independent.co.uk/arts-entertainment/films/features/the-big-match-what-happened-when-good-socialist-ken-loach-met-eric-cantona-a-legend-of-one-of-the-worlds-richest-football-clubs-1669047.html>

Chapman, James (2005) *Past and Present: National Identity and the British Historical Film.* London and New York: I.B. Tauris.

Clegg, Brian (2007) *The Man Who Stopped Time: The Illuminating Story of Eadweard Muybridge – Pioneer Photographer, Father of the Motion Picture, Murderer.* Washington, DC: Joseph Henry Press.

Coffey, Wayne (2005) *The Boys of Winter: The Untold Story of a Coach, a Dream, and the 1980 U.S. Olympic Hockey Team.* New York: Crown Publishing Group.

Collins, Jim. (1993) 'Genericity in the nineties: Eclectic irony and the new sincerity'. In Collins, Jim, Radner, Hillary and Preacher, Ava (eds.) *Film Theory Goes to the Movies.* New York: Routledge.

Combs, James E. (1984) *Polpop: Politics and Popular Culture in America.* Bowling Green, OH: Bowling Green University Popular Press.

Congressional Budget Office (2011) 'Trends in the distribution of household income between 1979 and 2007'. Accessed 2 November 2011 at <http://cbo.gov/ftpdocs/124xx/doc12485/10-25-HouseholdIncome.pdf>

Conklin, John E. (2008) *Campus Life in the Movies: A Critical Survey from the Silent Era to the Present.* Jefferson, NC: McFarland.

Cook, Pam (1982) 'Masculinity in crisis?', *Screen* 23 (3/4): 39–46

Corn, Elliott J., and Goldstein, Warren (1993) *A Brief History of American Sports.* New York: Hill and Wang.

Creed, Barbara (1998) 'Film and psychoanalysis'. In Hill, John and Gibson, Pamela Church (eds.) *The Oxford Guide to Film Studies.* Oxford: Oxford University Press.

Crick, Emily (2007) 'Cricket and Indian national consciousness', *Institute of Peace and Conflict Studies Research Papers,* June: 1–12. Accessed 17 May 2012 at <http://www.ipcs.org/pdf_file/issue/560458831IPCS-ResearchPaper9-EmilyCrick.pdf>

Crosson, Seán (2013) '"Ar son an náisiúin": The National Film Institute of Ireland's All-Ireland Films', *Éire-Ireland,* Special Issue on Irish Sport, 48 (1&2).

Croteau, David, and Hoynes, William (2003) *Media Society: Industries, Images and Audiences.* Thousand Oaks, CA: Pine Forge Press.

Crowther, Bosley (1948) 'The Screen; "The Babe Ruth Story", Starring William Bendix as baseball hero, opens at Astor', *The New York Times,* 27 July. Accessed 5 June 2011 at <http://movies.nytimes.com/movie/review?res=940CEFDA143EE53ABC4F51DFB1668383659EDE >

Cullen, Jim. (2004) *The American Dream: A Short History of an Idea That Shaped a Nation*. London: Oxford University Press.

Cup, The (2011) 'Production notes'. Accessed 26 April 2012 at <http://static.thecia.com. au/reviews/t/the_cup-production-notes.pdf>

Cusack, Carole M. and Digance, Justine (2009) 'The Melbourne Cup: Australian identity and secular pilgrimage', *Sport in Society: Cultures, Commerce, Media, Politics*, 12 (7): 876–889.

Davis, Lennard J. (2005) 'Why "Million Dollar Baby" infuriates the disabled', *Chicago Tribune*, 2 February. Accessed 5 June, 2012 at <http://articles.chicagotribune. com/2005-02-02/features/0502020017_1_mission-ranch-inn-disability-film>

Debruge, Peter (2010) 'The Fighter', *Variety*, 10 November. Accessed 3 June 2011 at <http://www.variety.com/review/VE1117944024/>

Devine, Jeremy (1999) *Vietnam at 24 Frames a Second: A Critical and Thematic Analysis of Over 400 Films About the Vietnam War*. Austin, TX: University of Texas Press.

DeVitis, Joseph L. and Rich, John Martin (1996) *The Success Ethic, Education, and the American Dream*. New York: State University of New York Press.

Didinger, Ray and Macnow, Glen (2009) *The Ultimate Book of Sports Movies: Featuring the 100 Greatest Sports Films of All Time*. Philadelphia, PA: Running Press Book Publishers.

Dissanayake, Wimal (2000) 'Issues in world cinema'. In Hill, John and Church Gibson, Pamela (eds.) *World Cinema: Critical Approaches*. Oxford: Oxford University Press.

Dittmar, Linda and Michaud, Gene (1990) 'America's Vietnam war films: Marching towards denial'. In Dittmar, Linda and Michaud, Gene (eds.) *From Hanoi to Hollywood: The Vietnam War in American Film*. New Brunswick, NJ: Rutgers University Press.

Dunning, Eric (1986) 'Sport as a male preserve: Notes on the social sources of masculine. identity and its transformations'. In Elias, Norbert, and Dunning, Eric (eds.) *Quest for Excitement: Sport and Leisure in the Civilizing Process*. Oxford: Basil Blackwell.

Dyer, Richard (1977 [1999]) 'Entertainment and Utopia'. In During, Simon (ed.) *The Cultural Studies Reader* London and New York: Routledge.

Dyer, Richard (1996) 'Don't look now: The male pin-up'. In Merck, Mandy, Caughie, John, Creed, Barbara and Kuhn, Annette (eds.) *The Sexual Subject: A Screen Reader in Sexuality*. London and New York: Routledge.

Ebert, Roger (2010) 'The Fighter', *Chicago Sun Times*, 15 December. Accessed 10 March 2012 at <http://rogerebert.suntimes.com/apps/pbcs.dll/article?AID=/20101215/REVIEWS/ 101219988>

Edelman, Rob. (2007) 'The baseball film to 1920,' *Base Ball*, 1 (1): 22–35.

Edgington, K., Erskine, Thomas, and Welsh, James M. (2010) *Encyclopedia of Sports Films*. Lanham, MD: Scarecrow Press.

Edinger, Edward (1976) 'The tragic hero: An image of individualism'. *Parabola*, 1 (Winter): 66–74.

Edwards, Harry, (1973) *The Sociology of Sport*. Homewood, IL: Dorsey Press.

Eisenstein, Sergei, Pudovkin, Vsevolod and Alexandrov, Grigori (1928 [1999]) 'Statement on sound'. In Braudy, Leo and Cohen, Marshall (eds.) *Film Theory and Criticism: Introductory Readings*. New York and Oxford: Oxford University Press.

Elias, Norbert, 'An Essay on Sport and Violence'. In Elias, Norbert, and Dunning, Eric (eds.) *Quest for Excitement: Sport and Leisure in the Civilizing Process*. Oxford: Basil Blackwell.

Faludi, Susan (1992) *Backlash: The Undeclared War Against Women*. London: Chatto & Windus.

Fiske, John (1992) 'British cultural studies and television'. In Allen, Robert C. (ed.) *Channels of Discourse, Reassembled*. London: Routledge.

Frazier, Adam (2010) 'The Fighter', *Counting Down the Hours*, 20 December. Accessed 19 December 2011 at <http://afrazier.blogspot.com/2010/12/fighter.html>

Free, Marcus (2010) 'Disunited damning: From *The Damned United* novel to *The Damned United* film', *Sport in Society*, 13 (3): 539–548.

Garcia, Maria (n.d.) 'He got game', *Film Journal International*. Accessed 1 June 2012 at <http://www.filmjournal.com/filmjournal/esearch/article_display.jsp?vnu_content_id=1000698276#>

Gates, Henry Louis (2004) 'Breaking the silence', *New York Times*, 1 August. Accessed 15 June 2011 at <http://www.nytimes.com/ref/opinion/henrylouisgatesjr-bio.html>

Gaudreault, André. (2000) 'The diversity of cinematographic connections in the intermedial context of the turn of the 20th century'. In Popple, Simon, and Toumlin, Vanessa (eds.) *Visual Delights: Essays on the Popular and Projected Image in the 19th Century*. Trowbridge: Flicks Books.

Gehring, Wes D. (1988) *Handbook of American Film Genres*. New York: Greenwood.

Gellner, Ernest (1983) *Nations and Nationalism*. Oxford: Basil Blackwell.

Giardina, Michael D. (2005) *Sporting Pedagogies: Performing Culture and Identity in the Global Arena*. Frankfurt am Main: Peter Lang.

Gilbey, Ryan (2011) '*The Fighter* is a boxing film that packs a punch outside of the ring', *New Statesman*, 3 February. Accessed 22 December 2011 at <http://www.newstatesman.com/film/2011/02/fighter-micky-dicky-boxing>

Giroux, Henry (1995) 'Animating youth: the disnification of children's culture,' *Socialist Review* 24 (3): 23–55.

Giroux, Henry (2002) *Breaking into the Movies: Film and the Culture of Politics*. Oxford: Blackwell.

Giroux, Henry (2006) *Stormy Weather: Katrina and the Politics of Disposability*. Boulder, CO: Paradigm Publishers.

Goffman, Erving (1963) *Stigma: Notes on the Management of Spoiled Identity*. Englewood Cliffs, NJ: Prentice-Hall.

Gokulsing, K.M. and Dissanayake, W. (2004) *Indian Popular Cinema: A Narrative of Cultural Change*. Stoke on Trent: Trentham Books.

Goldstein, Patrick (2011) 'Hollywood finds that some bombs can make millions worldwide', *Los Angeles Times*, 1 February. Accessed 10 March 2011 at <http://www.kansascity.com/2011/02/01/2623349_the-strange-trajectory-of-hollywood.html>

Gooptu, Sharmistha (2004) 'Cricket or cricket spectacle? Looking beyond cricket to understand Lagaan', *International Journal of the History of Sport*, 21 (1): 533–548.

Gorman, Clem (1990) *The Larrikin Streak*. Sydney: Pan Macmillan.

Gorn, Elliott and Goldstein, Warren (1993) *A Brief History of American Sports*. Champaign, IL: University of Illinois Press.

Gramsci, Antonio (1971) *Selections from the Prison Notebooks of Antonio Gramsci*, Hoare, Quintin and Nowell-Smith, Geoffrey (eds. and trans.). London: Lawrence and Wishart.

Grant, Barry Keith (2006) *Film Genre: From Iconography to Ideology*. London: Wallflower.

Grindon, Leger (Summer 1996) 'Body and soul: The structure of meaning in the boxing film genre', *Cinema Journal*, 35 (4): 54–69.

Gruneau, Richard S. (1993) 'The critique of sport in modernity: Theorizing power, culture, and the politics of the body'. In Dunning, Eric, and Maguire, Joseph A. (eds) *The Sports Process: A Comparative and Developmental Approach*. Champaign, IL: Human Kinetics.

Gruneau, Richard S. (1999) *Class, Sports, and Social Development*. Champaign, IL: Human Kinetics.

Guerrero, Ed (1993) *Framing Blackness: The African American Image in Film*. Philadelphia, PA: Temple University Press.

Gunning, Tom (1986) 'The cinema of attraction,' *Wide Angle*, 8 (3–4): 63–70.

Gunning, Tom (1989) '"Primitive" cinema – a frame-up? Or, the trick's on us,' *Cinema Journal* 28 (2): 3–13.

Gunning, Tom (1995) 'Tracing the individual body: photography, detectives and early cinema.' In Carney, Leo and Schwartz, Vanessa R. (eds) *Cinema and the Invention of Modern Life*. Berkeley, CA: University of California Press.

Hall, Stuart (1982) 'The rediscovery of "ideology": return of the repressed in media studies'. In Gurevitch, Michael, Bennett, Tony, Curran, James and Woollacott, Janet (eds.) *Culture, Society and the Media*. London: Methuen.

Haney, Craig (2003) 'The psychological impact of incarceration: Implications for postprison adjustment'. In Travis, J. and Waul, M. (eds.) *Prisoners Once Removed: The Impact of Incarceration and Reentry on Children, Families, and Communities*. Washington, DC: The Urban Institute.

Hansen, Miriam. (1994) *Babel and Babylon: Spectatorship in American Silent Film*. Cambridge, MA: Harvard University Press.

Harman, Gilbert (1975 [1999]) 'Semiotics and the cinema: Metz and Wollen'. In Braudy, Leo and Cohen, Marshall (eds.) *Film Theory and Criticism: Introductory Readings*. New York: Oxford University Press.

Heritage, M. (2011), 'The Fighter: movie review', *The Movie Pipe,* February 2011. Accessed 22 December 2011 at <http://filmpipe.tumblr.com/post/2975184253/movie-review-the-fighter-is-a-2010-biographical>

Higson, Andrew, (1989) 'The concept of national cinema', *Screen* 30 (4): 36–46.

Higson, Andrew (1995) *Waving the Flag: Constructing a National Cinema in Britain*. Oxford: Clarendon.

Higson, Andrew (2000) 'The limiting imagination of national cinema'. In Hjort, Mette and MacKenzie, Scott (eds.) *Cinema and Nation*. London: Routledge.

Hill, John. (1992) 'The issue of national cinema and British film production'. In Petrie, Duncan (ed.) *New Questions of British Cinema*, London: BFI.

Hirschhorn, Clive (1981) *The Hollywood Musical*. New York: Crown Publishers.

Hjort, Mette and MacKenzie, Scott (2000), 'Introduction', *Cinema and Nation*. London: Routledge.

Hobsbawm, Eric (1992) *Nations and Nationalism since 1780: Programme, Myth, Reality*. Cambridge: Cambridge University Press.

Hobsbawm, Eric and Ranger, Terence (eds) (1983) *The Invention of Tradition*. Cambridge: Cambridge University Press.

Holson, Laura M. (2006) 'More than ever, Hollywood studios are relying on the foreign box office' *The New York Times*, 7 August. Accessed 30 February 2011 at <http://www.nytimes.com/2006/08/07/business/worldbusiness/07movie.html>

Holt, Richard. (1990) *Sport and the British: A Modern History*. London: Oxford University Press.

hooks, bell (1995) 'Doing it for daddy'. In Berger, M., Wallis, B. and Watson, S. (eds.) *Constructing Masculinity*. New York: Routledge.

Horkheimer, Max and Adorno, Theodor W. (1944 [1979]) *Dialectic of Enlightenment,* trans. John Cumming. London: Verso.

Hornby, Nick (1992) *Fever Pitch*. London: Gollancz.

Howard Reid, John (2006) *Success in the Cinema: Money-making Movies and Critics' Choices*. Morrisville, NC: Lulu Press.

Inness, Sherrie A. (ed.) (2004) *Action Chicks: New Images of Tough Women in Popular Culture*. New York: Palgrave Macmillan.

Iverson, Gunnar (1998) 'Norway'. In Soila, Tytti, Söderbergh-Widding, Astrid and Iverson, Gunnar (eds.) *Nordic National Cinemas*. London: Routledge.

Jaafar, Ali (2009) 'Hollywood biz without borders', *Variety*, 17 April. Accessed 10 June 2012 at <http://www.variety.com/article/VR1118002564>

Jarvie, Ian, (2000) 'National cinema: A theoretical assessment'. In Hjort, Mette and MacKenzie, Scott (eds.) *Cinema and Nation*. London: Routledge.

Johnson, Barbara (1980) *The Critical Difference: Essays in the Contemporary Rhetoric of Reading*. Baltimore, MD: Johns Hopkins University Press.

Johnson, Heather Beth (2006) *The American Dream and the Power of Wealth: Choosing Schools and Inheriting Inequality in the Land of Opportunity*. Boca Raton, FL: CRC Press.

Jones, Glen (2005) '"Down on the floor and give me ten sit-ups": British sports feature film', *Film & History*, 35 (2): 29–40.

Jones, Stephen G. (1992) *Sport, Politics and the Working Class: Organised Labour and Sport in Interwar Britain*. Manchester: Manchester University Press.

Kamali Dehghan, Saeed (2010) 'Iran jails director Jafar Panahi and stops him making films for 20 years', *The Guardian*, 20 December. Accessed 10 June 2012 at <http://www.guardian.co.uk/world/2010/dec/20/iran-jails-jafar-panahi-films>

Kapuscinki, R. (1990) *Soccer War*. London: Granta.

Kaufman, Millard. (2008) 'A vehicle for Tracy: The road to Black Rock', *The Hopkins Review*, 1 (1): 70–88.

King, C. Richard and Leonard, David J. (eds.) (2006) *Visual Economies of/in Motion: Sport and Film*. Frankfurt am Main: Peter Lang.

King, Geoff (2002) *Film Comedy*. New York: Columbia University Press.

Kleinhans, Chuck (1985) 'Working class film heroes: Junior Johnson, Evel Knievel and the film audience'. In Steven, Peter (ed.) *Jump Cut: Hollywood, Politics and Counter Cinema*. New York: Praeger.

Koehler, Robert (2005) 'Cinderella man', *Variety*, 19 May. Accessed 30 May 2011 at <http://www.variety.com/review/VE1117927190?refcatid=31>

Koszarski, Richard (1994) *An Evening's Entertainment: The Age of the Silent Feature Picture, 1915–1928*. Berkeley, CA: University of California Press.

Lafalaise, Eric (2011) 'Oscars 2011: The Fighter (David O. Russell, 2010)', *Kinoreal*, 14 April. Accessed 23 December 2011 at <http://www.kino-real.com/2011/04/fighter-david-o-russell-2010.html>

Leach, Jim (2004) *British Film*. Cambridge: Cambridge University Press.

Leonard, David J. (2008) '"Do you believe in miracles?": Whiteness, Hollywood, and a post-9/11 sports imagination'. In Briley, Ron, Schoenecke, Michael K. and Carmichael, Deborah A. (eds.) *All-Stars and Movie Stars: Sports in Film and History*. Lexington, KY: University Press of Kentucky.

Leonard, Wilbert M. (1997) 'Racial composition of NBA, NFL and MLB teams and racial composition of franchise cities', *Journal of Sport Behavior*, 20 (4): 424–434.

Levitas, Ruth (1990) *The Concept of Utopia*. New York; London: Philip Allan.

Levy, Ariel (2006) *Female Chauvinist Pigs: Women and the Rise of Raunch Culture*. New York: Free Press.

Lewis, Michael (2006) *The Blind Side: Evolution of a Game*. New York: W. W. Norton and Company.

Leydon, Joe (2002) 'The Rookie', *Variety*, 17 March. Accessed 30 May 2011 at <http://www.variety.com/review/VE1117917257?refcatid=31>

Leydon, Joe (2004) 'Miracle', *Variety*, 1 February. Accessed 30 May 2011 at <http://www.variety.com/review/VE1117922978?refcatid=31 >

Leydon, Joe (2009) 'The Blind Side', *Variety*, 16 November. Accessed 30 March 2011 at <http://www.variety.com/review/VE1117941608?refcatid=31>

Linteau, Paul-André, Durocher, René, Robert, Jean-Claude and François Ricard (1991) *Quebec Since 1930*, trans. Robert Chodos and Ellen Garmaise. Toronto: James Lorimer & Company.

Longmore, Paul K. (2001) 'Screening stereotypes: Images of disabled people'. In Enns, Anthony, and Smit, Christopher R. (eds.) *Screening Disability: Essays on Cinema and Disability*. Lanham, MD: University of America Press.

Lopez, Daniel (1993) *Film by Genre*. Jefferson, NC: McFarland & Co.

Lopez, John (2011) 'Q&A: Melissa Leo on *The Fighter, Red State*, and *Kathryn Bigelow*', *Massachusetts Film Office*, 4 February. Accessed 20 December 2011 at <http://www.mafilm.org/2011/02/05/qa-melissa-leo-on-the-fighter-red-state-and-kathryn-bigelow/>

Lovece, Frank (2010) 'Winning combination: Mark Wahlberg and David O. Russell champion "The Fighter"', *Film Journal International*, 3 December. Accessed 4 January 2012 at <http://www.filmjournal.com/filmjournal/content_display/news-and-features/features/movies/e3i685a5fab231b85c01788ae456fd2ac23>

Lukow, Gregory, and Steve Ricci (1984) 'The audience goes "public": Inter-textuality, genre and the responsibilities of film literacy'. *On Film*, l2 (3): 28–36.

Majumdar, Boria (2001) 'Politics of leisure in colonial India, "Lagaan": Invocation of a lost history', *Economic and Political Weekly*, 36 (35): 3399–3404.

Manchel, Frank (1980) *Great Sports Movies*. New York: Franklin Watts.

Mangan, J.A. (ed.) (1992) *The Cultural Bond: Sport, Empire, Society*. London: Frank Cass.

Marchesani, Nicole (2011) 'Real Steel (2011) -vs- Rocky (1976)', *Movies SmackDown*, 9 October. Accessed 19 December 2011 at <http://www.moviesmackdown.com/2011/10/real-steel-vs-rocky.html>

McCann, Sean (2007) 'Dark passages: Jazz and civil liberty in the post-war crime film'. In Krutnik, F., Neale, S., Neve, B. and Stanfield, P. (eds.) *'Un-American Hollywood': Politics and Film in the Blacklist Era*. New Brunswick, NJ: Rutgers University Press.

McDonald, Ian (2007) 'Situating the sport documentary', *Journal of Sport & Social Issues*, 31 (3): 208–225.

McDonald, Mary G. and Andrews, David L. (2001) 'Michael Jordan: Corporate sport and postmodern celebrityhood'. In Andrews, David L. and Jackson, Steven J. (eds.) *Sport Stars: The Cultural Politics of Sporting Celebrity*. London: Routledge.

McGrath, Patrick J. (1993) *John Garfield: The Illustrated Career in Films and on Stage*. Jefferson, NC: McFarland & Co.

McKernan, Luke (1996) 'Sport and the first films.' In Williams, C. (ed.) *Cinema: the Beginnings and the Future,* London: University of Westminster Press.

McKernan, Luke (2005) 'Sports films'. In Abel, Richard (ed.) *Encyclopedia of Early Cinema* London and New York: Routledge.

McKiernan, Jason (2009) 'Varsity blues', filmcritic.com, 13 January, 2009. Accessed 1 June 2012 at <http://www.filmcritic.com/reviews/1999/varsity-blues/>

McNamee, Stephen J. and Miller, Robert K. (2009) *The Meritocracy Myth*. Lanham, MD: Rowman & Littlefield.

Mediatwin (2011) 'The Fighter (Review)', The Mediatwin Blog, 1 February. Accessed 22 December 2011 at <http://www.mediatwin.me/the-fighter-review>

Melançon, Benoît (2009) *The Rocket: A Cultural History of Maurice Richard*, trans. Fred A. Reed. Vancouver, BC: Greystone Books.

Messner, Michael (1988). 'Sports and male domination: The female athlete as contested ideological terrain', *Sociology of Sport* 5 (3): 197–211.

Metz, Christian (1974a [1971]) *Language and Cinema*, trans. D.J. Umiker-Sebeok. The Hague: Mouton.

Metz, Christian (1974b) *Film Language: A Semiotics of the Cinema*, trans. Michael Taylor. New York: Oxford University Press.

Miller, Toby (2006) 'A risk society of moral panic: The US in the twenty-first century', *Cultural Politics*, 2 (3): 299–318.

Mishra, Vijay (2002) *Bollywood Cinema: Temples of Desire*. London: Routledge.

Monaco, James (2000) *How to Read a Film: The World of Movies, Media and Multimedia, Language, History, Theory*. Oxford: Oxford University Press.

Moran, Albert and Vieth, Errol (2006) *Film in Australia: An Introduction*. Sydney: Cambridge University Press.

Morrison, Blake (2004). 'Back to reality'. *The Guardian*, Friday Review Section, 5 March, p. 4.

Mosher, Stephen David (1983). 'The white dreams of God: The mythology of sport films' *Arena Review*, 7 (2): 15–19.

Mulvey, Laura (1975 [1999]) 'Visual pleasure and narrative cinema'. In Braudy, Leo and Cohen, Marshall (eds.) *Film Theory and Criticism: Introductory Readings*. New York: Oxford University Press.

Murray, Scott (ed.) (1995) *Australian Film 1978–1994: A Survey of Theatrical Features*. Melbourne: Oxford University Press.

Musser, Charles. (1994) *The Emergence of Cinema: The American Screen to 1907*. Berkeley, CA: University of California Press.

Nandy, Ashis (2000) *The Tao of Cricket: On Games of Destiny and Destiny of Games*. Delhi: Oxford University Press India.

Naremore, James (1998) *More Than Night: Film Noir in Its Contexts* Berkeley, CA: University of California Press.

National Poverty Center (n.d.) 'Poverty in the United States', University of Michigan, Gerald R. Ford School of Public Policy. Accessed 15 June 2011 at <http://npc.umich.edu/poverty/>

Neale, Steve (2000) *Genre and Hollywood*. London and New York: Routledge.

Negra, Diane (2006) *The Irish in Us: Irishness, Performativity and Popular Culture*. Durham, NC: Duke University Press.

Negra, Diane (2009) 'Irishness, anger, and masculinity in recent film and television'. In Barton, Ruth (ed.) *Screening Irish-America: Representing Irish-American in Film and Television*. Dublin: Irish Academic Press.

Nixon, Howard L. (1984) *Sport and the American Dream*. Champaign, IL: Leisure Press/Human Kinetics.

Noverr, D.A. and Ziewacz, L.E. (1983). *The Games They Played: Sports in American History, 1865-1980*. Chicago: Nelson-Hall.

Oates, Joyce Carol (1987) *On Boxing*. New York: Dolphin/Doubleday.

Obama, Barack (2011a) 'The country we believe in', delivered at The George Washington University, Washington, DC, 13 April, 2011. Accessed 1 June 2011 at <http://blogs.wsj.com/washwire/2011/04/13/text-of-obama-speech-on-the-deficit/tab/print/>

Obama, Barack, (2011b) 'Remarks by the President at Irish Celebration in Dublin, Ireland', delivered at College Green, Dublin, Ireland, 23 May 2011. Accessed 5 June 2011 at <http://thecritical-post.com/blog/2011/05/president-obamas-speech-in-ireland-at-college-green-dublin-23-may-2011-transcript-text-tcpchicago/>

Olson, Elder (1968) *The Theory of Comedy*. Bloomington, IN: Indiana University Press.

Olson, Scott Robert, (1999) *Hollywood Planet: Global Media and the Competitive Advantage of Narrative Transparency*. London: Routledge.

O'Neill, Mark E. and Phillips, Murray G. (2010) 'Sport, film, and Australian cultural identity: Reading hero to a nation', *Sport History Review* 41 (1): 1–16.

Orbach, Barak Y. (July 2010) 'The Johnson–Jeffries fight and censorship of black supremacy', *New York University Journal of Law & Liberty* 5 (2): 270–346.

Ott, John. (2005) 'Iron horses: Leland Stanford, Eadweard Muybridge, and the industrialised eye', *Oxford Art Journal*, 28 (3): 407–428.

Parrish, Michael (1992) *Anxious Decades: American in Prosperity and Depression, 1920–1941.* New York and London: W.W. Norton.

Pearson, Demetrius W., Curtis, Russell L., Haney, C. Allen, and Zhang, James J. (2003) 'Sport films: Social dimensions over time, 1930–1995', *Journal of Sport and Social Issues,* 27 (2): 145–161.

Phillips, Murray G. and Osmond, Gary (2009) 'Filmic sports history: Dawn Fraser, swimming and Australian national identity', *International Journal of the History of Sport,* 26 (14): 2126–2142.

Pike, Andrew and Cooper, Ross (1980) *Australian Film 1900–1977: A Guide to Feature Film Production.* Melbourne: Oxford University Press.

Ponto, Arya (2010) '*The Fighter* review', *Just Press Play,* 12 December. Accessed 23 December 2011 at <http://www.justpressplay.net/reviews/7225-the-fighter.html>

Poulton, Emma and Roderick, Martin (2008) 'Introducing sport in films', *Sport in Society* 11 (2/3): 107–116.

Rader, B.G. (2008) *Baseball: A History of America's Game,* 3rd edn. Champaign, IL: University of Illinois Press.

Ramsaye, Terry (1926) *A Million and One Nights: A History of the Motion Picture Through 1925.* New York: Simon & Schuster.

Raskin, Eric (2011) '"Real Rocky" Wepner finally getting due', espn.com, 25 October 2011. Accessed 5 January 2012 at <http://espn.go.com/boxing/story/_/page/IamChuckWepner/chuck-wepner-recognized-rocky-fame>

Ray, Robert B. (1985) *A Certain Tendency of the Hollywood Cinema, 1930–1980.* Princeton, NJ: Princeton University Press.

Reade, Eric (1970) *Australian Silent Films: A Pictorial History of Silent Films from 1896 to 1929.* Melbourne: Lansdowne Press.

Reiss, Steven A. (1991) 'Sport and the redefinition of American middle-class masculinity', *International Journal of the History of Sport,* 8 (1): 16–22.

Rickard, John (1998) 'Lovable larrikins and awful ockers'. *Journal of Australian Studies* 56: 78–85.

Ridgeway, Cecilia L. (2011) *Framed by Gender: How Gender Inequality Persists in the Modern World.* Oxford: Oxford University Press.

'Robert' (2011) 'Distant relatives: *Midnight Cowboy* and *The Fighter'*, *The Film Experience,* 3 February. Accessed 19 December 2011 at <http://thefilmexperience.net/blog/2011/2/3/distant-relatives-midnight-cowboy-and-the-fighter.html>

Robson, Tom (2010) 'Field of American dreams: individualist ideology in the U.S. baseball movie', *Jump Cut: A Review of Contemporary Media* 52. Accessed 1 November 2011 at <http://www.ejumpcut.org/currentissue/RobsonBaseball/text.html>

Rockett, Kevin (2004) *Irish Film Censorship: A Cultural Journey from Silent Cinema to Internet Pornography.* Dublin: Four Courts Press.

Rowe, David (1998) 'If you film it, will they come? Sports on film.' *Journal of Sport & Social Issues,* 22 (4): 350–359.

Rudnick, Lois (1991) 'The new woman.' In Heller, Adele and Rudnick, Lois (eds) *1915, The Cultural Moment: The New Politics, the New Woman, the New Psychology, the New Art and the New Theatre in America.* New Brunswick, NJ: Rutgers University Press.

Russell, Bertrand. (1926, [2003]) *On Education Especially in Early Childhood.* London: Routledge.

Saez, Emmanuel (2010) 'Striking it richer: The evolution of top incomes in the United States', Institute for Research on Labor and Employment Working Paper, University of California, Berkeley. Accessed 13 June 2011, <http://www.econ.berkeley.edu/~saez/atkinson-piketty-saezJEL10>

Sakbolé *et al.* (1996) 'Le documentaire africain/The African documentary', *Ecrans d'Afrique*, 16: 45–55. Accessed 10 June 2012 at <http://www.africultures.com/revue_africultures/articles/ecrans_afrique/16/16_45.pdf>

Salam, Ziya Us (2001) 'Cinema: Lagaan', *The Hindu*, 22 June. Accessed 16 May 2012 at <http://hindu.com/2001/06/22/stories/09220227.htm>

Santoli, Michael (2008). 'The magic's back: Disney's bright future' *Barron's Online*, 26 February. Accessed 21 April 2011 at <http://www.smartmoney.com/investing/economy/the-magics-back-disneys-bright-future-22615/>

Sarris, Andrew (1980) 'Why sports movies don't work' *Film Comment*, 16 (6): 49–53.

Sarris, Andrew. (1998) *"You Ain't Heard Nothin' Yet": The American Talking Film – History and Memory, 1927–1949*. New York: Oxford University Press.

Schatz, Thomas (1981) *Hollywood Genres: Formulas, Filmmaking, and the Studio System*. New York: Random House.

Schatz, Thomas (1991 [2004]) 'Film genre and the genre film'. In Braudy, Leo and Cohen, Marshall (eds.) *Film Theory and Criticism: Introductory Readings*. New York: Oxford University Press.

Schirato, T. and Webb, J. (2004) *Reading the Visual*. Sydney: Allen & Unwin.

Schuker, Lauren A.E. (2010) 'Plot change: Foreign forces transform Hollywood films' *The Wall Street Journal*, 2 August. Accessed 25 January 2011 at <http://online.wsj.com/article/SB10001424052748704913304575371394036766312.html>

Scott, A.O. (2000) 'Strong, modest and sincere behind all the giddy cheer', *New York Times*, August 25, 2000. Accessed 2 November 2011 at <http://movies.nytimes.com/movie/review?res=980DE2D81431F936A1575BC0A9669C8B63>

Scott, A.O. (2010a) 'Guys, kiss Mom and come out fighting', *New York Times*, 9 December 2010. Accessed 4 January 2012 at <http://movies.nytimes.com/2010/12/10/movies/10fighter.html?pagewanted=all>

Scott, A.O. (2010b) 'Hollywood's class warfare', *New York Times*, 22 December, 2010. Accessed 19 December 2011 at <http://www.nytimes.com/2010/12/26/movies/26scott.html>

Scott, David (2010) 'Boxing and masculine identity'. In Dine, Philip and Crosson, Seán (eds.) *Sport, Representation and Evolving Identities in Europe*. Frankfurt am Main: Peter Lang.

Scraton, Sheila and Flintoff, Anne (eds.) (2002) *Gender and Sport: A Reader*. London: Routledge.

Shanahan, Donald (2011) 'Movies that epitomize the American Dream (part 6)', Examiner.com, 29 September. Accessed 21 December 2011 at < http://www.examiner.com/film-in-chicago/editorial-movies-that-epitomize-the-american-dream-part-6>

Sikov, Ed (2010) *Film Studies: An Introduction*. New York: Columbia University Press

Silk, Michael, Schultz, Jaime and Bracey, Bryan (2008) 'From mice to men: Miracle, mythology and the "Magic Kingdom"', *Sport in Society*, 11 (2): 279–297.

Singer, Matt (2011) 'Comparing fact and fiction in "The Fighter"', *The Independent Film Channel*, 5 January. Accessed 22 December 2011 at <http://www.ifc.com/news/2011/01/comparing-fact-and-fiction-in.php.>

Simmons, Bill (2010) 'Sports movies continue to evolve', espn.com, 23 December. Accessed 4 November 2011 at <http://sports.espn.go.com/espn/page2/story?page=simmonsnfl2010/week16picks>

Sklar, Robert (1992) *City Boys: Cagney, Bogart, Garfield*. Princeton, NJ: Princeton University Press.

Smith, Adam (2011) 'The Fighter [review]', *Empire*, 1 February 2011. Accessed 4 January 2012 at <http://www.empireonline.com/reviews/ReviewComplete.asp?FID=136326>

Smith, Earl. (2009) *Race, Sport and the American Dream*, 2nd edn. Durham, NC: Carolina Academic Press.

Stoddart, T.B. and Sandiford, K. (eds.) (1998) *The Imperial Game: Cricket, Culture and Society*. Manchester: Manchester University Press.

Street, Sarah (2003) 'National Cinema'. In MacFarlane, Brian (ed.) *The Encyclopedia of British Film*, London: Methuen/BFI.

Streible, Dan. (2008) *Fight Pictures: A History of Boxing and Early Cinema*. Berkeley, CA: University of California Press.

Swanson, R.A., and Spears, B. (1995). *History of Sport and Physical Education in the United States*, 4th edn. Madison, WI: Brown & Benchmark.

Sweeney, Kevin W. (2007) *Buster Keaton: Interviews* Jackson, MS: University Press of Mississippi.

Syed, Matthew (2010) 'What makes the perfect sports film?' *The Times*, 5 February. Accessed 20 January 2011 at <http://entertainment.timesonline.co.uk/tol/arts_and_entertainment/film/article7015598.ece>

Tasker, Yvonne (2011) 'Bodies and genres in transition: *Girlfight* and *Real Women Have Curves*'. In Gledhill, Christine (ed.) *Gender Meets Genre in Postwar Cinemas* Urbana, IL: University of Illinois Press.

Tomlinson, A. (1988) 'Images of sport: Situating *Chariots of Fire*', *British Society of Sports History Bulletin*, 8: 27–41.

Trimble, Patrick (1996) 'Babe Ruth: The media construction of a 1920s sport personality' *Colby Quarterly*, 32 (1): 45–57.

Tucker, Rufus S. (1922) 'Distribution of men physically unfit for military service', *Journal of the American Statistical Association*, 18 (139): 377–384.

Tudor, Deborah V. (1997) *Hollywood's Vision of Team Sports: Heroes, Race, and Gender*. New York and London: Garland Publishing.

Tulloch, John (1981) *Legends on the Screen: The Australian Narrative Cinema 1919–1929*, Sydney: Currency Press.

Turner, Graeme (2000) 'Cultural studies and film'. In Hill, John and Church Gibson, Pamela (eds.) *Film Studies: Critical Approaches*. Oxford: Oxford University Press.

Umphlett, Wiley Lee (1984) *The Movies Go to College: Hollywood and the World of the College-Life Film*. Rutherford, NJ: Fairleigh Dickinson University Press.

U.S. Census Bureau (2011a) 'Poverty, USA'. Accessed 22 September 2011 at <http://www.census.gov/hhes/www/poverty/about/overview/index.html>

U.S. Census Bureau (2011b) 'State and county quickfacts, USA'. Accessed 14 June 2011 at < http://quickfacts.census.gov/qfd/states/00000.html>

Wallenfeldt, J.H. (1989) *Sports Movies*. New York: CineBooks.

Wang, Benjamin (2002) 'The cold war, imperial aesthetics, and area studies'. *Social Text* 72 (3): 46–65.

Ward, Tony (2010) *Sport in Australian National Identity: Kicking Goals*. London: Routledge.

Warren, Val (1979) *Lost Lands, Mythical Kingdoms, and Unknown Worlds*. New York: Simon and Schuster.

Waterson, Johnny and Naughton, Lindie (1992) *Irish Olympians 1896–1992*. Dublin: Blackwater Press.

Wells, Paul (1999) 'The documentary form: Personal and social "realities"'. In Nelmes, Jill (ed.) *An Introduction to Film Studies*. London: Routledge.

Whannel, Garry (2008) 'Winning and losing respect: Narratives of identity in sport films', *Sport in Society: Cultures, Commerce, Media, Politics*, 11 (2–3): 195–208.

White, Armand (2010) 'Fighting for class', *New York Press*, 7 December. Accessed 22 December 2011 at <http://www.nypress.com/article-21937-fighting-for-class.html>

White, Leanne (2011) 'The role of the horse in Australian tourism and national identity'. In Frew, Elspeth Ann and White, Leanne (eds.) *Tourism and National Identities: An International Perspective.* London: Routledge.

Wickham, Phil (n.d.) '*This Sporting Life* (1963)', BFI Screenonline. Accessed 23 April 2012 at <http://www.screenonline.org.uk/film/id/440653/index.html>

Williams, Randy (2006) *Sports Cinema: 100 Movies The Best of Hollywood's Athletic Heroes, Losers, Myths, and Misfits.* Montclair, NJ: Limelight Editions.

Wolff, Edward N. (1995) *Top Heavy: The Increasing Inequality of Wealth in America and What Can Be Done about It* New York: New Press.

Wolz, Birgit (2004) *E-motion Picture Magic: A Movie Lover's Guide to Healing and Transformation.* Lakewood, CO: Glenbridge Publishing.

Wood, Robin (1977 [2004]) 'Ideology, genre, auteur'. In Braudy, Leo and Cohen, Marshall (eds.) *Film Theory and Criticism: Introductory Readings.* New York: Oxford University Press.

Wood, Robin (1985) 'An introduction to the American horror film'. In Nichols, Bill, (ed.) *Movies and Methods Vol. II.* Los Angeles, CA: University of California Press.

Wood, Robin (1987) 'Returning the look: Eyes of a Stranger'. In Waller, Gregory Albert (ed.) *American Horrors: Essays on the Modern American Horror Film.* Champaign, IL: University of Illinois Press.

Wright, Erik O. (1998) 'Class analysis'. In Levine, Rhonda (ed.) *Social Class and Stratification: Classic Statements and Theoretical Debates.* Lanham, MD: Rowman & Littlefield.

Wright, Melanie J. (2006) *Religion and Film: An Introduction.* London and New York: I.B. Tauris.

Zhang, Yingjin (2004) *Chinese National Cinema.* New York: Routledge.

Zhang, Zhen (2005) *An Amorous History of the Silver Screen: Shanghai Cinema, 1896–1937.* Chicago, IL: University of Chicago Press.

Zhou, Xuelin (2007) *Young Rebels in Contemporary Chinese Cinema.* Hong Kong: Hong Kong University Press.

Zipes, Jack (1999) 'Breaking the Disney spell'. In Tatar, Maria (ed.) *Classic Fairy Tales: Texts, Criticism.* New York: Norton.

Žižek, Slavoj (1997) 'Multiculturalism, or the cultural logic of multinational capitalism', *New Left Review* 225 (September/October): 28–51.

FILMOGRAPHY

127 Hours (2010) Danny Boyle. Century City, Los Angeles, CA: Fox Searchlight Pictures.

Accident (1967) Joseph Losey. London: London Independent Producers.

A Day at the Races (1937) Sam Wood. Beverly Hills, CA: Metro-Goldwyn-Mayer.

Ae Fond Kiss … (2004) Ken Loach. London: Sixteen Films.

Africa United (2010) Deborah 'Debs' Gardner-Paterson. Paris: Pathé.

Against all Odds (1984) Taylor Hackford. Culver City, CA: Columbia Pictures.

Air Up There, The (1994) Paul Michael Glaser. Walt Disney Studios, Burbank, CA: Hollywood Pictures.

A League of Their Own (1992) Penny Marshall. Culver City, CA: Columbia Pictures.

Ali (2001) Michael Mann. Culver City, CA: Columbia Pictures.

All Rounder (1984) Mohan Kumar. Mumbai: Emkay Productions.

American Flyers (1985) John Badham. Burbank, CA: Warner Bros.

Anand Math (1952) Hemen Gupta. Mumbai: Filmistan.

A Night at the Opera (1935) Sam Wood. Beverly Hills, CA: Metro-Goldwyn-Mayer.

Any Given Sunday (1999) Oliver Stone. Burbank, CA: Warner Bros.

Arthur's Hallowed Ground (1984) Freddie Young. London: Channel Four Television Corporation.

A Shot at Glory (2001) Michael Corrente. West Hollywood, CA: Butchers Run Films.

A Tribute to Maurice Richard, The Rocket (2005) Mathieu Roy. Montréal, Québec: Cinémaginaire.

Awwal Number (1990) Dev Anand. Mumbai: Navketan Films.

Babe Ruth Story, The (1948) Roy Del Ruth. Los Angeles, CA and New York: Allied Artists.

Band Plays On, The (1934) Russell Mack. Beverly Hills, CA: Metro-Goldwyn-Mayer.

Battling Butler (1926) Buster Keaton. Beverly Hills, CA: Metro-Goldwyn-Mayer.

Bend it like Beckham (2002) Gurinder Chadha. Century City, Los Angeles, CA: Fox Searchlight Pictures.

Big Boss, The (1971) Lo Wei. Kowloon, Hong Kong: Golden Harvest.

Big Race, The (1934) Fred C. Newmeyer. Hollywood, CA: Showmen's Productions.

Blades of Glory (2007) Josh Gordon and Will Speck. Universal City, CA: DreamWorks Pictures.

Blind Side, The (2009) John Lee Hancock. Burbank, CA: Warner Bros.

Blood of Heroes, The (1989) David Webb Peoples. Los Angeles, CA: New Line Cinema.

Blue Chips (1994) William Friedkin. Hollywood, CA: Paramount Pictures.

Blue Crush (2002) John Stockwell. Los Angeles, CA: Universal Pictures.

Body and Soul (1947) Robert Rossen. Los Angeles, CA & New York: Allied Artists.

Bodyline: It's Not Just Cricket (1984) Denny Lawrence, Lex Marinos, George Ogilvie and Carl Schultz. Sydney: Network Ten.

Boxer, The (1997) Jim Sheridan. Los Angeles, CA: Universal Pictures.

Breaking Away (1979) Peter Yates. Century City, Los Angeles, CA: 20th Century Fox.

Bring It On (2000) Peyton Reed. Los Angeles, CA: Universal Pictures.

Bring It On: All or Nothing (2006) Steve Rash. Los Angeles, CA: Universal Pictures.

Bronenosets Potyomkin (*Battleship Potemkin*) (1925) Sergei Eisenstein. Moscow: Goskino.

Brown of Harvard (1926) Jack Conway. Beverly Hills, CA: Metro-Goldwyn-Mayer.

Bull Durham (1988) Ron Shelton. Los Angeles, CA: Orion Pictures.

Burglar and the Lady, The (1914) Herbert Blaché. New York: Sun Photoplay Co.

Caddyshack (1980) Harold Ramis. Burbank, CA: Warner Bros.

Chain Kulii Ki Main Kulii (2007) Kittu Saluja. Kolkata: Saregama Film.

Champ, The (1931) King Vidor. Beverly Hills, CA: Metro-Goldwyn-Mayer.

Champ, The (1979) Franco Zeffirelli. Beverly Hills, CA: Metro-Goldwyn-Mayer.

Champion, The (1915) Charlie Chaplin. Chicago, IL: Essanay Studios.

Champion (1949) Mark Robson. Century City, Los Angeles, CA: United Artists.

Chariots of Fire (1981) Hugh Hudson. Century City, Los Angeles, CA: 20th Century Fox.

Chasing Dreams (1982) Therese Conte and Sean Roche. Los Angeles: Prism Entertainment.

Cinderella Man (2005) Ron Howard. Los Angeles, CA: Universal Pictures.

City Lights (1931) Charlie Chaplin. MGM Tower, Century City, Los Angeles: United Artists.

Coach Carter (2005) Thomas Carter. Hollywood, CA: Paramount Pictures.

College (1927) James W. Horne and Buster Keaton. Century City, Los Angeles, CA: United Artists.

College Hero, The (1927) Walter Lang. Culver City, CA: Columbia Pictures.

Cool Runnings (1993) Jon Turteltaub. Burbank, CA: Walt Disney Pictures.

Cricketer, The (1985) Bush Mehay. London: East End Films.

Cup, The (2011) Simon Wincer. Melbourne: Village Roadshow.

Damned United, The (2009) Tom Hooper. Culver City, CA: Columbia Pictures.

Das Wunder von Bern (*The Miracle of Bern*) (2003) Sönke Wortmann. Geiselgasteig: Bavaria Film International.

Dawn! (1979) Ken Hannam. Australia: Aquataurus Film Corp.

Days of Thunder (1990) Tony Scott. Hollywood, CA: Paramount Pictures.

Death Race (2008) Paul W.S. Anderson. Los Angeles, CA: Universal Pictures.

Death Race 2000 (1975) Paul Bartel. Los Angeles, CA: New World Pictures.

Dial M for Murder (1954) Alfred Hitchcock. Burbank, CA: Warner Bros.

Die Angst des Tormanns beim Elfmeter (*The Goalkeeper's Fear of the Penalty*) (1972) Wim Wenders. Berlin: Filmverlag der Autoren.

Dil Bole Hadippa! (2009) Anurag Singh. Mumbai: Yash Raj Films.

DodgeBall: A True Underdog Story (2004) Rawson Marshall Thurber. Century City, Los Angeles, CA: 20th Century Fox.

Dogtown and Z-Boys (2001) Stacy Peralta. New York: Sony Pictures Classics.

Downhill (1927) Alfred Hitchcock. London: Gainsborough Pictures.

Downhill Racer (1969) Michael Ritchie. Hollywood, CA: Paramount Pictures.

Down the Stretch (1936) William Clemens. Burbank, CA: Warner Bros.

Dragon: The Bruce Lee Story (1993) Rob Cohen. Los Angeles, CA: Universal Pictures.

Drop Kick, The (1927) Millard Webb. Burbank, CA: First National Pictures.

Fan, The (1996) Tony Scott. Culver City, CA: TriStar Pictures.

Fat City (1972) John Huston. Culver City, CA: Columbia Pictures.

Fever Pitch (1997) David Evans. London: Channel Four Films.

Field of Dreams (1989) Phil Alden Robinson. Universal City, California: Universal Studios.

Fighter, The (2010) David O. Russell. Hollywood, CA: Paramount Pictures.

Fighting Gentleman, The (1932) Fred C. Newmeyer. USA: Monarch Film Corporation.

Final Test, The (1953) Anthony Asquith. London: Rank Organisation.

Flåklypa Grand Prix (Pinchcliffe Grand Prix) (1975) Ivo Caprino. Stockholm: Sandrew Metronome.

Flesh and Fury (1951) Joseph Pevney. Los Angeles, CA: Universal Pictures.

Flying Scotsman, The (2006) Douglas Mackinnon. London: Verve Pictures.

For Love of the Game (1999) Sam Raimi. Universal City, California: Universal Studios.

Forrest Gump (1994) Robert Zemeckis. Hollywood, CA: Paramount Pictures.

Forward Pass, The (1929) Edward F. Cline. Burbank, CA: First National Pictures.

Freshman, The (1925) Fred C. Newmeyer and Sam Taylor. Buffalo, NY: Pathé Exchange.

Friday Night Lights (2004) Peter Berg. Los Angeles, CA: Universal Pictures.

Futuresport (1998) Ernest Dickerson. Culver City, CA: Columbia/TriStar.

General, The (1926) Clyde Bruckman and Buster Keaton. Century City, Los Angeles, CA: United Artists.

Gentleman Jim (1942) Raoul Walsh. Burbank, CA: Warner Bros.

Glory Road (2006) James Gartner. Burbank, CA: Walt Disney Pictures.

Gmar Gavi'a (Cup Final) (1992) Eran Riklis. Jerusalem: Israel Broadcasting Authority.

Go-Between, The (1971) Joseph Losey. London: EMI Films.

Golden Boy (1939) Rouben Mamoulian. Culver City, California: Columbia Pictures.

Good Bye Lenin! (2003) Wolfgang Becker. Berlin: X Verleih AG.

Grand Prix (1966) John Frankenheimer. Beverly Hills, CA: Metro-Goldwyn-Mayer.

Great White Hope, The (1970) Martin Ritt. Century City, Los Angeles, CA: 20th Century Fox.

Grifters, The (1990) Stephen Frears. New York: Miramax Films.

Hardball (2001) Brian Robbins. Hollywood, CA: Paramount Pictures.

Harder They Fall, The (1956) Mark Robson. Culver City, CA: Columbia Pictures.

Hattrick (2007) Milan Luthria. Mumbai: UTV Motion Pictures.

Headin' Home (1920) Lawrence C. Windom. USA: Kessell & Baumann.

He Got Game (1998) Spike Lee. Burbank, CA: Touchtone Pictures.

Here Comes Mr Jordan (1941) Alexander Hall. Culver City, CA: Columbia Pictures.

Hoop Dreams (1994) Steve James. Los Angeles, CA: Fine Line Features.

Hoosiers (1986) David Anspaugh. Los Angeles, CA: Orion Pictures.

Horse Feathers (1932) Norman Z. McLeod. Hollywood, CA: Paramount Pictures.

Hustler, The (1961) Robert Rossen. Century City, Los Angeles, CA: 20th Century Fox.

If.... (1968) Lindsay Anderson. UK: Memorial Enterprises.

Invincible (2006) Ericson Core. Burbank, CA: Walt Disney Pictures.

Iqbal (2005) Nagesh Kukunoor. Mumbai: Mukta Searchlight Films.

Irish in Us, The (1935) Lloyd Bacon. Burbank, CA: Warner Bros.

Iron Man (1931) Tod Browning. Los Angeles, CA: Universal Pictures.

It Ain't Hay (1943) Erle C. Kenton. Los Angeles, CA: Universal Pictures.

Jackie Robinson Story, The (1950) Alfred E. Green. Los Angeles, CA: Eagle-Lion Films.

Jazz Singer, The (1927) Alan Crosland. Burbank, CA: Warner Bros.

Jerry Maguire (1996) Cameron Crowe [2005 Collector's Edition DVD]. Culver City, CA: TriStar Pictures.

Kabhi Ajnabi The (1985) Vijay Singh. India: Sabah Video.

Kansas City Bomber (1972) Jerrold Freedman. Beverly Hills, CA: Metro-Goldwyn-Mayer.

Karate Kid, The (1984) John G. Avildsen. Culver City, CA: Columbia Pictures.

Kentucky (1938) David Butler. Century City, Los Angeles, CA: 20th Century Fox.

Kes (1969) Ken Loach. London: Woodfall Film Productions.

Kid from Brooklyn, The (1946) Norman Z. McLeod. New York: RKO Pictures.

Kid Galahad (1937) Michael Curtiz. Burbank, CA: Warner Bros.

Killing, The (1956) Stanley Kubrick. Century City, Los Angeles, CA: United Artists.

King's Speech, The (2010) Tom Hooper. New York: The Weinstein Company.

Knockout, The (1914) Charles Avery. Edendale, CA: Keystone Studios.

Knute Rockne All American (1940) Lloyd Bacon. Burbank, CA: Warner Bros.

Lady Vanishes, The (1938) Alfred Hitchcock. London: Gainsborough Pictures.

Lagaan (2001) Ashutosh Gowariker. Mumbai: Aamir Khan Productions.

Lamb (1963) Paulin Soumanou Vieyra. Bénin, Sénégal: Cinémathèque Afrique.

Les Triplettes de Belleville (*Belleville Rendez-vous*) (2003) Sylvain Chomet. Paris: Diaphana Films.

Le voyage dans la lune (*A Trip to the Moon*) (1902) Georges Méliès. Paris: Gaston Méliès Films.

Loneliness of the Long-Distance Runner, The (1962) Tony Richardson. London: Woodfall Film Productions.

Longest Yard, The (1974) Robert Aldrich. Hollywood, CA: Paramount Pictures.

Longest Yard, The (2005) Peter Segal. Hollywood, CA: Paramount Pictures.

Looking for Eric (2009) Ken Loach. London: Sixteen Films.

Love Guru, The (2008) Marco Schnabel. Hollywood, CA: Paramount Pictures.

Main Event, The (1979) Howard Zieff. Burbank, CA: Warner Bros.

Major League (1989) David S. Ward. Hollywood, CA: Paramount Pictures.

Major League II (1994) David S. Ward. Burbank, CA: Warner Bros.

Man from Snowy River, The (1982) George T. Miller. Century City, Los Angeles, CA: 20th Century Fox.

Man with a Movie Camera (1929) Dziga Vertov [2000 BFI edition]. Kiev: VUFKU.

Maryland (1940) Henry King. Century City, Los Angeles, CA: 20th Century Fox.

Match, The (1999) Mick Davis. London: United International Pictures.

Maurice Richard (2005) Charles Binamé. Toronto: Alliance Atlantis.

Meerabai Not Out (2008) Chandrakant Kulkarni. Mumbai: Pritish Nandy Communications.

Melbourne Cup, The (1896) Marius Sestier.

Mermaid, The (1911) unknown.

Mighty Ducks, The (1992) Stephen Herek. Burbank, CA: Walt Disney Pictures.

Mike Bassett: England Manager (2001) Steve Barron. London: Entertainment Film Distributors.

Milky Way, The (1936) Leo McCarey. Hollywood, CA: Paramount Pictures.

Million Dollar Baby (2004) Clint Eastwood. Burbank, CA: Warner Bros.

Million Dollar Mermaid (1952) Mervyn LeRoy. Beverly Hills, CA: Metro-Goldwyn-Mayer.

Miracle (2004) Gavin O'Connor. Burbank, CA: Walt Disney Pictures.

Moneyball (2011) Bennett Miller. Culver City, CA: Columbia Pictures.

Mother India (1957) Mehboob Khan. Mumbai: Mehboob Productions.

Murderball (2005) Henry Alex Rubin and Dana Adam Shapiro. New York: TH!NKFilm.

My Name is Joe (1998) Ken Loach. London: Sixteen Films.

Nacho Libre (2006) Jared Hess. Hollywood, CA: Paramount Pictures.

National Velvet (1944) Clarence Brown. Beverly Hills, CA: Metro-Goldwyn-Mayer.

Natural, The (1984) Barry Levinson. Culver City, CA: TriStar Pictures.

Naya Daur (1957) B.R. Chopra. Mumbai: B.R. Films.

Night Train to Munich (1940) Carol Reed. Century City, Los Angeles, CA: 20th Century Fox.

North Dallas Forty (1979) Ted Kotcheff. Hollywood, CA: Paramount Pictures.

Nü lán 5 háo (Woman Basketball Player No. 5) (1957) Xie Jin. Shanghai: Tian Ma Film Studio.

Number One (1969) Tom Gries. Century City, Los Angeles, CA: United Artists.

Offside (2006) Jafar Panahi. Tehran: Jafar Panahi Film Productions.

Olympia (1938) Leni Riefenstahl [Triad Productions Corporation DVD, 2008]. Berlin: Olympia-Film.

On the Waterfront (1954) Elia Kazan. Culver City, CA: Columbia Pictures.

One in a Million (1936) Sidney Lanfield. Century City, Los Angeles, CA: 20th Century Fox.

Other Girl, The (1916) Percy Winter. New York: Raver Film Corporation.

Other Side of the Mountain, The (1975) Larry Peerce. Los Angeles, CA: Universal Pictures.

Outside Edge (1994–96) Nick Hurran. London: Carlton UK Productions.

Palooka (1934) Benjamin Stoloff. Century City, Los Angeles, CA: United Artists.

Pat and Mike (1952) George Cukor. Beverly Hills, CA: Metro-Goldwyn-Mayer.

Patiala House (2011) Nikhil Advani. Mumbai: Hari Om Entertainment.

Payoff, The (1935) Robert Florey. Burbank, CA: Warner Bros.

Personal Best (1982) Robert Towne. Burbank, CA: Warner Bros.

Phar Lap: Heart of a Nation (1983) Simon Wincer. Century City, Los Angeles, CA: 20th Century Fox.

Phörpa (The Cup) (1999) Khyentse Norbu. New York: Palm Pictures.

Pinch Hitter, The (1917) Charles Miller and/or Victor L. Schertzinger. New York: New York Motion Picture Company.

Players (1979) Anthony Harvey. Hollywood, CA: Paramount Pictures.

Playing Away (1987) Horace Ové. London: Channel Four Films.

Pride of St. Louis, The (1952) Harmon Jones. Century City, Los Angeles, CA: 20th Century Fox.

Pride of the Yankees, The (1942). Sam Wood [2002 MGM DVD]. New York: RKO Pictures.

Prince from Avenue A, The (1920) John Ford. New York: Universal Film Manufacturing Company.

Prizefighter and the Lady, The (1933) W.S. Van Dyke and Howard Hawks. Beverly Hills, CA: Metro-Goldwyn-Mayer.

Program, The (1993) David S. Ward. Burbank, CA: Touchstone Pictures.

P'tang, Yang, Kipperbang (1982) Michael Apted. London: Channel 4 Television Corporation.

Quarterback, The (1926) Fred C. Newmeyer. Hollywood, CA: Paramount Pictures.

Queen of the Sea (1918) John G. Adolfi. New York: Fox Film Corporation.

Radio (2003) Michael Tollin. Culver City, CA: Columbia Pictures.

Raging Bull (1980) Martin Scorsese [2005 MGM DVD]. Century City, Los Angeles, CA: United Artists.

Real Steel (2011) Shawn Levy. Universal City, CA: DreamWorks Pictures.

Remember the Titans (2000) Boaz Yakin. Burbank, CA: Walt Disney Pictures.

Riding Giants (2004) Stacy Peralta. New York: Sony Pictures Classics.

Ring, The (1927) Alfred Hitchcock. Borehamwood, Hertfordshire, England: British International Pictures.

Rocky (1976) John G. Avildsen. Century City, Los Angeles, CA: United Artists.
Rocky II (1979) Sylvester Stallone. Century City, Los Angeles, CA: United Artists.
Rocky III (1982) Sylvester Stallone. Century City, Los Angeles, CA: United Artists.
Rocky IV (1985) Sylvester Stallone. Century City, Los Angeles, CA: United Artists.
Rocky Balboa (2006) Sylvester Stallone. Beverly Hills, CA: Metro-Goldwyn-Mayer.
Rollerball (1975) Norman Jewison. Century City, Los Angeles, CA: United Artists.
Rollerball (2002) John McTiernan. Beverly Hills, CA: Metro-Goldwyn-Mayer.
Roma, città aperta (Rome, Open City) (1945) Roberto Rossellini. Rome: Minerva Film spa.
Rookie, The (2002) John Lee Hancock. Burbank, CA: Walt Disney Pictures.
Rudo y Cursi (2008) Carlos Cuarón. Los Angeles, CA: Universal Pictures.
Running Brave (1983) D.S. Everett and Donald Shebib. Burbank, CA: Buena Vista Pictures.
Say Salaam India (2007) Subhash Kapoor. Mumbai: Speaking Tree Films.
Seabiscuit (2003) Gary Ross. Los Angeles, CA: Universal Pictures.
Senna (2010) Asif Kapadia. Los Angeles, CA: Universal Pictures.
Set-Up, The (1949) Robert Wise. New York: RKO Pictures.
She's the Man (2006) Andy Fickman. Universal City, CA: DreamWorks.
Slap Shot (1977) George Roy Hill. Los Angeles, CA: Universal Pictures.
Slugger's Wife, The (1985) Hal Ashby. Culver City, CA: Columbia Pictures.
Social Network, The (2010) David Fincher. Culver City, CA: Columbia Pictures.
Somebody Up There Likes Me (1956) Robert Wise. Beverly Hills, CA: Metro-Goldwyn-Mayer.
So This Is College (1929) Sam Wood. Beverly Hills, CA: Metro-Goldwyn-Mayer.
Soul Surfer (2011) Sean McNamara. Culver City, CA: TriStar Pictures.
Space Jam (1996) Joe Pytka. Burbank, CA: Warner Bros.
Speedy (1928) Ted Wilde. Hollywood, CA: Paramount Pictures.
Spirit of Youth, The (1938) Harry L. Fraser. Globe Pictures Corp.
Sporting Life, This (1963) Lindsay Anderson. London: Rank Organisation.
Step Into Liquid (2003) Dana Brown. Santa Monica, CA: Artisan Entertainment.
Strangers on a Train (1951) Alfred Hitchcock. Burbank, CA: Warner Bros.
Stumped (2003) Gaurav Pandey. Mumbai: Reel Life Entertainment.
Sunset Boulevard (1950) Billy Wilder. Hollywood, CA: Paramount Pictures.
Sweetie (1929) Frank Tuttle. Hollywood, CA: Paramount Pictures.
Swell Head (1935) Benjamin Stoloff. Culver City, CA: Columbia Pictures.
Swimming Upstream (2003) Robert J. Emery. Beverly Hills, CA: Crusader Entertainment.
Take Me Out to the Ballgame (1949) Busby Berkeley. Beverly Hills, CA: Metro-Goldwyn-Mayer.
Talladega Nights: The Ballad of Ricky Bobby (2006) Adam McKay. Culver City, CA: Columbia Pictures.
Taris, roi de l'eau (Jean Taris, Swimming Champion) (1931) Jean Vigo. Paris: Gaumont Franco-Film Aubert (GFFA).
Tarzan and the Golden Lion (1927) J.P. McGowan. New York: Robertson-Cole Pictures Corporation.
Tarzan and the Great River (1967) Robert Day. Hollywood, CA: Paramount Pictures.
Tarzan and the Jungle Boy (1968) Robert Gordon. Hollywood, CA: Paramount Pictures.
Tarzan and the Valley of Gold (1966) Robert Day. Los Angeles, CA: American International Pictures.
Tarzan, the Ape Man (1932) W.S. Van Dyke. Beverly Hills, CA: Metro-Goldwyn-Mayer.
There is Only One Jimmy Grimble (2000) John Hay. London: Sarah Radclyffe Productions.
They Made Me a Criminal (1939) Busby Berkeley. Burbank, CA: Warner Bros.

This Sporting Life (1963) Lindsay Anderson. London: Rank Organisation.
Tiger Town (1983) Alan Shapiro. Burbank, CA: Walt Disney Television.
Ti yu huang hou (Queen of Sports) (1934) Yu Sun. Hong Kong: Lian Hua Film Company.
Tokyo Olympiad (1965) Kon Ichikawa. Tokyo: Toho Company.
Tooth Fairy (2010) Michael Lembeck. Century City, Los Angeles, CA: 20th Century Fox.
Touching the Void (2003) Kevin MacDonald. Paris, France: Pathé.
Triumph des Willens (Triumph of the Will) (1935) Leni Riefenstahl. Berlin: Universum Film AG.
Trobriand Cricket (1975) Gary Kildea and Jerry Leach. Government of Papua New Guinea/ University of Cambridge Museum of Archaeology & Ethnography.
United We Stand (2009) Toby Reiz [DVD]. London: Feasible Films Production. Included on DVD edition of *Looking for Eric* (Ken Loach, 2009).
Upside of Anger, The (2005) Mike Binder. Los Angeles, CA: New Line Cinema.
Varsity Blues (1999) Brian Robbins. Hollywood, CA: Paramount Pictures.
Venus of the South Seas (1924) James R. Sullivan. New York: Lee-Bradford Company.
Victory (2009) Ajit Pal Mangat. Mumbai: Victory Moving Pictures.
Waterboy, The (1998) Frank Coraci. Burbank, CA: Touchstone Pictures.
When Saturday Comes (1996) Maria Giese. UK: Guild/Pint O'Bitter Productions.
Whip It (2009) Drew Barrymore. Century City, Los Angeles, CA: Fox Searchlight Pictures.
Wildcats (1986) Michael Ritchie. Burbank, CA: Warner Bros.
Winning (1969) James Goldstone. Los Angeles, CA: Universal Pictures.
Winning Team, The (1952) Lewis Seiler. Burbank, CA: Warner Bros.
World's Greatest Athlete The (1973) Robert Scheerer. Burbank, CA: Walt Disney Pictures.
Wrestler, The (2008) Darren Aronofsky. Los Angeles, CA: Fox Searchlight Pictures.
Yesterday's Hero (1979) Neil Leifer. Los Angeles, CA: Cinema Seven Productions.
Zendegi va digar hich (And Life Goes on...) (1992) Abbas Kiarostami. Tehran: Institute for the Intellectual Development of Children & Young Adults (Kanoon).

Avildsen, John G. (2005) 'DVD Commentary', *Rocky* (1976), *Sylvester Stallone Rocky Anthology* (Ultimate Edition 6 Disc Box Set), Sony Pictures Home Entertainment.
Scorsese, Martin (2004) 'DVD Commentary', *The Set-Up* (1949), Turner Entertainment Co. and Warner Bros. Entertainment Co.
Shire, Talia (2005) 'DVD Commentary', *Rocky* (1976), *Sylvester Stallone Rocky Anthology (Ultimate Edition 6 Disc Box Set)*, Sony Pictures Home Entertainment.
Wise, Robert (2004) 'DVD Commentary', *The Set-Up* (1949), Turner Entertainment Co. and Warner Bros. Entertainment Co.

INDEX